CONTEMPORARY SOCIAL PROBLEMS IN BRITAIN

Contemporary Social Problems in Britain

Edited by

ROY BAILEY and JOCK YOUNG

SAXON 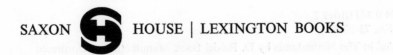 HOUSE | LEXINGTON BOOKS

Published by

SAXON HOUSE, D. C. Heath Ltd.
Westmead, Farnborough, Hants, England

Jointly with

LEXINGTON BOOKS, D. C. Heath & Co.
Lexington, Mass. U.S.A.

ISBN 0 347 01017 2
LC No. 73–3729

Printed in The Netherlands by D. Reidel Book Manufacturers, Dordrecht

Contents

Contents

Notes on Contributors

PETER ARCHARD completed his first degree in sociology at the University of Leeds. At present he is a research worker with the Alcoholics Recovery Project, Camberwell, London. His PhD research is on 'The Subculture of the Skid Row Alcoholic'.

JOHN AULD graduated in sociology from the University of Leicester in 1969 and is now a post-graduate research student at the London School of Economics where he is registered for a PhD on 'Drug Use and Bohemianism'.

ROY BAILEY graduated from the University of Leicester in 1963. He began teaching at Enfield College of Technology (now a constituent college of Middlesex Polytechnic, London) in 1964 where he was senior tutor. He was responsible, at that time, for the development of sociology at the College. In 1967 he moved to the University of Bradford as Lecturer in Sociology. He is currently Head of the Department of Applied Social Studies at Sheffield Polytechnic. He is a member of the editorial board of *Economy and Society*, a social science journal, and a committee member of the National Deviancy Conference.

MIKE BRAKE After a career in the theatre as a ballet dancer Mike Brake went to Leeds University as a mature student, graduating in 1967 with a BA in psychology and sociology. He then attended the London School of Economics completing an MSc in 1968. Since then he has lectured on the sociology of deviance in the UK and California and has conducted research on sexual deviants and adolescent subcultures. He is a Lecturer in Sociology at Bradford University where he is writing a book on youth culture.

MIKE FEATHERSTONE graduated Durham University 1967 with a BA in sociology and politics. He has been a Lecturer in Sociology at Teesside Polytechnic since 1967. At present he is engaged in writing a critique of the theoretical assumptions of human ecology. An article, 'Persons Believed Missing: A Search for a Sociological Explanation' will appear in the forth-coming collection of British Sociological Association Conference papers edited by P. Rock and M. MacIntosh *Social Control, Deviancy and Dissent*. The article was written in collaboration with Mike Hepworth of Aberdeen University, with whom a research project into Missing Persons is being conducted with a view to future publication.

MIKE HEPWORTH worked as a Careers Advisory Officer in Warwickshire after graduating in social studies at the University of Hull in 1961. Since then he has held teaching posts in further and higher education and is presently Lecturer in Sociology at the University of Aberdeen. A committee member of the National Deviancy Conference, his main research interests are the sociology of privacy and secrecy and symbolic aspects of social deviance. His preliminary study of blackmail was published in *Images of Deviance* edited by Stanley Cohen and he has recently completed a book, *Blackmail: Publicity and Secrecy in Every Day Life*. He has also written, in collaboration with Mike Featherstone, a paper, 'Persons Believed Missing'. Currently he is planning, with Mike Featherstone, a research project which will form the basis of a book-length study of missing persons. He is also writing papers on privacy and secrecy including an exploratory comparative analysis of criminal and religious confessions.

IAIN MANSON graduated in Sociology from Enfield College of Technology and then completed an MSc in social psychology at the London School of Economics. His research interests are currently in the sociology of sex. He is lecturing at the Institute of Education, London University. He is joint author with Jerry Palmer of a forthcoming book on pornography, *The Dirty Old Man on the Last Tube*.

JERRY PALMER completed his BA, MA and PhD at the University of Southampton. His MA thesis was concerned with aspects of J.-P. Sartre and his PhD on seventeenth-century classicism. His current research interests centre around the sociology of literature. He is also London correspondent for VPRO Radio/TV Hilversum and De Groene Amsterdammer. He is teaching at present at the City of London Polytechnic. He has written several articles and is currently completing a book with Iain Manson.

FRANK PEARCE completed a degree in sociology at the University of Leeds in 1967. He then went to the University of Kent as a research student. Currently he is a Senior Lecturer in Sociology at the Polytechnic of North London. He has also lectured at California State College at Los Angeles. He has published articles on 'Corporate Crime' and on the 'Mass Media Treatment of Homosexuality'. At present he is working on a number of projects including a book, *Crime, Politics and the State*, and a study of the Press Council.

KEN PLUMMER completed his first degree at Enfield College of Technology in 1967. He spent a year engaged in various social-work projects before taking up teaching, first at Kingston Polytechnic and then at Middlesex

Polytechnic, where he is currently lecturing in sociology. He is registered with the London School of Economics and is completing his PhD research on sexual variations this year (1973). His interests lie in the areas of interactionist theory, sexual behaviour and deviancy and he is the author of various articles. His first book is to be published in 1974.

ANDREW ROBERTS is currently an undergraduate at Middlesex Polytechnic reading a social science degree. He worked as research assistant with Frank Pearce on a number of projects. His research interest at the present time is on the history of madness.

JOCK YOUNG completed his first degree, MSc and PhD at the London School of Economics. In 1966 he went to teach at Enfield College of Technology where he is currently a Senior Lecturer in Sociology. For some years he has been carrying out research on drug-taking in various social settings. He is currently engaged on a research project sponsored by the Social Science Research Council, 'The Student Culture Project'. He is the author of several books: *The Drug-takers*, *The New Criminology*, *Subculture Analysis* and *Media as Myth*. He is also one of the founder members of the National Deviancy Conference.

Acknowledgements

We should like to thank all the contributors to this volume not only for the work and time they spent on their essays, but perhaps more significantly for their patience and tolerance with us as editors. Our thanks go also to our friends and colleagues of the National Deviancy Conference. Their work and interest in these and related areas has proved a major stimulus for the development of the approach that these essays utilise.

Our thanks must also be expressed to Gill Humberstone for her patient typing of the manuscript, and often retyping as we 'changed our minds'.

ROY BAILEY
JOCK YOUNG

Introduction

Our aims in bringing together this selection of readings are threefold. First, we have chosen original articles which epitomise the approach advocated by the new deviancy theory. Such an approach originated in the work of the American Society for the Study of Social Problems in the early sixties and was developed later in the decade by a British group centring around the National Deviancy Conference.

Characteristic of this approach is that social problems are not regarded as pathological aberrations, indicative of disturbed personalities, but as meaningful attempts to solve problems faced by individuals in specific parts of the social structure. As a corollary of this it is necessary that social problems are viewed in a historical context as the product of individuals who are conscious, however inarticulately, of their social predicament and evolving patterns of behaviour which can only be understood in terms of their past culture and history. The deviant actor must be granted a conscious past, a present perceived problem and a future praxis. Although the individual is free to actively pursue solutions to his problems he nevertheless exists in a world of circumstances not of his own making. His freedom is limited by conditions and opportunities not of his own choice.

Thus the deviant's reflections on his situation and his creative attempts to transcend the social encumbrances which beset him must be followed. It is necessary to delineate the nature of the total society which has engendered these problems and placed obstacles to their resolution. Both the subjective machinations of the individual and the objective social structure which impinges upon him must form vital interrelated strands in any analysis of deviancy. Further, the interplay between the deviant's tentative attempts to achieve his aims and the manoeuvred responses of the social control agencies which surround him must be examined. The moral career of the individual is to be examined in terms of patterns of interaction with his social surroundings. History, consciousness, meaning and career within the interstices of a comprehensive understanding of the total society are the mainstays of such an analysis. It is in terms of such criteria that articles have been selected for this volume.

Our second aim has been to focus attention on British material set against a comparative perspective. For the British reader this attempts to fill a gap in the literature on social problems which, apart from a few isolated endeavours, has largely utilised American material. For the American student of social problems, it provides a useable yardstick against which American findings can be contrasted.

Finally we have endeavoured to demonstrate the wide applicability of modern deviancy analysis. All too often handbooks on social problems have concentrated on somewhat narrow definitions of their objects of study—usually crime and delinquency. We have included articles on areas beyond this definition, such as pornography and missing persons. As areas of study these latter issues are important in their own right but they have been sadly neglected in the literature.

We believe that the range of material brought together in this book will be of use both to undergraduate students in social studies and professional social workers. At the same time, it will provide relevant material for post-graduates working within the field of social problems.

Student Drug Use and Middle-Class Delinquency

Jock YOUNG

Subcultural theory demands that deviant behaviour be seen in terms of means to resolve particular problems—that is, unachieved aspirations—which confront the actor and which cannot be resolved by normal activities. It attempts to make understandable the behaviour of the actor in terms of his subjective perception of his predicament and the structural forces which impinge upon him.[1] It is opposed to theories that view deviant behaviour as the manifestation of a meaningless physical and/or psychological pathology. In terms of student drug use, therefore, it must examine the relevant socially induced frustrations which present themselves to certain segments of the student population and detail the attempts to solve this problem through the conjoint creation of a subcultural solution involving drug use. For this reason the focus of analysis must dwell preponderantly on the subculture *not* on the drug itself, out of social context. For the dosage, mode of administration, expectations and interpretations which surround drug use —indeed the effects themselves—are dependent on the culture in which it is used.[2] I wish to argue that student marihuana smoking is an adjunct of bohemian subcultures and that the primary task of sociology is to explain the origins of such bohemian solutions.

For empirical evidence I will refer continually to a study of the origins and change in student drug use which my colleagues and I undertook over the years 1968 to 1971. This involved questionnaires, structured interviews and direct observation and utilised a large panel study.[3] I do not, however, intend to focus directly on the results of this research as I have done so elsewhere, and my intention in this article is primarily theoretical.

David Matza[4] has argued at length against the idea of the delinquent contraculture. Oppositional subcultures are, he suggests, unlikely to occur amongst young people as they are, because of their age, encircled by their elders. Authentic oppositional subcultures can arise, but only amongst adults who are partially isolated from the rest of society. But certain groups of young people are precisely in this position of being isolated from adults and society in general, namely students (who are, of course, largely of middle-class origin). Students, unlike their working-class contemporaries, often live away from home and have, as universities grow, little contact with anyone

1

except their peers. As John Rex put it, 'by virtue of the systems of social relations in which he moves as compared with his non-student contemporary, he finds himself cut off from his fellow men, alienated from his society.'[5] This is not to suggest that all students will, because of their isolated position, form contracultures. Rather, that the insulation from the rest of society provides a potentiality for contraculturation which will be realised by sections of the student population who are subject to certain tensions. For, as J. Yinger has outlined, the movement from subculture to contraculture occurs when: (*a*) there is *frustration*—that is a motivation to deviate— and (*b*) there is *weak social control*—that is, because of isolation, it is possible to resolve these tensions in a deviant fashion.[6] Precisely such a thesis has been evolved by Frank Musgrove in his book, *Youth and the Social Order*, in which he says that societies in which young people are segregated and suffer acute status frustration are those in which deviance will be most prevalent.[7]

I have described the potentiality for students to become deviant, but what has yet to be explained is: (*a*) the particular set of frustrations that lead to this deviance, and (*b*) why drugs in particular are chosen as vital components in the content of the ensuing culture.

Origins of student bohemianism

Subcultural theorists such as Cohen[8] and Cloward and Ohlin[9] have based their analysis of the *motivation* for deviancy among lower-class delinquents on their own variations of the Mertonian paradigm situation, namely situations where the socially inculcated aspirations of the actors are not met by the objective possibilities of their social situation. For Cloward and Ohlin this deprivation is economic; for Cohen it is in terms of the inability to realise middle-class status. All the various theorists who base themselves on the Mertonian notions of anomie phrase the disparity between aspirations and possibilities in terms of values such as success (in terms of money) and status, that is in terms of ends which are external to the actual work or study of the individual. They regard these activities instrumentally rather than as ends in themselves with their own implicit satisfactions. But any adequate study of the satisfactions (or, conversely, deprivations) that individuals obtain from their work or studies must be couched in terms *both* of instrumentality *and* of expressivity: that is, the material or status gains that derive from the job itself.[10] In other words Mertonian anomie—the disparity between aspirations and actuality— must be reformulated in terms of instrumentality *and* expressivity.

If one asks why a man goes out to work every day, or why a student

spends years of study to obtain a degree, the answer must be in terms
of:

(*a*) Intrinsic benefits of the work itself: what I will term the 'expressive'
satisfaction, and
(*b*) Extrinsic benefits of the work: what I will term the 'instrumental'
satisfaction.

The *degree* of commitment of a person to his work will be proportional
to the instrumental and expressive satisfaction which he obtains from it, and
the *type* of commitment will vary with whether the satisfactions derived from
the job are preponderantly instrumental or expressive. Moreover, these
satisfactions or deprivations have to be understood in *relative* terms. That
is—in the phrasing of Mertonian anomie theory—in terms of the disparity
between the socially inculcated aspirations of the actor and the institutionalised means available for him to realise them.

As far as young people are concerned, this analysis must be couched as
follows:

(*a*) If they are at work, in terms of the degree of realisation of their expressive and instrumental aspirations
(*b*) If they are students, in terms of the degree of expressive satisfaction
gained from their studies and the *anticipated* instrumental satisfaction (or
deprivation) perceived by them as available in their future work roles.

The subcultural theorists' emphasis solely on instrumental satisfaction and
deprivation is understandable for two main reasons:

(*a*) The major instrumental benefit is, of course, money and although
people are willing to work in situations where their expressive aspirations
are not met, they obviously always require some financial payoff.
(*b*) Some segments of the population have very low expressive aspirations
as regards work. The lower working class is a prime example. Thus, examples
of lower-working-class delinquency, which has been the major focus of
analysis, do not necessitate examination of expressive factors in the work
situation. For middle-class youth, however, expressive satisfaction or deprivation experienced during studies would be a much more cogent factor.

I have suggested that we must understand a student's commitment to this
course in terms of two factors:

(*a*) The *intensity* of commitment, that is the degree to which his aspirations
are met by the course.

(*b*) The *direction* of commitment, that is whether this commitment is of a predominantly expressive, instrumental or mixed nature.

From this it is possible to create a typology of commitment as in Table I.

TABLE I
Typology of Commitment to Course

Type	Instrumental Commitment	Expressive Commitment
I	+	+
II	+	−
III	−	+
IV	−	−

Key
+ = positive commitment, that is where instrumental or expressive aspirations are met.
− = negative commitment, that is where instrumental or expressive aspirations are not met.

From this typology it can be postulated, in the tradition of subcultural theory stemming from Merton, that the solutions which students evolve to meet these problems of commitment will vary with the nature of the commitment. That is, that sub- or contraculturation will emerge along the lines of this typology. To be specific, the following hypotheses can be made about the nature of student subcultures:

1. The nature of the student culture is a function of the satisfactions or frustrations arising from the course. This explains the *origins* of conformity or deviancy.
2. The degree of deviancy of a student culture will be inversely proportional to the degree of commitment to a course. If a student perceives that he is obtaining substantial benefits from his course he will be loath to jeopardise them by engaging in culpable deviant behaviour. This explains the *costs and benefits* of conformity or deviancy.
3. If a student does not obtain expressive satisfaction from his work he will find it in his leisure. This explains the *focus* of conformity or deviancy.

4

Thus the origins, degree and focus of conformity and deviancy are explicable in terms of the student's perceived satisfactions and deprivations.

I will illustrate, using various student groups as examples, each of the four cells in the typology.

Type I   Here the course is perceived as both expressively and instrumentally rewarding. The individual's life is focused on work and his leisure is seen chiefly as a means of relaxation. The student forms conformist *subcultures* because he has little grievance with the course and much to lose if he acts deviantly. An example here would be the medical student. I will term this the 'academic subculture'.

Type II   Here work is perceived as being instrumentally satisfactory but expressively inadequate. The life of such individuals is focused on leisure. Course work is considered merely as a means to earn in the future a reasonable salary and respected status. Their leisure activities are, however, non-deviant as any activities deemed socially undesirable might prejudice their degree and, with it, their future job chances.[11] The most notable example of this are many engineering students. I will term this the 'careerist subculture'.

Type III   Here work is perceived as being expressively satisfying but is considered inadequate from an instrumental point of view. There is a tendency for these individuals to take up a radical position within their subject and college. It is here the student militant would be found. Individuals are essentially work-focused but if alienation from the course is sufficient they may form cultures of an intellectual nature focused on their leisure time.[12] A considerable proportion of sociology students may well fall into this category. I will term this the 'radical contraculture', as the student is motivated in a deviant direction and has little to lose from deviant activities.

Type IV   Here both expressive and instrumental commitment are missing. These individuals focus automatically on leisure activities and have a considerable tendency to deviance as they have least to lose by being deviant. It is here that the 'bohemian contraculture' evolves.

Commitment, involvement and anomie

At this juncture it is necessary to elaborate the basis of commitment. I have suggested that commitment will be minimal when neither expressive nor instrumental benefits accrue to the student. This absence of commitment can, however, occur in two situations:

(a) Where both aspirations and perceived benefits are low. That is, the student neither asks for nor receives benefits. He is, therefore, not bound into the course: he has nothing to lose by nonconformity. I will term this 'low involvement' with the course.
(b) Where aspirations are high but where benefits are low. This is *anomie* of the Mertonian sort. This is a motivation for deviancy, a source of discontent.

The bohemian student's placing in type IV, involving low expressive and instrumental commitment, may be a result of a combination of expressivity that is either non-involved or anomic and instrumentality that is either non-

TABLE II

Types of Minimal Commitment

Type	Instrumental	Expressive
A	low involvement	low involvement
B	low involvement	high anomie
C	high anomie	low involvement
D	high anomie	high anomie

involved or anomic. There are four possibilities all of which would ensure a type IV commitment (see Table II).

In my survey of student marihuana users it was found that type B commitment was most common, that is student bohemians experienced high expressive anomie and had only low income involvement. I will show later how this is directly understandable in terms of their class backgrounds.

Comparisons with working-class adolescents

David Downes, in his study of working-class adolescents in Stepney and Poplar, notes how they have exceedingly low aspirations at work, either instrumentally or expressively. He writes:

What has been achieved (in their case) is an opting-out of the joint middle- and skilled-working-class value-system whereby work is extolled as a central life issue, and whereby the male adolescent of semi- and unskilled origin is enjoined to either 'better himself' or 'accept his station in life'. To insulate himself against the harsh implications of this creed in a 'dead-end job', in a 'dead' neighbourhood, extricates himself from the belief in work as of any importance beyond the simple provision of income, and deflects what aspirations he has left into areas of what has been termed 'non-work' (rather than leisure).[13]

This process of lowering instrumental and denying expressive aspirations in work is called 'dissociation' by Downes.

Cotgrove and Parker concur on this:

Satisfaction from work and the significance attached to it will depend not only on the nature of the work, but also on the expectations which the individual brings to his job. These in turn will be the result of complex processes of selection and socialisation, which begin with 11+ with entry to the grammar or modern school, each of which carries its stream of children on to broad groups of occupations. ... For the less able child in the lower forms of the modern school, the dominant picture which emerges is one of school as a source of boredom and frustration. In many schools the imposition of dull, mechanical tasks, which lack any apparent significance or relevance to the life of the child, effectively train him to accept the routine demands of industry. The transition from school to work involves little more than a change of routine. Many expect little from work and are satisfied with what they find, even though the work is repetitive and makes few demands. The secondary modern boy leaving school at 15 has received early training in dissociating himself from the demands which 'they' make upon him. *He simply doesn't care.* It is not surprising that psychologists have discovered that many are content to carry out routine tasks. Dissatisfaction is a measure of the gap between aspiration and achievement. *For many? No such gap exists—their expectations and aspirations are centred on the world outside the factory.*[14]

From this description it is clear that this group of working-class adolescents fit well the type IV category of commitment outlined earlier. That is, there is a lack of both instrumental and expressive benefits. Further, it is clear that this is a type of minimal commitment where there is low instrumental and expressive involvement (type A in Table II); anomie is absent because nothing is asked of work. The dissociation of bohemian students is not as extreme as this. It involves, it is true, a parallel lack of involvement in instrumental demands from their study and a complete dissociation from both expressive and instrumental demands of *future* work roles. But a function of their intensive socialisation in the educational system has been to raise some hopes and expectations of the expressive possibilities of higher education. The students still demand, at this stage in their bohemian career, something of their courses and are thus capable of experiencing expressive anomie. Later on, expressive demands also tend to be rejected and complete dissociation ensues. This leads eventually to a total disengagement from their course, a well-argued disdain for work and a complete focus on leisure activities. Because of its more articulate and self-conscious nature I will term this process 'ideological dissociation' to distinguish it from the less-reflective disengagement characteristic of lower-working-class adolescents.

The deprived middle class

On the face of it, it might seem strange to talk of deprivation among middle-class youth. After all they have, in absolute terms, much greater access to both instrumental and expressive benefits. Indeed, traditional subcultural theory places the problem of deprivation firmly within the ranks of the lower classes. Thus Cloward and Ohlin write:

> The middle-class person can generally take advantage of educational opportunities despite their cost; his family may be in the position to finance the beginnings of his profession or business, or at least to put him in touch with established and successful people who can give him an 'edge'. In these and other ways, middle-class youth enjoy greater access to success goals. Although the lower-class boy may yearn to rise in the social structure, the obstacles are great.[15]

This, I would argue, ignores the effect of *relative* deprivation on individuals. Middle-class youth may well have an easier access to success goals in absolute terms than their contemporaries in the working class but this does not necessarily lead to contentment. In contrast there is much evidence to show that in Britain at least working-class youth have very realistic aspirations.[16] This realism is explained by Downes as being a result of what R. H. Turner called the sponsored system of education. He contrasts two types of mobility via education: the *contest* where there is prolonged competition for mobility and massive participation (as in America) and the *sponsored*—as in Britain—where a small portion of individuals are selected for mobility at an early age and there is freedom from competition thereafter.[17] Downes links the prevalence of dissociation amongst British working-class youth with the existence of sponsored mobility. Thus he writes: 'For the British boy, dissociation is engendered and strengthened by the earliness at which selection (and rejection) takes place: the result is a certain fatalism towards the roles of school and work to which he has been allocated, and an overt stress on fulfilment through leisure comes early.[18] Thus, whereas the American system engenders aspirations that are totally unrealistic, the British system creates the pattern of realistic aspirations mentioned above.

But what happens to the small percentage of individuals who are selected by the educational system for mobility.[19] Is the situation as sponsored and free from competition as Turner suggests? A. H. Halsey, in a critique of Turner's article,[20] suggests that only the minority public-school system in Britain fits Turner's category of sponsored mobility as he has delineated it. In contrast, the state grammar-school system, although sponsored in that selection is early, exhibits prolonged and intensive competitive aspects chiefly in the competition for university places. Middle-class young people are in an analogous position to the lower-class youths described by Cloward and Ohlin. They have absorbed the democratic competitive ideology of the educational system [21] and are faced with limited objective chances of realising these aspirations. There is no doubt, also, that the competition occurring in grammar schools for university places is matched by the competition in universities for good degrees in order to obtain desirable jobs.[22] Moreover, students of certain subjects, especially when they are studying at institutions that are labelled by the outside world as 'second rate', face particularly severe problems of adjustment.

It is not absolute chances of success, then, that determine instrumental deprivation or satisfaction but *relative* chances—chances compared to those of others who are seen in a similar competitive situation. This accords completely with the theory of relative deprivation that was elaborated by Merton.[23] But why do middle-class young people have higher expressive aspirations *vis-à-vis* their future work or present studies than their contemporaries in the working class have? I would suggest that this is because:

(*a*) Educational ideology engenders the notion of vocation and of scholastic ideals—that a subject is worth studying as an end in itself. At the same time because of the necessity of getting a good degree in order to have a competitive position in the job market, many students find themselves in a position of 'cramming' a set syllabus rather than exploring a subject according to their personal interests.[24]

(*b*) Because of anticipation of future career prospects many students choose subjects which prove to offer only instrumental satisfactions.

(*c*) Many students have a conception of university as offering chances of

9

'finding oneself' and determining one's true vocation, particularly when they have just left grammar school.[25] Often they find that university does not meet these lofty expressive aspirations.

Class background and bohemianism

I have argued that students are likely to experience deprivation and that the specifically bohemian orientation to a course lacks both instrumental and expressive satisfactions. Such a position was corroborated in the survey but it was further discovered that the specific type of bohemian commitment was that of high expressive anomie and low income involvement, and that this related closely to students who had a non-commercial middle-class background. How can such a result be meaningfully explained?

Richard Flacks, in his study of student activists, notes that their background was:

> disproportionately the sons and daughters of highly educated parents; in a large proportion of cases, their parents have advanced graduate and professional degrees; a very high percentage of activists' mothers are college graduates; the parents tend to be in occupations for which higher education is a central prerequisite: professions, education, social service, public service, the arts; both businessmen and blue- and white-collar workers tend to be under-represented among the parents of activists; family interests—as they are expressed in recreation, or in dinner-table conversation, or in formal interviews—tend to be intellectual and 'cultural' and relatively highbrow; these are families in which books were read, discussed and taken seriously, in which family outings involved museums and concert-halls rather than ball-parks and movies, etc. They were families in which 'values' were taken seriously— conventional religion and morality were treated with considerable scepticism, while at the same time strong emphasis was placed on leading a principled, socially useful, morally consistent life. They were, finally, families in which education was regarded with considerable reverence and valued for its own sake, rather than in utilitarian terms.
>
> In short, the student movement originated among those young people who came out of what might be called the 'intellectual' or 'humanist' subculture of the middle class.[26]

This ongoing tradition is not new to Western society:

> For more than a century, at least, small groups of intellectuals have

10

expressed their revulsion with industrial capitalism, and the commercialism, philistinism, and acquisitiveness they saw as its outcome. By the turn of the century, what had largely been an expression of genteel criticism was supplanted by a more vigorous and intense revolt by some educated youth—expressed through bohemianism and through a variety of political and social reform movements. Indeed, opposition to Victorian morality and business culture has been characteristic of American intellectuals in this century, and the emergence of large numbers of humanistic youth out of relatively intellectual families is an indication of the impact this opposition has had on the society. What was once the protest of tiny pockets of intellectuals and artists has become a mass phenomenon, in part because the ideas of these earlier critics and reformers were taken up in the universities and became part of the world-view of many members of the educated middle class.[27]

It is the growth of the professional middle class concomitant with the welfare state that has increased this humanistic tradition. As Frank Parkin notes, in a British context:

... any industrial society could be said to have certain values which occupied a certain position in the normative order, in the sense that they were the values upheld by the major institutions of society. While there is an overall tendency for acceptance of these values to be more complete among higher social strata than among lower, it seems clear that exposure to certain forms of advanced education has the effect of undermining such total acceptance among middle-class members. To this extent, it could be said that the minority of the non-manual stratum which has undergone formal education and intellectual training beyond the sixth form constitutes a permanent source of potential opposition to certain commonly accepted socio-political values. ...[28]

Here Flacks concurs:

... occupations which are structurally not bound into the private, corporate economy—for example, occupations associated with education, social service, social planning, and other intellectual or human service work... embody values which tend to be critical of the culture and of the going system and tend to have an ethic which emphasises collective welfare rather than private gain. It is important to recognise that the current student activists were born into the social stratum defined by these occupations, and many students with activist sympathies end up in these occupations. In a certain sense, then, the student movement

11

may be seen as an outgrowth of a new level of occupational differentiation, i.e. the development of a distinct stratum organised around these
occupations. This stratum is one of the most rapidly growing occupational sectors, and its political impact can already be seen, not only
on the campus, but in such developments, as the 'new politics' movement during the recent elections.[29]

This class typically views the commercial middle class as non-creative,
boring and philistine. The expressive demands of their children, from education, is therefore rooted in their background:

> The rootedness of the bohemian and quasi-bohemian subcultures, and
> the spread of their ideas with the rapid increase in the number of college
> graduates, suggests that there will be a steadily increasing number of
> families raising their children with considerable ambivalence about
> dominant values, incentives and expectations in the society. In this
> sense, the students who engage in protest or who participate in 'alienated'
> styles of life are often not 'converts' to a 'deviant' adaptation, but people
> who have been socialised into a developing cultural tradition.[30]

But this notion of a continuing humanistic tradition should not blind us
to the creative role of these students in terms of their *raising* and *transforming*
their parents' expressive aspirations. It is not merely, as Frank Parkin has
suggested, that society inculcates young middle-class people with ideals that
they find lacking in the real world.[31] What has happened is that bohemianism
has taken parts of a humanistic culture, accentuating and adding to it, to
a point where it is qualitatively different.[32] This process is thus not merely
anomie of a static sort (the inability of 'objective' opportunities to meet
socially inculcated aspirations)—although this is certainly part of the process
—it also involves the creation of aspirations which the social structure is
unable to meet.

But what of the low level of instrumental aspirations? The reasons for
this are, I believe, simple if viewed in a historical context. The upper-middle-
class student who has grown up since the war has been conscious merely
of a neo-Keynesian plain, where income has gradually risen and the material
comfort of people like his parents has been taken for granted. As Flacks
puts it:

> ... widespread restlessness about becoming committed to conventional
> careers and life-styles is evident on the American campus. This has been
> particularly surprising for those of us who remember the decade of the
> fifties and the prevailing feeling of that era—namely, that affluence was

producing a generation which would be particularly conformist, complacent, status-conscious, and bourgeois.

It is now apparent that the opposite may be equally true. Although people with high status and material security may typically be motivated to maintain their position, it is also the case that being born into affluence can foster impulses to be experimental, risk-taking, open to immediate experience, unrepressed. For some at least, growing up with economic security in families of secure status can mean a weakening of the normal incentives of the system and can render one relatively immune to the established means of social control, especially if one's parents rather explicitly express scepticism about the moral worth of material success. Postwar affluence in our society, then, has had the effect of liberating a considerable number of young people from anxieties about social mobility and security, and enabled them to take seriously the quest for other values and experiences. To such youth, established careers and adult roles are bound to be unsatisfying. What is the sense, after all, of binding oneself to a large organisation, of submitting to the rituals, routines and disciplines of careerism, of postponing or foregoing a wide range of possible experience—when there is little chance of surpassing one's father, when the major outcome of such efforts is to acquire goods which one has already had one's fill of, when such efforts mean that one must compromise one's most cherished ideals?[33]

The spiral of increasing consumption and production written into economics and notions of human nature would seem to have found its own limit.[34] In a class structure with wide variation in income and taste this assertion may be, to an extent, presumptuous. But certainly for segments of the upper-middle classes in advanced industrial countries the marginal pecuniary inducement which alienated labour can provide is insufficient. More leisure and unalienated work are preferred to the maximisation of income and consumption powers.

All the above, it might be argued, would be true of the backgrounds of both student militants and bohemians. And, indeed, both Flacks and Parkin, writing respectively about student activism in America and the CND movement in Britain, seem to make no distinction between the two. However, the survey data indicate that the student bohemian stems from a more *homogeneous* liberal middle-class background than does the militant. This was because the student revolutionaries included a mixture of upper-middle-class and working-class students. Either upward mobility *or* liberal middle-class background increased the tendency to radicalism. The lower-middle-class student from a commercial background is less likely to be militant or bohemian. Thus in terms of background the upper-middle-class liberal student is most likely to be bohemian or revolutionary, the commercial upper-middle-class or lower-middle-class student to be conservative, and the working-class student to be revolutionary. What this would seem to suggest is that the ideological path faced by the affluent, liberal middle-class student leads two ways: either to bohemianism or to Marxism. There is no necessary one-to-one relationship between structural position, perceived problem and subcultural solution. To expect there to be such a relationship would:

(a)   Deny the historical consciousness of individuals, their experimentation with life-styles, and their rejection of one life-style for another in a process of learning from life and adapting new solutions.[35]
(b)   Demand a complete determinism which would deny man's creative potentiality.
(c)   Deny that bohemianism and militancy may be polar alternatives, choices which the same group finds itself facing and which provide solutions which interact with and sustain each other. I could not do better than quote from Stuart Hall's analysis of the two poles of the underground:

> What the existence of the beats and of the hippies reminds us is that there has been a ceaseless dialectic at work in the growth of the 'generational underground' in the United States—one which, though different in many important ways from other parallel developments elsewhere, may nevertheless offer us a *paradigm*. This dialectic may now be seen as a movement between two poles —two 'moments'—in the materialisation of the revolutionary project. Those poles may be defined roughly as the *expressive* and the *activist*. (The slogan raised during the recent events in May in Paris also catches the same contradictory extremes: 'imagination au pouvoir'.) The hippies, like the beats before them, are prototypes of what Herbert Blumer calls an 'expressive social movement'. Their appearance in 1966-7 marked the temporary ascendancy of the expressive over the activist in the dialectic of generational revolt (in fact, of course, both 'moments' developed simultaneously and overlapped). There is no rigid separation between these 'moments'—indeed, it is central to the argument that they belong together and are alternative manifestations of a common mood, critique, style and form of revolutionary activity. Nevertheless, around each 'pole' one can group apparently different clusters of ideas, feelings, concepts. The expressive includes the stress on the personal, the psychic, the subjective, the cultural, the private, the aesthetic or bohemian elements in the spectrum of political emotions and attitudes. The activist 'pole', by contrast, stresses the political, the social, the collective, the engagement or

commitment to organising, the public end of the spectrum. The expressive 'moment' gives emphasis to the development of a revolutionary *style*: the activist 'moment' puts the emphasis on the development of a revolutionary *programme of issues*. The expressive often provides the language through which is tapped the subterranean, anarchic, rebellious psychic fuel—the id-forces—of rebellion: the activist phase provides the social, shaping, organising, driving thrust.[36]

Up to now I have outlined:

(*a*)   Why students have a high potentiality for forming contracultures—because of their relative isolation.
(*b*)   Why segments of middle-class youth have a motivation for deviance —because of a coincidence of expressive frustration and instrumental disinterest.

Now I wish to explain:

(*a*)   The nature of the values held by such bohemian cultures (the subcultural solution).
(*b*)   The relationship between these values and drug-taking.

Nature of bohemian culture

Bohemian cultures involving the use of drugs are often seen in the literature as being retreatist. Thus Cloward and Ohlin write: 'The participants in these drug subcultures have become alienated from conventional roles, such as those required in the family or occupational world. They have withdrawn into a restricted world in which the ultimate values consist in the "kick".'[37]
    I should like to examine the reasons why this retreatist response is said to be taken and what the nature of the response is supposed to be.

Aetiology of the retreatist response

Merton   Retreatism arises because of continued failure to reach culturally inculcated goals by legitimate measures and inability to use illegitimate means because of internalised prohibitions.

Cloward and Ohlin   These writers amend Merton's formulation suggesting that internalised prohibitions may not be necessary to bring about retreatism but rather failure in the use of illegitimate means to success, either of a criminal or a violent nature, may be a more cogent factor. This failure in both legitimate and illegitimate spheres is called 'double failure' by them.

If I am correct in my analysis of the motivation of student bohemianism, the reasons for what I have called ideological dissociation are as follows:

(a)   They have scorned the instrumental rewards offered by the system.
(b)   The system has failed to offer them expressive rewards concomitant with their aspirations.
(c)   They have set up an alternative value system which is leisure-focused and includes amongst its activities illegitimate means (namely drugs) to obtain the desired expressive ends.

This process of ideological dissociation is system-blaming—that is, it views the system as having failed the bohemian not the individual as a failure at achieving agreed cultural ends.[38] Indeed, as the bohemians have set up an alternative value system with its own 'legitimate' means they might more appropriately be described in Mertonian terms as 'rebels' rather than retreatists. That is, they have substituted new success goals and means rather than withdrawing from all idea of success and social meaning.

To counter this the subcultural theorists would argue that the principal characteristic of retreatist subcultures is that they are individualistic adaptations; they are characterised by a *lack* of culture rather than a *different* culture.

Nature of the retreatist response

Merton   For Merton the problem of the individual's continued inability to realise goals by both legitimate and illegitimate measures is resolved by 'abandoning both precipitating elements, the goals and the norms. The escape is complete, the conflict is eliminated and the individual is asocialised.'[39] The retreatist acts on impulse, he is hedonistic and sensual and essentially asocial.

Cloward and Ohlin   Although agreeing with Merton up to a point they argue that the druguser must to some extent affiliate with others and form a social group as:
(a)   Obtaining drugs necessitates social relationships—there must be an illegal market.
(b)   As Becker has argued, the novice must learn the lore of druguse.[40] But

16

despite this they deny drugusers the status of a subculture proper because they see the 'kick' as an essentially private experience and competition between drugusers for drugs as inherently divisive.

E. H. Powell. In an article on American bohemianism, Powell argues that it is a product of anomie.[41] It is, he writes, quoting Durkheim, characterised by 'a thirst for novelties, unfamiliar pleasures, nameless sensations, all of which lose their savour once known'.[42] It is, then, a normlessness typified by mindless impulsive behaviour.

Descriptions by psychologists
It is interesting to note how the sociological description of retreatism parallels the psychologists' notion of psychopathy. For example:

(*a*) 55 per cent of the drug addicts at the US Public Health Service Hospital were classified as manifesting 'psychopathic diathesis'. They exhibited marginal economic adjustment, unstable mental history and were tolerant to all forms of thrill seeking and vice.[43]
(*b*) For Isidor Chein *et al.*, the addicts, which they studied in New York, are seen to be irresponsible and pleasure seeking, desirous of shelving their adult responsibilities. They suffer from an unrealistic ego, a weak superego and inadequate masculine identification.[44] (All these attributes suggest of psychopathy.)

Thus psychologists and sociologists would seem to concur that retreatism is an asocial condition. As E. H. Powell puts it: 'The prototype of the beatnik is the psychopath—the man dissociated from his own feelings and therefore requiring even more violent jolts to jar him out of his own lethargy.'[45]

What I want to suggest is that this composite portrait of the drug subculture is a product of:

1. Generalisation from clinical cases in a hospital or prison setting.
2. Generalisation from certain types of drugtakers consuming certain drugs to all drugtakers.

For instance, it may be true that the heroin addict in America who is lower class may, at least on the surface, fit this asocial pattern.[46] But it is certainly not true of the marihuana user (with which this chapter is particularly concerned), or the middle-class addict,[47] or the criminally successful American addict.[48]
(*c*) As H. Becker astutely recognised, the labels 'anomie', 'asocial', and 'undersocialised' are often used—though chiefly unintentionally because of

17

misperception and ethnocentrism—as a weapon by certain groups against others, which are, in fact, not normless but merely possess different norms to those of the evaluating group.[49] The verbalisations involved in this 'normative reaction to normlessness' are familiar to us all:

> They are acting like animals.
> They are not human.
> They are philistines: They have no culture.

Gwynn Nettler comments on this use of anomie: 'to call all deviant norms non-norms is inadequate sociological description. It also denies authenticity to the disgruntled.'[50] One should instead talk of the development of a new status system calibrated in terms of different values.[51]

An almost solitary exception to the general asocial description of drug subcultures is that of H. Finestone,[52] who describes in detail the development of an alternative status system by lower-class young Negroes in Chicago. Central tenets of this culture are:

1   Disdain for work.
2   Short-term hedonism, preoccupation with the 'kick'.
3   Emergence of an expressive culture centring around jazz.
4   Money must be got through manipulation ('the hustle') rather than hard work.
5   Image of 'the cat' as rejected by 'squares' yet as superior to them.
6   All activity must be voluntary. It must possess all the freedom of 'play'.

Finestone notes how these values are an almost complete inversion of those of middle-class America. I want to argue, further, that the values of bohemian cultures are related to those of the wider society in a special sort of way, namely that they are an accentuation of what David Matza has termed the *subterranean* values of society.

Theory of subterranean values

Matza and Sykes suggest that coexisting alongside the workaday values of society are series of values, which they term subterranean, manifesting themselves chiefly in leisure activities.

The values they detail are as follows:

(*a*)   *Short-term hedonism*: excitement, a search for 'kicks'.

18

(*b*)   *Disdain for work*: money must be earned easily and manipulatively through the 'hustle' and spent 'conspicuously'.
(*c*)   *Violence*: masculinity must be asserted through toughness and violence.

Society, they argue, provides certain institutionalised times for the expression of such values. Thus we have the world of leisure, of holidays, festivals and sports or—to cite a particularly apposite example—the Saturnalia of the ancient world. Thus they write: 'The search for adventure, excitement and thrill is a subterranean value that ... often exists side by side with the values of security, routinisation and the rest. It is not a deviant value, in any full sense, but must be held in abeyance until the proper moment and circumstances for its expression to arrive.'[53] They see the juvenile delinquent as an individual who accentuates these subterranean values, who presents 'a disturbing reflection or caricature' of society's values, who has an imbalance of values, overstressing the subterranean component and disdaining the values of the workaday world and who, finally, has a bad sense of timing; he expresses these values at normatively incorrect times and places.

Whereas I would agree with Matza and Sykes's conception of the bifurcation existing within the value system of society, their analysis would seem to have two major shortcomings:

(1)   Their actual tabulation of subterranean values is of an insufficiently generalised nature; one can differentiate two levels of values:

(*a*)   *General subterranean values* which are values opposite to those of the workaday world. These correspond to a high level of generality.
(*b*)   *Specific subterranean values* which are the specific manifestation of the general values in a particular social group.

Thus one of the most prominent general subterranean values is ego-expressivity and its behavioural manifestation in lower-class delinquents is violence, a reflection partly of the general subterranean value and partly of the significant place of masculinity through violence in lower-class *adult* culture. The manifestion of ego-expressivity is very different, for example, in Finestone's cats who are expressly against violence. Here it is displayed in the aesthetics of dress and behaviour.

I want to suggest that the general subterranean values are as in Table III (where they are presented as contrasts with workaday values).

The formal values are, of course, concomitant with the structure of modern industry, namely the large-scale bureaucracy embodying a system of economic rationality, high division of labour and finely woven rules of behaviour.[54]

TABLE III
The Formal and Subterranean Values

	Formal Work Values	Subterranean Values
I	deferred gratification and planning	short-term hedonism
II	conformity to bureaucratic rules	ego-expressivity
III	routine, predictability	new experience, excitement
IV	instrumental attitude to activities	activities regarded as ends in themselves
V	hard, productive work seen as a virtue	disdain for work

(2)   Matza and Sykes make little attempt to explain why certain groups decide to accentuate subterranean values at the expense of workaday norms. They, in fact, tend to portray all young people as equally committed to subterranean values. This ignores, as Downes suggests, the fact that commitment to the various forms of youth culture, embodying subterranean values, is more prevalent in certain segments of youth than in others. I have suggested that portions of middle-class youth are more committed to subterranean values than others and this is because of:

(*a*)   Lack of expressive and instrumental commitment.
(*b*)   Insulation from the rest of society which allows the *possibility* of the development of a subterranean tradition.

It is these two factors which give rise to the emergence of bohemian cultures among the middle-class young. Moreover, the content of the culture is understandable in terms of:

(*a*)   The general subterranean values.
(*b*)   The specific subterranean values—that is, the manifestation of the general values in terms of the initial culture (or culture of origin) of the middle-class student.

David Matza has, in a paper published the same year as 'Juvenile Delinquency and Subterranean Values' (1961), sketched the outline of such a bohemian culture.[55] Table IV utilises his framework, analysing its relevance to contemporary British subcultures and illustrating how the general subterranean values are manifested in forms specific to middle-class youth.

TABLE IV

Bohemian Values

General Subterranean Value	Specific Subterranean Values of Bohemianism
1. ego-expressivity	(a) *romanticism:* artistic originality and spontaneity.
	(b) *expressive authenticity:* the direct unfettered expression of mood.
2. new experience/excitement	(a) artistic spontaneity
	(b) pursuit of the unconventional personal experience, sometimes hedonistic, sometimes transcendental.
3. short-term hedonism	sexual excess, use of drugs, lack of planning or deferment of impulse.
4. non-instrumentality	*spontaneity* in artistic and personal endeavours.
5. disdain for work and workaday values	(a) *dedicated poverty:* that is a renunciation of monetary values.
	(b) *primitivism:* certain folk groups are seen as possessing subterranean values and representing the opposite of formal values, e.g. the lower-class Negro.
	(c) *mediaevalism:* rejection of bureaucratic-industrial society; man is seen to have fallen from grace but there is no vision of redemption in the future.
	(d) *monasticism:* formation of insulated communities.

21

The bohemianism of contemporary middle-class youth parallels to a high degree the values listed by Matza.[56] Ideological dissociation results in the creation of a 'new' value system, by accentuation of the subterranean values of society, and at the same time evades feelings of failure by disdaining the monetary success value of the larger society. These Bohemians, like the delinquents of Cloward and Ohlin, do not regard themselves as individuals who have failed, but collectively judge the system as having failed them. But their response is not the seeking of illegitimate means to monetary success goals as in Cloward and Ohlin's criminal subculture, but the creation of a value system less likely to fail them in terms of their expressive needs.

Drugs and subterranean values

In *The Drugtakers* I analysed the factors which determined the social valuation of a particular form of drugtaking. I concluded that it was not the drug *per se*, but the reason why the drug was taken that determined whether there would be an adverse social reaction to its consumption. The crucial yardstick in this respect is the ethos of productivity. If a drug either stepped up work efficiency or aided relaxation after work it was approved of; if it was used for purely hedonistic ends it was condemned (see Table V).

TABLE V

Drug Use and Perceived Motivations

Perceived Motivation for Use of Drug	Drugs
1. to aid productivity	caffeine (coffee and tea) cigarettes (nicotine) amphetamine use by soldiers, students, astronauts, etc.
2. to relax after work	'social' drinking prescribed barbiturates cigarettes (nicotine)
3. purely hedonistic ends	'problem' drinking marihuana, heroin, non-prescribed amphetamines

For a moment let us focus on the legitimate psychotropic drugs, remembering that 15p in every pound of British consumer spending is devoted to the purchase of alcohol and tobacco alone, not counting coffee, tea and prescribed barbiturates, amphetamines and tranquillisers.

Kessel and Walton see the function of drinking as a means of relieving the tensions created by the need in advanced industrial societies for conforming to an externally conceived system of rules.

> In simple cultures, where literacy does not exist, everyone has his place, with an importance and a dignity that the group recognises. As social differentiation increases in complex cultures more rules are required. Those individuals who find themselves hard pressed to fulfil the requirements imposed on them become anxious because they must suppress and inhibit some of their urges in order to conform.
>
> Rules check individual behaviour. As a society's rules become more complex, and especially where their enforcement is harsh and punitive, the individual has to limit the extent to which he can act solely in accord with his own wishes. In practice, restrictions are most stringent where they relate to aggressive and sexual behaviour. The threat of retaliatory punishment evokes anxiety in a person whenever sexual or hostile urges are aroused. Because these are vigorous urges, a powerful conflict situation is set up in the individual. From time to time recourse may be had to alcohol to facilitate release of these proscribed urges.[57]

I would agree with the above authors up to a point. It is true that alcohol is used to break down the inhibitions inculcated by modern society but it does not result in an asocial response consisting of indiscriminate aggressive and sexual urges. Rather it leads to a social area where hedonistic and expressive *values* come to the fore, replacing the bureaucratic rules of the workplace. Alcohol, in short, is used as a *vehicle* which enhances the ease of transition from the world of formal values to the world of subterranean values. And the same is true for many of the myriad other psychotropic drugs used by humanity. As Aldous Huxley put it:

> That humanity at large will ever be able to dispense with Artificial Paradises seems very unlikely. Most men and women lead lives at the worst so painful, at the best so monotonous, poor, and limited that the urge to escape, the longing to transcend themselves if only for a few moments, is and has always been one of the principal appetites of the soul. Art and religion, carnivals and saturnalia, dancing and listening to oratory—all these have served, in H. G. Wells's phrase, as Doors in the Wall. And for private, for everyday use there have always been chemical intoxicants. All the vegetable sedatives and narcotics, all the euphorics that grow on trees, the hallucinogens that ripen in berries or can be

squeezed from roots—all, without exception, have been known and systematically used by human beings from time immemorial. And to these natural modifiers of consciousness modern science has added its quota of synthetics—chloral, for example, and benzedrine, the bromides, and the barbiturates.

Most of these modifiers of consciousness cannot now be taken except under doctor's orders, or else illegally and at considerable risk. For unrestricted use the West has permitted only alcohol and tobacco. All the other chemical Doors in the Wall are labelled Dope, and their unauthorised takers are Fiends.[58]

These doors in the wall open into the world of subterranean values. They allow us to step out into a world free of the norms of workaday life not—let me repeat—into an asocial world. For there are norms of appropriate behaviour when drunk or 'stoned' just as there are norms of appropriate behaviour when sober. For the effects of drugs, although physiologically induced, are socially shaped. We have definite expectations or roles of appropriate and reprehensible behaviour while 'under the influence'. It may be that some individuals imbibe so much that they completely lose control, but this merely underlines my argument because loss of control is defined precisely in terms of deviation from the appropriate norms of drug-induced behaviour.

It is fallacious to think of these episodes as escapes from reality. Instead we must view them as escapes into *alternative* forms of reality. For social reality is socially defined and constructed and the world of subterranean values, however ambivalently it is viewed by 'official' society, is as real as the world of factories, workbenches and conveyor belts. In fact many authors, like Huxley, would argue that the world behind the doors in the wall is more substantial and realistic than that of the formal world.

Alcohol, then, is a common vehicle for undermining the inhibitions built up by our socialisation into the work ethic. It is the key to an area of subterranean values which are, however, in our society tightly interrelated and subsumed by the work ethic. It is as if the door in the wall merely led onto an antechamber of the world of work, a place to relax and refresh oneself before the inevitable return to 'reality'. But other drugs in the hands of groups who disdain the ethic of productivity, are utilised as vehicles to more radical accentuations of subterranean reality. It is drug use of this kind that is most actively repressed by the forces of social order. For it is not drugtaking *per se* but the culture of drugtakers which is reacted against: not the notion of changing consciousness but the type of consciousness that is socially generated.

24

Bohemianism and drugs

The culture of delinquent youth is created when a body of young people are cut off from access to the material rewards which the system has to offer. The good job, the suburban house and the new car are not within their legitimate reach. Thus work and school are not only boring and stifling, they are also meaningless in the instrumental sense of being inadequate as a means of obtaining valued material goods. The response of the bohemian student is fundamentally different. Initially at least he is well capable of leading a materially successful life. But in practice he finds the rewards offered him are insufficient to warrant his conformity to the work ethic. Instead, like the delinquent, he focuses his life on his leisure, but unlike the delinquent his dissociation is a matter of choice rather than a realistic bowing to the inevitable. Moreover, his disdain for society is of an articulate and ideological nature. He evolves social theories which uphold subterranean values as authentic guides to action, and which attempt to solve the problem of the domination of the ethos of productivity.

Fit between pharmacology and culture

The major drug used by hippie communities all over the world is undoubtedly marihuana. Far behind this in frequency of use, but of almost equal importance in the pharmacopoeia of bohemia, is LSD. In *The Drugtakers* I suggested that to solve a particular problem using drugs one would expect them:

(*a*)   To have properties which are roughly pharmacologically related to the problem.
(*b*)   To be accessible.
(*c*)   To be in turn shaped to fit these problems by the culture of the group.

Marihuana is a mild and LSD an exceedingly strong hallucinogen. The major effects of hallucinogens are almost invariably reported, although there is wide cross-cultural variation. The three principal effects are: a lengthening of the experience of time, a disjunction between concepts and 'reality' and an increased awareness of the tenuous nature of the self.

The bohemian seeks his identity through the pursuit of subterranean values. He is intent on creating a culture which is hedonistic in the short term, spontaneous, expressive, exciting and unalienated. Hallucinogenic drugs facilitate such aims admirably. The lengthening of the time experience allows minute examination of the moment and a sensation of directness and immediacy.

Further, the manner in which the hallucinogens make transparent the

25

relative nature of seemingly absolute standards of conduct make them attractive to a culture that views contemporary man as alienated and social mores as mere games to be played. Culture is a game because it consists of rules created by man and sustained only by his adherence. It is alienating because these rules are thought of as existing apart from, and superordinate to, individual desires for self-expression. Identity is therefore sought in a subterranean reality. Moreover, the drugs that are vehicles to this realm promise insight into the social basis of identity; they invite an exciting exploration, a 'trip' through the esoteric pathways of the psyche.

Accessibility

Marihuana is available in Britain:

(a)   In areas with long-standing bohemian cultures.
(b)   In areas where there are large concentrations of West Indians.

Both long-standing bohemian and West Indian communities tend to occur in deteriorated neighbourhoods and these are precisely the types of area where there are many bed-sitters, where large numbers of middle-class youth and particularly students live. Moreover, the culture of West Indians is attractive to emergent bohemian groups because it emphasises precisely the same subterranean values (witness Finestone's account of lower-class Negroes in Chicago mentioned earlier). 'In the modern rendition of bohemianism', writes Matza, 'the mantle of idealised folk has largely fallen on the lower-class negro'.[59]

Conclusions

1.   Certain segments of middle-class youth, especially students, face exceptional frustrations of an expressive nature at the same time as having relatively little instrumental involvement with their course.
2.   These high expressive and low instrumental demands represent an accentuation of the culture of the noncommercial middle-class wherein a high proportion of these students originate.
3.   These expressive ideals are exacerbated by long exposure to competitive and democratic ideals of the educational system.
4.   The potentiality for the formation of contracultures among these youths is related to their isolation from adult society and to their lack of payoffs from their study situation.

5. A major subcultural solution to these problems is bohemianism which is leisure focused and which originates through a process of ideological dissociation involving the genesis of new ends and institutionalised means of obtaining them.

6. These ends and means are derived from the accentuation of the subterranean component of the dominant value system and a rejection of the formal component.

7. Drugs are used as vehicles in all cultures for the transition from the formal to the subterranean value systems.

8. Legal psychotropic drug use represents an adjunct to the conventional balance between formal and subterranean values.

9. The bohemian value system, involving as it does a qualitatively different appraisal of subterranean values, will seek drugs which enhance this conception of reality and will not resort to those drugs which are under the hegemony of the wider culture.

10. The drug marihuana is of most prevalent use in bohemian cultures because it is most physiologically suitable for this task and because it is highly accessible in the type of area where individuals who are actually involved or beginning to be involved in the culture are likely to reside.

Notes

[1] For an excellent discussion of the subcultural approach see Downes, David Malcolm *The Delinquent Solution: A Study in Subcultural Theory* (Routledge & Kegan Paul, London 1966). Especially ch.1.

[2] I develop such a sociological interpretation of drug use in *The Drugtakers: The Social Meaning of Drug Use* (Paladin, London 1971).

[3] See Young, J., 'The Student Drugtaker: The Subculture of Drug Use in a London College' (London University unpublished PhD thesis) and Young, J., and Crutchley, J., 'Student Drug Use', *Drugs and Society* vol. II, pp. 11–15.

[4] Matza, David *Delinquency and Drift* (Wiley, New York/London 1964).

[5] Rex, J. 'Students and Revolution', *New Society* II, p. 792 (30 May 1968).

[6] Yinger, J., 'Contraculture and Subculture', *American Sociological Review* vol. XXV (October 1960).

[7] Musgrove, F. *Youth and the Social Order* (Routledge & Kegan Paul, London 1964), ch. 7.

[8] Cohen, A. K. *Delinquent Boys: The Culture of the Gang* (Free Press, New York 1955).

[9] Cloward, R., and Ohlin, L. *Delinquency and Opportunity* (Free Press, New York).

[10] See, for instance, Morris Rosenberg's excellent *Occupations and Values*

(Free Press, New York 1957). I would disagree, however, with his formulation of the instrumental and expressive benefits that derive from a job as *alternatives* as I prefer to view them as two separate dimensions of satisfaction or deprivation.

[11] They have, in Becker's terms, made 'sidebets' in their commitment to future occupational roles which constrains their out-of-work activities. See Becker, H. S., 'Notes on the Concept of Commitment', *American Journal of Sociology* vol. LXVI (1960), pp. 32 et seq.

[12] Becker and Carper, in their analysis of student identification with their future professions, describe precisely such a group. The philosophy students they studied were instrumentally frustrated because of chronic job shortages, yet remained committed to an 'intellectual ideal'. Their theoretical orientation was basically hostile to the predominant school of thought within their department. See Becker, H. S., and Carper, J. W., 'The Development of Identification with an Occupation', *American Journal of Sociology* vol XLI (1956), pp. 289 et seq.

[13] Downes, op. cit., pp. 236–7.

[14] Cotgrove, S. and Parker, S., 'Work and Non-work', *New Society* vol. XLI (11 July 1963), pp. 18–19.

[15] Cloward and Ohlin, op. cit., p. 85.

[16] See Wilmott, P. *Adolescent Boys of East London* (Penguin, Harmondsworth 1969), Downes, op. cit., Musgrove, op. cit.

[17] Turner, R. H., 'Modes of Ascent Through Education', in *Education, Economy and Society: A Reader in the Sociology of Education*, ed. Halsey, A. H., Floud, Jean, and Anderson, C. Arnold (Free Press, New York/Collier-Macmillan, London 1965), ch. 12.

[18] Downes, op. cit., p. 261.

[19] 15 per cent of young people aged 17 were at school in 1962. 5.8 percent go to university and these are overwhelmingly of middle-class background, in the ratio 6.5:1. See Robbins Report Pt I p. 11; Pt II p. 54. (Higher Education *Report of the Prime Minister's Committee on Higher Education* HMSO, London 1963).

[20] Halsey, A. H., 'A Criticism of Turner's Sponsored Mobility vs. Contest Mobility', *American Journal of Sociology* vol. XXVI (1961), p. 454.

[21] Talcott Parsons has outlined the nature of such inculcation of democratic ideology by the educational system in 'The School Class as a Social System' in *Education, Economy and Society*, op. cit.

[22] Ferdynand Zweig's study of student attitudes in Manchester and Oxford bears this out. See *The Student in the Age of Anxiety* (Heinemann, London 1963).

[23] Merton, R. K., *Social Theory and Social Structure*, revised ed. (Free Press, New York 1957).

[24] See, for example, 'The Fate of Idealism in a Medical School', Becker, H., and Geer, B., *American Sociological Review* vol. XXIII (1958), pp. 50–6.

[25] Incidentally, the attitudes of pupils in grammar schools are of an overwhelmingly instrumental nature (see Musgrove, Frank *The Family, Education and Society*, Routledge & Kegan Paul, London 1966). This only serves in many cases to intensify their expressive aspirations at university.

[26] Flacks, Richard, 'Social and Cultural Meanings of Student Revolt', *Social Problems* vol. XVII (Winter 1970), p. 346.

[27] Ibid. p. 350.

[28] Parkin, Frank *Middle Class Radicalism* (Manchester University Press, Manchester 1968), p. 178.

[29] Flacks, op. cit., pp. 355–6.

[30] Flacks, R., 'The Liberated Generation', *Journal of Social Issues* vol. XXIII (1967), p. 63.

[31] Parkin, op. cit., pp. 173–4.

[32] What makes one culture not merely an accentuation of another but qualitatively different is a moot point depending on the definer. But relevant definers, here, would be the mass media and the liberal professions, both of whom, themselves, tend to see it as contracultural although they are quick to claim its more positive and large-scale influences as subcultural (i.e. hippies are merely acting out our own cherished ideals). It is problems of this order that make David Matza's claim that delinquents are a *subculture* who simply accentuate general subterranean values, an oversimplification.

[33] Flacks, R., 'Social and Cultural Meanings of Student Revolt' *Social Problems*, vol. XVII (Winter 1970), pp. 349–50. See also the parallel remarks made by Jurgen Habermas on the West German Student Movement in *Towards a Rational Society* (Heinemann, London 1971).

[34] See Galbraith, John Kenneth *The New Industrial State* (Penguin, Harmondsworth 1969).

[35] The fashion in which the same Negroes in American ghettos systematically try delinquent, retreatist ('righteous dope fiend'), religious (Black Muslim), and political (Black Panther) solutions in response to the same 'objective' problems gives some indication of the need to discuss the open-ended, problematic and historical nature of the subcultural project. See Malcolm X *Autobiography* (Penguin, Harmondsworth 1964), Ellison, R., *The Invisible Man* (Penguin, Harmondsworth 1965), Seale, B. *Seize The Time* (Arrow Books, London 1970).

[36] Hall, S. 'The Hippies', in *Student Power*, ed. Nagel, J. (Merlin Press, London 1969), pp. 198–9.

[37] Cloward and Ohlin, op. cit., p. 20.

[38] For a discussion of the factors which lead to system-blaming rather than

self-blame for failure, see Cloward and Ohlin op. cit., p. 121.

39 Merton op. cit., pp. 153–4.

40 Becker, H. S., 'Marihuana Use and Social Control', *Social Problems* vol. III (1955) p. 35.

41 'Beyond Utopia' ch. 19 of *Human Behaviour and Social Processes* ed. Rose, A. M. (Houghton Mifflin, Boston/Routledge & Kegan Paul, London 1962).

42 Durkheim, E. *Suicide*, tr. Spaulding, John, A. and Simpson, George (Free Press, New York 1951), p. 256. This interpretation by Durkheim of expressive cultures reflects his profound antiromanticism. For a discussion of this see Young, J., 'New Directions in Subcultural Theory', in *Contributions to Sociology* ed. Rex, J. (Routledge & Kegan Paul, London 1973).

43 Cited by Ausubel, D. *Drug Addiction* (Random House, New York 1958), p. 43.

44 Chein, I. *et al. Narcotics, Delinquency and Social Policy* (Tavistock, London 1964).

45 Powell, op. cit., p. 367.

46 For instance see the descriptions of such addicts in Trocchi, A. *Cain's Book* (Calder, London 1963) and Burroughs, W. *The Naked Lunch* (Corgi, London 1968).

47 See Winick, C., 'Physician Narcotic Addicts', *Social Problems* vol. IX (1964), pp. 174–86.

48 See Sutter, Alan 'The World of the Righteous Dope Fiend', *Issues in Criminology* vol. II (1966), pp. 177–222. The righteous dope fiend certainly does not fit this picture although Sutter's 'garbage junkie' may well do so.

49 See Becker, H., 'The Normative Reaction to Normlessness', *American Sociological Review* vol. XXV (December 1960).

50 Nettler, G., 'Anomie, Comment on McClosey and Schaar', *American Sociological Review* vol. XXX (October 1965).

51 For a discussion of conflict strategies utilised in order to deem alternative realities asocial see Young, *The Drugtakers*, op. cit., ch. 3.

52 Finestone, H. 'Cats, Kicks and Color' in *The Other Side: Perspectives on Deviance* ed. Becker, Howard S. (Free Press, New York/Collier-Macmillan, London 1964).

53 Matza, D., and Sykes, G., 'Juvenile Delinquency and Subterranean Values', *American Sociological Review* vol. XXVI (1961), p. 716.

54 For a more developed treatment of the theory of subterranean values see Young, J., 'The Hippie Solution: An Essay in the Politics of Leisure', in *Politics and Deviancy* ed. Taylor, I., and Taylor, L. (Penguin, Harmondsworth, 1973).

55 Matza, D., 'Subterranean Traditions of Youth', *Annals of the American Academy* (1961), pp. 102 et seq.

[56] There are, however, certain discrepancies: contemporary British bohemianism is both mediaevalist in its perception of civilisation's fall from grace and radical in that it envisages possible utopian futures. It is monastic in that it insulates itself from the outside world yet it is evangelist in that it desires to convert the uncommitted. It despises monetary success in itself but at the same time it idealises individuals who make considerable sums of money in a manner concomitant with subterranean values—pop singers, for example. Now, Matza separates out three major subterranean traditions: the delinquent, the radical and the bohemian, contemporary British (and American). Bohemianism, in that it is to some extent evangelistic and utopian, has tendencies towards Matza's radicalism, and, in that it is ambivalent about conspicuous consumptions, shares some common ground with delinquency. I discuss these contradictions in 'The Hippie Solution' and in Van Zanten, N., and Young, J. *The Romantic Movement: A Social History of Bohemianism* (forthcoming).
[57] Kessel, Neil, and Walton, Henry *Alcoholism* (Penguin, Harmondsworth 1965), p. 413.
[58] Huxley, Aldous *The Doors of Perception*, in *The Doors of Perception and Heaven and Hell* (Penguin, Harmondsworth 1959), pp. 51–2.
[59] Matza, op. cit., p. 112.

Cultural Revolution or Alternative Delinquency: an Examination of Deviant Youth as a Social Problem

MIKE BRAKE

> The young people of today love luxury. They have bad manners, they scoff at authority and lack respect for their elders. Children nowadays are real tyrants, they no longer stand up when their elders come into the room where they are sitting, they contradict their parents, chat together in the presence of adults, eat gluttonously and tyrannise their teachers.
>
> *Socrates*

A considerable interest since the Second World War in the reputably wild social life of the young has led to them being defined as a social problem. Their reputed affluence, means that, as Friedenberg says,

> ... only as a customer ... are adolescents favourably received. Otherwise they are treated as a problem, and potentially as a threatening one. ... Adults attribute to them a capacity for violence and lust, in this respect teenagers serve the rest of us as the occasion both for wish fulfilment and for self-fulfilling prophecy. Adolescents are grouped together by adults, and defined as a problem, and yet we must ask ourselves whether this problem refers to something in the adolescent, or whether it is making a statement about our society.[1]

The unfavourable attitude to youth has arisen because society, in order to continue the *status quo*, must socialise the young into certain sets of values—concerning, for example, the family and work—and into accepting certain positions in the social structure. If the young are not socialised into conventional political and ethical outlooks, if they are not programmed into regular work habits, then society as it is today cannot continue. Once the young are sufficiently bound to society by the responsibilities of maintaining dependants, and by financial commitment, then the situation takes care of itself. The young are, in addition, often in the vanguard of changes in moral behaviour, and as such subject to conservative backlash. The strength of

33

socialising pressures such as work and the family can be judged by the fact that most young people are fairly conventional in behaviour and values. The rest are categorised as social problems because, in this way, any implicit or overt criticism that they make of society has its legitimation removed.

In the last decade, a new residual category has been invented to deal with cultural and behavioural changes in the young. This is the mythical monster of youth culture, presented as some sort of commercialised temptress, leading the young astray from their proper concern with work and study. It has been described by scholars with moral indignation disguised as scientific detach-ment (in the manner usually reserved for the publications of colleagues) and has revealed only the sheltered lives led by the writers when young. Fortu-nately the position is beginning to change,[2] although it is not helped by the inaccurate stereotyping by the mass media.

Youth culture, I would argue, is not some structural monolith appealing to all ages and classes under 30, but a complex kaleidoscope of several adoles-cent subcultures, in which myth and reality possess a tortured relationship. They appeal to different groups and involve different age groups. They appeal to the young along traditional class lines similar to the adult culture. The self-images, values, behaviour and life-styles of these subcultures are quite different, and they involve people who mostly have nothing to do with the other groups involved. They reflect traditional class lines and, even more so, educational background.

The behaviour of the young has traditionally been explained in terms of neo-Freudian pathology with appeals to clinical psychology. The idea that the young may have different values, as opposed to an arrested development, was first suggested in a sociological sence by Parsons.[3] Teenage culture, as the concept was first known, was seen as an area of hedonistic irresponsi-bility which culminated in generational conflict. That teenage culture possessed class divisions was pointed out by Smith,[4] and Coleman first drew attention to the differential status rewards in the American high-school system, many of which are counter to the academic value system.[5] Jessie Bernard[6] pointed out the important fact that teenagers reflected the class cultures of their parents, and that class pervaded all aspects of the cultural elements of the teenage world. She also pointed out that the teenage culture was a leisure culture. However, most young people, as Berger shows,[7] pass more or less painlessly through to adulthood without being involved in teenage culture, or at least those aspects of it seen as deviant. Elkin and Westley[8] show that most youngsters do not become involved in what Yinger[9] describes as a contraculture, that is a culture oppositional to the adult normative system.

The earlier sociological work was concerned with the behaviour of delin-quent working-class youth. Delinquency, mainly in the form of theft and violence was seen as a phenomenon among young working-class males. The Chicago school[10] emphasised the ecological features which generated the culture of the slum and the ghetto. The street was seen as a subterranean high school for the street-corner peer group, with its cooperative solidarity and its group loyalty. The street acts as playground and mentor for the juvenile, who with little else to take pride in, makes it into a defensible territory. If you cannot get out you can keep others out. The traditional close face-to-face interaction in a working-class street, gossip (an informal telling system), the pub and the street market create the scenario for everyday life to be played against. The subcultural work of Cloward and Ohlin, Cohen and Miller[11] accurately emphasises the use of the delinquent subculture as a response to the low status imposed by middle-class institutions such as the school, with its emphasis on a meritocratic education system. However, the appearance of various cultural phenomena of a middle-class nature on the youth culture scene led to the problem of deviant behaviour among other youth groups. The 'social problem' of delinquency was joined by the 'social problem' of the dropout, and the politically militant student. Drug-taking and violent resistance to the authorities became of wide concern to the adult society. Explanations of a positivistic nature were offered; these argued that the deviant had somehow failed society, rather than the other way round.

It is a mistake to argue that all these phenomena are part and parcel of the same culture of youth. There is no general culture common to those under 30 as such. To argue this is to overlook the attachments young people from different aspects of the class structure have to the hopes, occupations, educational and vocational opportunities open to them. It overlooks the restrictions and pressures differentially experienced by those in different parts of the class structure. Certainly some strands of certain subcultures, such as the hippie or freak subculture appear superficially to be international, but in fact the subculture varies from country to country. The self-images of the young within the same country differ, as do their views of the world, their values and attitudes. These subcultures are in fact different worlds. The freak dropping mescaline before tripping out on acid rock has nothing to do with the skinhead boozing up before getting into a punch-up on the terraces while watching Spurs play at home. There are cultural differences: if you like reggae, you do not listen to the Grateful Dead. To argue that if you are, say, a freak then, because you are in the same age group as hell's angels, rockers, greasers or student radicals, you are part of the same culture is to say that Louis Armstrong and Herbie Hancock are soul brothers because they are black musicians.

A series of subcultures is more useful as a working concept if sociological analysis is to proceed beyond the mass-media stereotype. By a subculture, I mean a system of shared symbolic experiences, which evolve a set of sympathetic norms, that is set apart from the larger value system. These norms support and develop the thrust of a shared collective life-style which is set apart from the greater more traditional style of life in society.

The reasons for the development of these subcultures is interesting. Deviant behaviour among the young is an extension of the world they come into contact with, and around which they construct a series of meanings. These meanings differ according to the specific location of the actor in the social structure. 'Deviant behaviour ... is a meaningful attempt to solve the problems faced by a group or an isolated individual—it is not a meaningless pathology.[12] Subcultures arise then as attempts to solve certain problems in the social structure, which are created by contradictions in the larger society. To reduce these to some form of collective clinical pathology is to remove from the argument the contradictions inherent in the social system itself. Youth is not in itself a problem, but there are problems created, for example, by the conscription of the majority of the young into the lower strata of a meritocratic educational system and then allowing them only to take up occupations which are meaningless, poorly paid and uncreative. Working-class subcultures attempt to infuse into this bleak world, excitement and colour during the short respite between school and settling down into marriage and adulthood. In addition, youthful subcultures are not, as Berger[13] accurately suggests (much to the relief of over-thirties), just the domain of the young but of the youthful in outlook. Some subcultures, such as certain bohemian subcultures, continue along much wider age ranges, while others fade away as they become first the subculture of the 18-year-olds, then of younger and younger people until they become the contemptible bubble-gum or teenyboppers' culture. Youthful subcultures can be subdivided into four main areas:

(a) *Respectable or 'straight' youth.* This involves the majority of young people, most of whom pass through adolescence without any particularly overt deviant behviour.

(b) *Delinquent youth.* These are the typical young offenders against the law. Generally they are working class. The boys have been involved with violence or theft, and the girls have had their sexual behaviour used to bring them before the authorities. In this group are found mods and rockers, hell's angels and other motor-cycle gangs, skinheads and smoothies, and teddy boys.

(c) *Cultural rebels.* This group are adventurers in 'la vie de bohème'. Among them are found the fringes of the literary-artistic world, including beatniks, freaks and hippies who have come into contact with the law through drug use. They also include the mystical religious sects such as Krishna Consciousness, adherents of transcendental meditation, followers of Meher Baba and the primitive evangelical Jesus freaks.

(*d*)   *Politically militant youth*. These are the politically conscious young, al-most entirely of a leftwing orientation. They include ethnic groups like the Black Panthers and the Young Lords, civil-rights movements like SNCC, anti-Vietnam-war groups, pacifist groups like CND, and student groups such as SDS and the New Left.

Matza[14] suggested a similar typology but failed to differentiate the important intra-group differences, although he does point out the important aspect that subterranean values play in these groups.

An examination of what problems are solved by recruitment into various subcultures gives us some idea of the actor's entry into them. The problems arise from certain inherent contradictions of the socioeconomic structure which the actor becomes aware of. However, his subjectivistic perception and interpretation of these problems are limited by the parochial locale of the neighbourhood he lives in and his location in the class structure. The apparent range of voluntaristic selections he can make, in terms of choosing which subculture to adhere to, is in fact limited both subjectively and struc-turally. If you live on a working-class housing estate in East London, where all the other boys are skinheads, you do not, unless you are heavily into masochism, choose to become a hippie. The choices are less structured further up the scale, although one seldom meets middle-class skinheads (or if a skinhead is middle class he hides it). At the individual level it could be argued that a form of differential identification occurs in terms of selecting a youth culture. Glaser says[15]

> The image of behaviour as role-playing, borrowed from the theatre, presents people as directing their actions on the basis of their concep-tions of how others see them. The choice of another from whose per-spective we view our own behaviour is the process of identification. It may be with immediate others, or with distant and perhaps abstractly generalised others of our preference groups. ... Acceptance by the group with which one identifies oneself and conceptions of persecution by other groups are among the most common and least intellectual bases for rationalisation by criminals'.

and this does usefully suggest that the individual interacts with certain reference groups to create a self image. Reference groups involve; as Run-ciman shows, 'reference groups are bound up with relative deprivation.'[16] The choice of reference group—in this case adolescent subcultures—comes from parameters set by the social structure itself. People have to select a reference group because of problems created by contradictions in society. An example is the problem of coping with being black in a white racist society. It is not that a black person is part of a minority group that is important (in South Africa one is part of a majority if one is black), but that society creates an ideology where all that is beautiful, intelligent and desirable in a human is moulded in a white Caucasian image. A group like the Black Panthers will return to its members their pride and humanness. Such a group also creates the idea that one can actively do something about one's position, one is not some passive creature controlled fatalistically by something one has no power over. The reference group creates consciousness and solidarity. Similarly, working-class children in England internalise a sense of failure at school without realising that the educational system is structured to create a majority of failures. In order to cope with these cues of failure, working-class young people fatalistically accept school and work as something one has no interest in. A meaningful work life is an alien concept to them. What sort of problems do subcultures solve for the young?

(a) They offer a collective solution to structural problems created by the internal contradictions in the larger society.

(b) They offer a collective identity containing certain cultural elements of style, sets of values and ideologies, which differ from those offered by home, school and work.

(c) They offer, through expressive elements and leisure, a meaningful way of life which has been removed from the instrumental world of work.

(d) They offer, at an individual level, solutions to certain existential problems. Adolescence is a period of reshaping ideas and values, and also an important time for socialisation. Young people can shop around for certain elements of identity which they can incorporate into a self-image.

One common problem found in most adolescent subcultures is the problem of coping with disenchantment with the educational system. This is overcome by the process of what David Downes calls 'dissociation'.[17] The English working-class boy who has received no proper skills at school and who is prepared for a dead-end job does not revolt; what occurs

> ... is an opting out of the joint middle-class and skilled-working-class value system, whereby the lame adolescent of semi and unskilled origins is enjoined to either 'better himself' or to 'accept his station in life'. To insulate themselves against the harsh implications of this creed, the adolescent in a 'dead-end' job in a 'dead' neighbourhood extricates himself from the belief in work as of any importance beyond the simple provision of income, and deflects what aspirations he has left into areas of what has been termed 'non-work'.[18]

Downes quotes Cotgrove and Parker's point that

> Satisfaction from work and the significance attached to it will depend
> not only on the nature of the work, but also on the expectations that the
> individual brings to his job. ... For the less able child in the lower forms
> of the secondary modern school, the dominant picture that emerges is
> one of school as a source of boredom and frustration. ... Many expect
> little from work and are satisfied with what they find, even though the
> work is repetitive and makes few demands. The secondary modern boy
> leaving school at 15 has received early training in dissociating himself
> from the demands which 'they' make upon him. He simply does not
> care ... dissatisfaction is the measure of the gap between aspiration and
> achievement. For many, no such gap exists—their expectations and
> aspirations are centred on the world outside the factory.[19]

During the last year at school, Hargreaves[20] has shown that two subcultures
form, the higher streams identify with the academic pupil role while the lower
streams form a status mirror image, dissociating from school and forming
a 'deliquescent' subculture. These are the boys of whom

> It has become clear over the years that these children see school almost
> entirely in terms of the day-to-day and hour-to-hour tasks that we im-
> pose upon them. ... they were in school because they had to be. ... it is
> a place where *they* make you go, and where *they* tell you to do things,
> and where *they* try to make your life unpleasant if you don't do them,
> or don't do them right.[21]

Feeling no control over their school life, they invest their energy in the youth
subcultures to be found outside of school. It is culture which they use to
create some sort of identity.

> In the absence of work orientation, and job satisfaction, and lacking the
> compensation accruing from non-work ... the 'corner-boy' attaches
> unusual importance to leisure. There is no reason to suppose that the
> delinquent 'corner-boy' does not share the more general technically
> classless 'teenage culture', a culture whose active pursuit depends on
> freedom from the restraints of adult responsibility, but which reflects
> the 'subterranean values' of the adult world. ...[22]

Sugarman reports similar findings for his London schoolboy sample. Those
who dissociated from school identify with a role from the external youth
culture

This is the role of 'teenager' which is roughly an inversion of the official pupil role. In place of the officially expected deferred gratification, it puts an emphasis on spontaneous gratification or hedonism.[23]

Sugarman explains this

> Boys strongly committed to the teenager role and to the youth culture ... are on the whole rebelling against the norms imposed by the school, and performing academically below expectation. ... youth culture defined and measured in this sense is the culture of the mobile working class; the downwardly mobile and those who cherish hopes of mobility along channels where the criteria do not apply.
>
> It is no accident that the heroes of youth culture, pop singers, songwriters, clothes designers and others have mostly achieved their positions without long years of study, work or sacrifice. ... youth culture is the new opium of the teenage masses. ... it may not be true that all boys with bad conduct have long hair, at the same time it may also be true that all boys with long hair do have bad conduct.

These headmasterly comments not only fail to differentiate the complex strata of youth culture, but also fail to see the irony that songwriting, designing and the practice of musical instruments are difficult skills requiring technical mastery and time that are beyond the reach of the average working class kid.

Middle-class boys also dissociate from the educational system, but in their case it comes at the level of further education, not secondary. A boring curriculum preparing the student for a dreary and not very well paid job led to the dropout culture of the hippies. A demand for spontaneous hedonism led to the use of hallucinogenic drugs. In particular the use of psychedelic drugs meant the development of acid rock, communal life, pop art and the individual, mystical revolution.

There are noticeably different things about the middle-class and working-class subcultures. Middle-class education encourages greater articulation of criticism of the world and also develops individual autonomy in the sense that one is encouraged to believe one can get up on the received world and change it. Working-class subcultures are a temporary filling in of the time before marriage; they are temporary, part-time subcultures, but the middle-class subcultures can become a way of life in terms of full-time commitment. This is greatly aided by the use of the period spent at college or university. Working-class adolescents seldom leave home, except to get married and so they never explore alternative subcultures. The middle class go away to college, and develop both social and geographical exploratory journeys. It is they who go to Nepal, to San Francisco and the hip capitals of the world. The middle-class culture of the freak is then developed from the bohemian student culture, especially the culture of the art student.

Members of adolescent youth subcultures draw upon the subterranean norms of their class background. Working-class delinquents become involved in theft because on the one hand there is pressure through mass-media advertising to gain consumer goods (a process that is necessary for the continuation of capitalism) and on the other hand there is a value system which has an ambiguous and complicated attitude to theft. It is always possible, for example, to buy things in a working-class community which 'fell off a lorry'.

Violence grows in a culture which respects the machismo values of the hard man, and where fist fights continue into early middle age; where it is essential to be able 'to look after yourself'. The value system develops out of the violence done to the working class in the slums and ghettos. In a dreary life you go where the action is, fighting, gambling, football or nicking. You do not get off the pavement when you are three abreast, because you are fed up with being ordered about; you stare at people until they look away and if they do not you ask them what they are looking at. In this way fighting breaks out, but it partly breaks out because you are in a situation you can never financially afford to leave.[24] Middle-class youthful subcultures have developed differently. The control of physical aggression is part of middle-class life, and the response of middle-class deviants has been to develop nonviolence. The effect of the use of hallucinogenic drugs has been to escalate the values of love and peace, and develop metaphysical explanation as a means of analysing the world.

At this stage let us examine certain aspects of the thematic structure of youthful subcultures, and their development since the end of the Second World War.[25] A. Cohen has pointed out the importance of investigating 'The process of progressive involvement in, commitment to and movement among social roles, and the processes whereby one learns the behaviour that is significant of the roles'.[26] He suggests

An actor learns that the behaviour signifying membership in a particular role includes the kinds of clothes he wears, his posture, and gait, his likes and dislikes, what he talks about and the opinions he expresses...

These expressive and symbolic elements make up what I would call 'style'. Style, expressed in the cultural aspects of youthful subcultures, is important because it marks who does, and who does not, belong. It marks out the social world one wants to identify with, and accentuates to the outside world one's inner self-image. It indicates where one is at by the use of clothing;

41

for example, seventeenth-century dandies wore silk and lace to show they did not have to work, that they were aristocrats. Style is not merely fashion, because mass consumption kills style. When Woolworths starts selling hippie bells, then it means no hippie is wearing them. Let us examine the style in various youthful subcultures.

Delinquent youth

There developed during the fifties in working-class youth an open rejection of polite, middle-class values. This rebellious thrust negated the smug notion of well-integrated cultural pluralism and, while it was not political resistance, it did disturb the respectable sufficiently to cause a severe mass-media reaction. In England a distinct creator of style was the teddy boy. Possibly as a reaction to a dreary postwar England they developed the first postwar English working-class dandyism. Establishment psychiatry was shocked, seeing mother-dominated latent homosexuality in every working-class pub. The teds quickly became stigmatised as cosh boys,[27] and their hair—quiffed at the front with brushed back and sides—their long jackets, drainpipe trousers and bootlace ties struck terror throughout the country. At one time the British Army banned its soldiers from wearing ted gear out of uniform.

Another cultural shock developed at this time, and this was the birth of rock and roll, the white folks' R & B. The rise of the unrespectable had started.

In the United States the cult of sartorial elegance never developed as in England, except among young blacks. The whites tended to sport denim jeans and black leather jackets, but it was the black 'cool cat' and the hipster who were really into clothes. Among the poor, to be ostensibly and mysteriously well-off indicates that one has made the money scene, without being forced into respectability. In America delinquency was complicated by the fact that most of the poor were members of minority groups. The violent gangs became a source of terror to the respectable while a romanticised view of them grew up in the hipster. The hipster heroes were James Dean and the early Brando. Mailer argued 'the hipster came from the muted rebellion of the proletariat', but on the whole most people were responding to middle-class stereotypes of the romantic outsider type. The hipster in real life is to be found in the cool cat. Often black, a sharp dresser, he had a taste for foxy chicks but avoided relationships. He used the ghetto drug of total commitment—heroin. He dealt daily with the problems of employers, chicks, and the man by using his wits and his skilful conversation. He avoided violence, using his cool to remain above the 'gorilla' who, with his strong-arm tactics, was neither cool nor hip. He hustled bread by using a series of themes based on begging, borrowing and stealing. His superior taste was shown by an esoteric knowledge of progressive jazz and by sartorial elegance. Life's main purpose was the kick, the act tabooed by squares that heightens and intensifies. Finestone[28] describes this world as one in which

> the social type of the cat is an expression of one possible type of adaptation (of white society of working-class black youth) in which a segment of the population turns in upon itself and attempts to develop within itself criteria for the achievement of social status and a satisfactory life...

Conventional values are despised and attacked. The emphasis of the kick attacks the notion of planning and responsibility. Play becomes a dominant theme in every-day life. These are solutions to the problems of ghetto urban life in a white racist middle-class society.

Another predominant theme which has continued through to the present time is the motorbiker. In England this first came to the notice of the public as the trunk roads and motorways developed. The motorcycle has always been a working-class machine, and bikers are mainly working-class boys who like to ton up the bypasses and genuinely dice with death on very powerful machines. The rockers were the first noticeable collective English movement. They wore studded, black leather jackets, heavy boots, broad studded belts which were handy in a punch up, and oil-stained denims. Their self-image was butch, they had traditional manual working-class values, machismo chivalry, mechanical ability and great solidarity to their mates, and were dominating to their girlfriends. What little empirical work that has been done on them[29] suggested they were unskilled manual working-class boys, with a realistic appraisal that their future was unlikely to change. Their view of their lot was fatalistic, and they seem to come from Hargreaves's delinquent school subculture. They accentuated their class position by using a working-class mode of transport and by wearing traditional working clothes. The riders were helmetless, accentuating the danger; only decorative but functionally useless helmets were allowed.

The most notorious American group of bikers are the hell's angels. Coming from the San Francisco Bay area, they were of all ages and quickly became notorious for their riding and their violence. A statement by the American Motorcycle Association that 99 per cent of motorcyclists were decent led them to wear '1%' as a symbol. They have heavy ritualistic initiation ceremonies and a brief flirtation with them by Berkeley intellectuals ended when they beat shit out of a peace march. As Tom Wolfe says,

> One way or the other, the Hells Angels came to symbolise the side of

the (psychedelic) adventure that panicked the hip world. The Angels were too freaking real. Outlaws? They were outlaws by choice from the word go, all the way to Edge City.[30]

The English rocker is inseparable from the mod. In the late fifties in England there was a brief spate of Italianate fashion, and this concern with appearance continued with the Mods. They tended to be grammar schoolboys in the lower streams, or semi-skilled manual working-class workers. They changed the working-class male image, so that it was no longer poovy to be clean and elegant. They were not the development of a group identifying with the middle class, but the emergence of a working-class elite. The mod could be as smart and more fashionable than anyone, regardless of his background. His clothes, his smart, shiny scooter, his new dances and his music suddenly made him a member of the smartest working class in Europe, with Carnaby Street the fashion centre of the world.

This almost-feminine clothes consciousness was not found in the English skinhead of the sixties. Probably as a reaction against the middle-class student hippies, he wore a short, almost shaven haircut; he was clean shaven, sporting industrial work boots, levi jeans (showing his attachment to the manual working-class world), which were turned up to show the boots (a symbol of his readiness to get into 'bovver'), with a smart patterned and coloured shirt and coloured braces supporting the levis. There was a return to conservative working-class values and a passionate regard for football was allied to some unpleasant racism. However, this racism had been definitely (to my mind) fostered by Conservative politicians and was the result of the fear that Britain was changing and that jobs and housing would go to the immigrant. Sooner than solve the problem by building enough houses and creating enough jobs for all, society preferred to blame the kids.

Cultural rebels

The first major middle-class deviant who came to public attention through a bohemian life-style after the war was the beatnik. Beats, although hip, were not hipsters. Hipsters were operators; they held to the visible symbols of success and they hustled hard with that end in view. Beats, however, faded into the background; they dressed unobtrusively like most working men and were mainly distinguishable by their beards. They could be subdivided into the literary-artistic movement and the larger fringe subcultural group. They formed many of the values later taken up by the hippie movement, in that they withdrew from contact with the straight world, espoused poverty voluntarily (unlike working-class delinquents who had it thrust upon them) and cut themselves off from traditional square career systems. They were concerned with the present, and not the future, and they were very concerned with existential questions, which finally led them to take up individualism. They radically criticised society, but had no clear radical political analysis, and this led them into retreating from society and pursuing individual solutions to the problems created in the social structure.[31]

In the early sixties, the beat generation was replaced by a sartorial counter-revolution, conspicuous in its finery, which assaulted the senses, in contradiction to the quiet fading into the background of the beats. This was the rise of the beautiful people, the flower children, known to the straight world as hippies. The major variable in this subcultural movement was the use of psychedelic drugs led to San Francisco becoming the acid centre of the world. Owsley, a dropped out chemist together with Ken Kesey, the novelist, formed an itinerant acid development of acid rock, found in the music of the Grateful Dead (formed by Owsley) and the Jefferson Airplane.

Dr T. Leary was meanwhile literally blowing academic minds at Harvard University, by using LSD on human volunteers.

Haight Ashbury celebrated the Summer of Love in 1967. Thousands of young people tuned in, turned on and dropped out, and this was not restricted to the USA; London and Amsterdam became hip centres in Europe and the rise of the underground spread all over the Western world.

An aristocratic dissociation from work and school, from the grey world of the nine-to-fivers, led to the attempt to form an alternative culture. This culture, however, contains within itself several important contradictions. Poverty is espoused, but this only occurs among those to whom poverty is a novelty. Dropping out of school has occurred in the USA which has probably the easiest system in the world to drop back into. Dropping out rests on the idea that there is something to drop out from. The subjective world was explored through the use of hedonistic artefacts such as drugs. This was the most dangerous of the underground's weapons because it attacked the work ethic and the supporting ideology. Not working is only possible, however, in a social structure where there is surplus. The surplus of capitalism[32] provides for an articulate, intelligent, educated dropout minority. In the end, making a living led to an alternative career structure, often as vicious as the traditional one. The groovy jobs in the underground go to the skilled—sound engineers, journalists, musicians, designers, or others with similar highly developed skills—or to the moneyed. A lot of money is made out of the alternative culture, either legitimately through financing shops, groups, films and money-making enterprises like pop festivals, or illegitimately through dope dealing, with its large profits based on exploitation, and the ugly introduction of counter-culture organised crime. On one hand there is the retreat, only possible in a warm climate, to the rural commune, and on the other the growth of the alternative bourgeoisie (in most cases not so alternative).

These contradictions show themselves in many levels. They show themselves when a 15-year-old pregnant hippie's child suffers before birth from malnutrition, or at Altamont where thousands watched the hell's angels stab a young black to death. Such social problems have led to important countermeasures such as the free clinics, and the diggers' shops, but important problems remain. The contradictions show also in the political situation; for example in Taos County, New Mexico, groovy entrepreneurs bought up 70,000 acres which, after holding a large rock concert there, they 'liberated from capitalism and gave to the people'. That is to say, to the hippies. But Taos has many dispossessed Chicanos who have been fighting for the restoration of the same land. In addition, the local rednecks were not going to have any hippies near their property. This led to a confrontation that the original entrepreneurs had avoided by returning to their New York penthouses. City-bred freaks found themselves up against a hostile and dangerous local population. Their ecological vision was vehemently attacked by an old local inhabitant.

> 'But you're just escapees', he said, 'and can't you see there ain't no place to escape to? You're trying to run away from a system, not a place, and that system is here and there and everywhere. ... New Mexico is in America... Change America and you don't have to come to New Mexico.[33]

This sound commonsense has too often been answered by a return to the individual revolution. Astrology, mysticism, faeries and the occult have been used to explain the harsh reality of a war economy and an exploiting market. As the Beatles say in 'Revolution', 'You say that it's the institution, well, you know, you better free your mind instead.' Elektra Records have pointed out that they are not the tool of anyone's revolution; the revolution will be won by poetics and not politics. To show how we are all fighting the same struggle [34] Columbia records warn us 'The Man can't bust our music', and *Rolling Stone* puts ads on the back of the *New York Times* which cost $7,000 to appeal directly to the young corporation executive.

The politically militant

The radical critique and militant stance of young people in the last 20 years is mostly to be found among the intellectual faction of the student subculture. The roots of militancy can again be traced to structural contradictions. In

America it was a concern with the civil rights movement, and the Vietnam War, and in England the growth of CND and the fear of nuclear war. The civil rights movement developed because of the obvious contradiction that a country which claimed to be democratic refused enfranchisement, educational and economic equality to its impoverished classes. These classes were black, and nowhere was the struggle more evident than in the South. It was also a struggle between federal and local legislation, and it was a continuation of the Civil War. The 1955 bus boycott in Alabama was the beginning of direct action which led to sit-ins and militant passive resistance. Student bodies such as CORE and SNCC developed, and the violent reaction they met indicated to students the violence of racism.

The move from civil rights to the militant activism of Black Power was also reflected in the anti-War movement. The student movement was threatened by conscription, and the sizeable number of draft resisters, and the force of the anti-War demonstrations, began to have their effect on the consciousness of the young. Activism spread to the campus, and the movement began to give birth to the SDS and the New Left. Students began to criticise the economic system they lived in and the Berkeley rebellion of 1964 indicated that they had began to criticise the position of education in the state socialising process and their own role in society. The university was seen as refusing to take sides in a situation because it plainly had interests in the *status quo*. Consequently the inapplicability of the curriculum to modern life came under fire. The Berkeley Free Speech Movement, the uprising at Columbia, the harsh brutality of the police at the Chicago Convention and the slaughter of the Black Panther party all played their part in developing a radical critique. The student power movement took on an international flavour as it spread to Italy, West Germany, Japan and, of course, Paris of 1968.[35]

Several interesting effects occurred. There was a realisation that man had to actively change his situation in order to create any change, there was a concern not only with national government but also with the local community (the history of Berkeley is an interesting one in this case). Disillusion with the possibilities of change in the present structure led on the one hand to the extreme urban guerrilla tactics of the Weathermen and, on the other hand, to the local community as a source of action. The lack of a clearly defined class structure, combined with the myth of the affluent lower-middle class, led in America to the expansion of other themes of revolutionary consciousness. The psychedelic left of the Yippies and the Diggers, with their Agit-prop attitude to everyday life was a result of this, as was the Women's movement, Gay Liberation Front and eccentric fringes such as the Jocks for Joints in Berkeley (a movement created by marihuana-smoking athletes). This meant a concern with psychosocial attitudes, such as male chauvinism, and a counteraction to the puritanism of the New Left, and also the development of radical consumers' organisations in the local community, Digger free shops, free clinics, legal advice centres, tenants' associations, and claimants' unions. This concentration on the micro-structure admittedly has a flavour of the utopian Electric Village, but it does mean that small-scale attacks can be made on the local landlords and administrators, and consciousness of various kinds can be developed in a humanistic atmosphere.

It is hoped that this description of the development of themes in various youthful subcultures indicates that these subcultures are not related just to an age category. Some are transient solutions to specific problems, but some are of a more enduring nature and, as a result of them, the world will not be quite the same again. The threat of these various subcultures varies considerably. Berger has accurately put the position

> The concept of a 'transitional stage' is often employed as a palliative for society's functional problems of recruiting and integrating youth into adult worlds; if it is merely 'a stage they're going through' then adults need not frankly confront the problems their behaviour raises because, after all 'they'll grow out of it.'[36]

If, on the other hand, some of them are plainly not going to grow out of it, but are proud of what they are, and are not interested in the laws of a society they feel nothing in common with, then the situation is different. The youthful subcultures allow to other groups something the middle class have always had in the university, a space, both temporal and geographical, where they can ask questions about the world and themselves, and where they can experiment with ideas and identities. The subcultures are rebellious, but they could be revolutionary. It is this possible escalation of dissent into action which threatens society, and enrages the moral entrepreneurs. The challenging of morality leads to threatening the hegemony of the state, and it is this that is feared in the cries for law and order. As long as rebellion can be stigmatised as adolescent, then it can be kept out of adult society.

Notes

1 Friedenberg, Edgar Z. 'Adolescence as a Social Problem', in *Social Problems: A Modern Approach* ed. Becker, H. (Wiley, New York 1966).
2 For a more sympathetic view of youth culture see Downes, David Malcolm *The Delinquent Solution: A Study in Subcultural Theory* (Routledge & Kegan

Paul, London 1966), Young, Jock *The Drugtakers* (Paladin, London 1971) and Cohen, Phil, 'Subcultural Conflict and Working-Class Community' in *Working Papers in Cultural Studies 2* (Spring 1972) (University of Birmingham Centre for Contemporary Studies).

3 Parsons, Talcott, 'Age and Sex in the Social Structure of the United States', in *Essays in Sociological Theory* (Free Press, New York, 1954).

4 Smith, Ernest A., *American Youth Culture* (Free Press, New York 1962).

5 Coleman, James S. *The Adolescent Society* (Free Press, New York 1961).

6 Bernard, Jessie, 'Teen Age Culture: An Overview', *The Annals of the American Academy of Political and Social Science* (Philadelphia 1961).

7 Berger, Bennett, 'On the Youthfulness of Youth Cultures', *Social Research* (September 1963).

8 Elkin, Frederick, and Westley, William A., 'The Myth of Adolescent Subculture', *American Sociological Review* (December 1965).

9 Yinger, J. Milton, 'Contraculture and Subculture', *American Sociological Review* vol. XXV (October 1960).

10 See for example Thrasher, F. W. *The Gang* (University of Chicago Press, Chicago 1960) also T. P. Morris's review in *The Criminal Area* (Routledge & Kegan Paul, London 1958).

11 Cohen, A. K. *Delinquent Boys: The Culture of the Gang* (Free Press, New York 1965), Cloward, R. A., and Ohlin, L. E. *Delinquency and Opportunity* (Free Press, New York 1960/Routledge & Kegan Paul, London 1961), Miller, W. B. 'Lower Class Culture as a Generating Milieu of Gang Delinquency' *Journal of Social Issues* vol. XIV (1958).

12 Young, J. 'New Directions in Subcultural Theory' in *Contributions to Sociology* ed. Rex, John (Routledge & Kegan Paul, London 1973).

13 Berger, op. cit.

14 Matza, David, 'Subterranean Traditions of Youth', *Annals of the American Academy* (1961), pp. 102 et seq.

15 Glaser, Daniel, 'Criminality theories and behavioural images', *American Journal of Sociology* vol. LXI (March 1956).

16 Runciman, Walter Garrison *Relative Deprivation and Social Justice* (Routledge & Kegan Paul, London 1966).

17 Downes, op. cit.

18 Downes, op. cit., pp. 236–7.

19 Cotgrove, Stephen and Parker, Stan, 'Work and Non-Work', *New Society* vol. XLI (July 1963).

20 Holt, John *How Children Fail* Pelican Books 1969.

21 Holt, op. cit.

22 Downes, op. cit.

23 Sugarman, Barry, 'Involvement in Youth Culture, Academic Achievement and Conformity in School', *British Journal of Sociology* (June 1967).

[24] For a sensitive and vivid account of this process see Brown, Claude *Manchild in the Promised Land* (Penguin, Harmondsworth 1969) which describes life in the Harlem ghetto, and Daniel, Susie and McGuire, Pete (eds) *The Paint House: Words from an East End Gang* (Penguin, Harmondsworth 1972), which discusses the attitudes of East London skinheads.

[25] This is discussed in greater detail in my forthcoming book, *The Culture of Youth.*

[26] Cohen, Albert, 'The Sociology of the Deviant Act; Anomie Theory and Beyond', *American Sociology Review* vol. XXX (February 1965).

[27] Rock, Paul and Cohen, Stanley 'The Teddy Boy', in Bognador and Skidelsky *The Age of Affluence: The Fifties* (Macmillan, London 1965).

[28] Finestone, Harold 'Cats, Kicks and Color', *Social Problems* vol. V, no. 1 (July 1957).

[29] See Barker, Paul 'The Margate Offenders' *New Society* (30 July 1964), Maguire, Alec 'Emancipated and Reactionaries', *New Society* (28 May 1964) and Cohen, Stan, 'Mods, Rockers and the Rest: Community Reaction to Juvenile Delinquency', *Howard Journal of Penal Reform* vol. XII (1967). The last study gives an excellent explanation of the role of the mass media in spreading and whipping up public reaction to an adolescent subculture cult.

[30] Wolfe, Tom *The Electric Kool-Aid Acid Test* (Bantam, London 1969).

[31] One of the few sociological studies on beats has been written by Ned Polsky: *Hustlers, Beats and Others* (Aldine, New York 1967/Penguin, London 1971). Despite his intelligent comments on methodology the work is marred by his strong disapproval of beats, shown in remarks such as 'Their [the beats'] bedhopping 'genitality' comes about precisely because they are sexually impoverished—"orgastically impotent" in Reich's terms.'

[32] Jock Young discusses some of these contradictions in 'The Hippie Solution—An Essay in the Politics of Leisure', in *Politics and Deviancy* ed. Taylor, I., and Taylor, L. (Penguin, Harmondsworth 1973). Illuminating insights by Karl Marx on surplus value and surplus labour are analysed in Nicolaus, Martin 'The Unknown Marx', in *Ideology in the Social Sciences* ed. Blackburn, R. (Fontana, London 1972).

[33] Stewart, Jon, 'Truckin' towards Taos with Tootsie', *Organ Magazine* (1970).

[34] Lydon, Michael, 'Rock for Sale' *Ramparts* (1969). This article and the one by Jon Stewart cited in note 33 are both in *Conversations with the New Reality* Editors of *Ramparts*; (Harper and Row, New York 1971).

[35] The student movement is discussed in Skolnik, Jerry *The Politics of Protest* (Simon and Schuster, New York 1969) and Cockburn, R., and Blackburn, R. *Student Power* (Penguin, Harmondsworth 1969).

[36] Berger, op. cit.

The Social Regulation of Sexual Behaviour and the Development of Industrial Capitalism in Britain

Frank PEARCE and Andrew ROBERTS

The recent revival of interest in sexual liberation has resulted in a questioning of many British institutions. But the articulation of what sexual liberation means can only be achieved dialectically through specifying, criticising and surpassing the oppression generated by these institutions. This essay is an attempt to relate the sexual frustrations and discontents of those living in bourgeois society to the changing definitions of the nature of the family, the differing contents of public morality and the development of the capitalist mode of production[1] in Britain between 1800 and the 1960s. Surpassing requires action as well as contemplation and perhaps for this it is to the liberation movements that we should look.

Before moving into the substantive analysis, we shall mention briefly certain assumptions that we do not dwell on elsewhere. We do not assume that private conduct is necessarily directly determined by public definitions of what it should be but we do think that it is always affected by such definitions, albeit in a complex way. In this article we have used the development of legislation aimed at the control of male homosexual activities as a manageable indicator of social attitudes to sexuality. It seems likely that changing social attitudes have structured the nature, meaning and incidence of such behaviour. Thus, although we assume that all men and women are potentially bisexual[2] the likely patterning of their activities is determined from their earliest moments of sociality when gender identities are assigned to them with the attendant expectations concerning appropriate conduct for someone with their particular genital equipment. The dominant definitions effecting the social organisation of sexual contact, will constantly define likely options for them and will reinforce or undermine their changing self-concepts throughout their lives. In Britain the particular content of these dominant definitions has been limited to those available in the Christian literature of the time. Which of these competing views informs public morality depends on their 'fit' with the perceived needs of capitalism, with what the press calls 'the national interest'.[3] Because of Christianity's importance it is attended to in the first section of the paper.

Christianity and sexuality [4]

In Britain discussions of morality have, for over a thousand years, been defined in relationship to the opinions of the Christian church. Indeed, until comparatively recently ecclesiatical courts have had jurisdiction over certain kinds of sexual offenders. In order to understand the moral standards applied to sexual behaviour, an analysis of the changes in the Christian atti-tude towards sexuality is required, with some attempt to relate these to the changes in the economic structure of British society. Whatever particular interpretations that have been placed on the Christian definitions of morality they have tended to use as their referents a common corpus of early Christian writings. There seems little doubt that on the whole Christianity, following on from Judaism, has tended to view sexual activity as, at best, a necessary evil. The strong Christian dualism valued highly things of 'the spirit', since they were seen as the means of achieving salvation, and denigrated things of the flesh as potential impediments to such a goal. The extent to which the flesh could be controlled was seen as problematic since 'the spirit is willing but the flesh is weak'.

The 'weakness' was compounded by the need for sexual contact for procreation to be possible. But this did little more than excuse intercourse under certain conditions.

After the Norman invasion this view of sexuality informed the separate ecclesiastical courts set up by William the Conqueror. At first sexual licen-tiousness seems to have been limited by a system of public confession, fines and public stigmatisation. Soon, when penances were commuted to mone-tary payments, and when the clergy were seen to be often the worst offenders, the system lost credibility. Throughout the period that the system operated certain offences were always seen as graver than others. Sexual activity that could not lead to procreation was particularly strongly condemned. Aquinas described such activities as the sin against nature. He was referring to masturbation, bestiality, homosexual acts and deviations from the natural manner of heterosexual coitus. The 'penitentials' similarly condemned such acts and they were dealt with by the ecclesiatical courts.

The Reformation in Britain does not seem to have substantially altered the definition of acceptable/unacceptable sexual behaviour. Moreover the Anglican church tended to share the pre-Reformation pessimism about controlling men's lusts. The moral code imposed during the Puritan inter-regnum of 1649–60 was exceptional. It became a civil offence to commit adultery, an ineffective move because juries refused to convict on this charge. But the systems of ecclesiastical courts remained and were used as important sources of social control until the late eighteenth century, their formal authority extending up to at least the time of the 1908 Prevention of Incest Act. In rural England the alliance between landlord and magistrate (as secular authority) and the Anglican clergy (as spiritual authority) was strong. The parish was the local administrative unit.

The Kings of England had long disputed with the Church its claims to exclusive jurisdiction over certain areas of conduct and particular personnel. Henry VIII, early in his reign, made buggery a felony, without benefit of clergy:

> FOR ASMOCHE as there is not yet sufficient and condigne punys-shemente appoynted and lymetted by the due course of the laws of this realm for the detestable and abomynable vice of buggerie comytted with mankynde or beaste; It may therefore please the Kynges Hyghnes with the assent of his Lords Spuall and temporall and the Comyns of the present Parliament assembled, that it may be enacted by authorytie of the same, that the same offence be from hensforth adjudged felony ... (25 Hen. 8, c.6. An ACTE for the punysschemente of the vice of Buggerie. (1533.)

This act was the basis of policing activity against 'unnatural offences' well into the nineteenth century. Buggery was virtually identical with Aquinas's 'sins against nature' and included bestiality, homosexual sodomy and heterosexual sodomy. (Sodomy in this context refers to intercourse *per anum*.) However, there was no belief that men who engaged in any of these types of behaviour were unlikely to engage in 'normal' heterosexual intercourse; such behaviours were merely viewed as possible variants of sexual practice.

In Mary MacIntosh's words 'there was no homosexual role, with its associated preclusion of heterosexual activity and justificatory belief systems.'[5] Total and exclusive commitment to homosexual activity seems to have been a rare occurrence, except in the case of certain monks, until the late nineteenth century. Homosexuality as a term was not coined until 1869, and theories of 'inversion' such as those of Havelock Ellis had little currency until that time. A careful examination of tracts such as *Satan's Harvest Home* (1749) shows that while (homosexual) sodomy is viewed as an Italian vice, one particularly practised by Cardinals and Churchmen, those who practise it are still thought typically to get married and engage in heterosexual intercourse although feebly.[6]

In nearly all cases, the men engaged in homosexual relations in Hyde's book, *The Other Love*, are also married.[7] Furthermore there seems little evidence that their marriages, in themselves, were unhappy. Respectable companionship and children seemed as typical of these cases as others. There was generally a relative indifference to such activities. In 1811 only five people were convicted of buggery, although four of them were executed.

Puritanism and the bourgeoisie

The dominance of a puritan morality in the nineteenth century brought about important changes. Without wishing to be reductionist one can argue that puritanism was associated with the rising bourgeoisie and the ascendance of puritanism in the late eighteenth century and the nineteenth century accompanied the rise of the bourgeoisie.

The breakdown of the old local method of social control (the parish) consequent upon industrialisation and urbanisation showed general cause to many of the privileged for governmental control of morality. Agitation was led by those in the Puritan/Nonconformist traditions for action about Sunday observance, adultery, 'obscene' publications (1824 Vagrancy Act) and later in the century the repeal of the Contagious Diseases Acts. The Puritan view of the relationship between sex and morality can be seen in Bunyan's *Pilgrim's Progress* (1678). This text was not only used extensively by Nonconformists but was a standard text in the nineteenth-century Sunday schools, set up to help control the poor.

In Bunyan's view salvation necessarily demanded that the things of the world should be rejected since they were either intrinsically evil or acted as snares. Wife and children, for example, could be considered as impediments to salvation. Even more so is sensuality condemned. This is clearly expressed in the names given to the daughters of Adam who are offered to Christian in marriage. The three are called 'the Lust of the Flesh', 'the Lust of the Eyes' and 'the Bride of Life'.[8] Weber provides general support for such an interpretation of this view.

> In the opinion of various Pietistic groups the highest form of Christian marriage is that with the preservation of virginity, the next highest that in which sexual intercourse is only indulged in for the procreation of children, and so on down to those which are contracted for purely erotic or external reasons and which are, from an ethical standpoint, concubinage. On these lower levels a marriage entered into for purely economic reasons is preferred (because after all it is inspired by rational motives) to one with erotic foundations.[9]

The relationship between this ethic and the economic base of the bourgeoisie was well expressed by V. F. Calverton.

> The social milieu of the aristocracy encouraged freedom of sex impulse; the economic life of the bourgeoisie encouraged repression, or at least rigid restriction, of the sex impulse. In the literature and acts of the aristocracy, therefore, we discover in matters of sex description a candour and oft-times an extravagance of expression; in the literature of the bourgeoisie, on the other hand, we find a denial of things sexual, an avoidance of sex description and a condemnation of episode or diction, of status or painting suggestive of sex-reality.
>
> This sex attitude of the bourgeoisie, in this instance of the Puritan, is but an outgrowth of the social economics of its life. It is but a rationalisation of the economics of its existence. It is but a defence mechanism unconsciously designed to protect the private-property concept upon which it has thrived.[10]

Such a world view was important for this class when struggling to establish itself. It was also important in transforming and controlling the poor. E. P. Thompson has extensively documented the transformation of Merrie Englande with the spread of such a morality among the lower classes.[11] Temperate, devout men made the best workers. A Christian family was the surest foundation of this. For the bourgeoisie the family was essentially linked with consolidation of their private property, women had no property right, adultery was viewed in relation to the property right and a man could not be convicted of raping his wife.

For the poor the family had a disciplinary function. This can perhaps be best seen by examining the debate concerning the 1842 Act prohibiting the working of women and children in the mines. After the publication of the Children's Employment Commission (Mines) Parliamentary Report earlier that year there was little doubt that there was extensive concern over the health of the children, yet their conditions of work in the mines were not worse than elsewhere. What is often underplayed, however, is the importance given in the report and in the subsequent debates, to the position of women in the mines. The Report, the press (notably editorials in *The Times*), Parliament (for example, Lord Egerton) were most appalled at the effect of the working conditions—men and women's nakedness and the alleged promiscuity — on the moral character of those present. The women were 'corrupted' by such debauchery and were rendered incapable of being 'good' wives and mothers. A typical testimony from the report said:

I dare venture to say that many of the wives who come from the pits know nothing of sewing or any household duty, such as women ought to know — they lose all disposition to learn such things.

Such women would not produce respectable obedient workers who would be impervious to the appeal of Chartism. Any public activity that tended to undermine this morality was strongly condemned and effectively repressed. Thus, although, in the enthusiasm of the early stages of the French Revolution, writers such as Keats, Coleridge, Wordsworth, Godwin and Mary Wollstonecraft wrote of sensuality and were sceptical of marriage, the English counter-revolution was effective in crushing much of this revolt. Most of the poets 'changed their minds' and others, such as Byron, had to leave England.

Victorian morality

There was a general repression of discussion of sexual matters. This is clear if one reads Victorian newspapers and magazines, even sensational ones such as the *Illustrated Police News*. And although there was massive prostitution,

> If the nineteenth-century files of the two great periodicals, *Punch* and the *Illustrated Police News*, which were taken in almost all middle-class homes are examined not a single reference to prostitution will be found.[12]

Sex was only acknowledged as the necessary means by which procreation took place. Producing a family and managing the household were seen as women's main tasks, as was made clear in such publications as the *Household Companion*. Sex was a duty because chaste women were thought not to have any sexual desires. Acton expressed a typical opinion when he wrote:

> I should say that the majority of women (happily for society) are not much troubled by sexual feelings of any kind. As a general rule, a modest women seldom desires any sexual gratification for herself. She submits to her husband's embraces, but principally to gratify him; and were it not for the desire of maternity, would rather be relieved from his attention.[13]

The Victorian ideal was self-control yet two inconsistencies are already manifest. If there was such an ideal why were not men abstemious and why were there prostitutes? An answer was given to that question in the 1880s. The preamble to a report somewhat sympathetic to the repeal of the Contagious Diseases Act said:

There is no comparison to be drawn between prostitutes and the men who consort with them. With one sex the offence is committed as a matter of gain, with the other it is the irregular indulgence of a natural impulse.[14]

Obviously some women engaged in sex and also they were often thought to actually enjoy it. These women gained their sexual drive through the 'magical' contamination of their first sexual experience. As the *Westminster Review* said in 1850:

> Women's desires scarcely ever lead to their fall; for... the desire scarcely exists in a definite and conscious form until they have fallen.[15]

A belief in their enjoyment of sex and a clear distinction between them and respectable women was made. This distinction was based on their alleged immorality and, much more fundamentally, on their being outside the social and political 'community' in which the middle and upper classes moved. One did not apply the same standards to these women. They were there to be used. One of the great 'objectifiers' of the nineteenth century, the author of *My Secret Life*, who wrote constantly of all the (lowerclass) women that he had made use of, dismissed two servants because they were discovered to be having sexual relations.

> It would not have done to have passed over open fornication. Had I done so, the habit would have spread throughout the household.[16]

An equally clear differentiation of attitude was to be found in the attempts made to control venereal disease.[17] A Contagious Diseases Act was passed in 1864 which made it illegal for women *alleged* to be prostitutes to refuse to undergo medical inspection if so ordered by the magistrates in certain garrison and naval towns. In effect this Act meant that ordinary working-class women were liable to be picked up, branded as prostitutes (no conviction was necessary) and exposed to the humiliation of a painful medical inspection. Soldiers and sailors were not inspected. The Association for the Promotion of the Extension of the Contagious Diseases Act (1866) to the Civil Population of England was founded soon after to safeguard the health of the middle-class users of prositutes. However, the Acts and their supporters in turn engendered tremendous opposition particularly from working-class people and also from certain Evangelicals, notably Josephine Butler. After a long and bitter campaign raising the whole question of the 'double standard' and challenging the assumption that all women who had premarital intercourse were prostitutes, the Acts were suspended in 1883. Two years later the scandal about the trade over child prostitution was made public in W. T. Stead's 'The Maiden Tribute of Modern Babylon' articles in the *Pall Mall Gazette*, and struck another blow at prostitution. The articles brought effective pressure on the legislature to raise the age of consent to sixteen.

These changes in legislation occurred at the time of the third Reform Act of 1884, which increased the electorate from two to three million. Effective moves to question the effective division of the country into the predatory middle class (particularly males) and the utilisable lower classes (notably females) occurred at the time when it was necessary to begin to redefine the country's social and political community if the working class were to be incorporated effectively.

The relationships between men and women had been fragmented in a particularly cruel way. Husband and wife related to each other only in the context of the home. Responsibility, respectability and sometimes sentimentality characterised this particular haven. The wife was a crystal vase which would be shattered by any display of sensuality. Such purity symbolised the man's success and responsibility. Indeed the reason for late marriage in Victorian times, an important contributor to the demand for prostitution, was that it could not be undertaken until sufficient style and comfort could be achieved. The young man (and husband) still had excessive sexual energy and this animalistic instinct could, with no need of tenderness, be satisfied with the prostitute in a manner where its utility could be compared with the calculable price. Women were divided into two classes, the desexed respectable woman of the middle classes and the animalistic lower-class woman.

Man separated tenderness and respect from sexual gratification in dividing his time between one and the other. His actions protected himself from the dangers of sexual equality. The image of Samson and Delilah had long been with Western man. In trusting her and surrendering himself totally to her sensuality Samson lost his hair and strength. By coldly objectifying women, men made sure they would not lose something worse, even at the height of their sexual passion. The inability to achieve reciprocal sensuous relationships in Victorian times was perhaps most clearly expressed in the great vogue for flagellation. It is unlikely that even now man has put himself together again.

Further evidence of Victorian sexual fears can be seen in their attitude towards masturbation. This was morally wrong and unnatural since there was obviously no possibility of offspring. This sinful practice not only broke God's law but, as all vices should, produced terrible effects. As late as 1867 Henry Maudsley wrote of the connection between masturbation and insanity.

The habit of self-abuse notably gives rise to a particular and disagreeable form of insanity, characterised by intense self-feeling and conceit, extreme perversion of feeling and corresponding derangement of thought, in earlier stages, and later by failure of intelligence, nocturnal hallucinations and suicidal and homicidal propensities.[18]

The fears about masturbation and the preventive measures taken against it are now well documented. Its condemnation was linked with the general Victorian belief expressed by men such as Ashton, that man had only a limited reservoir of sexual energy which had to be conserved. The connection between such beliefs and the industrial capitalistic structure can be made by reflecting on a comment of Wayland Young.

> The more energy you draw from a machine, the less there is left: you must not overload it. The more money you draw from a bank or a firm, the less there is left: it must not overspend. Therefore, the more a man fucks, the weaker he gets.[19]

Challenges to the monolith

Since masturbation is usually a solitary activity there was little likelihood of any social movement advocating it. But such a movement could grow up around the issue of contraception, which obviously made possible non-procreative sexual release. Early in the nineteenth century radicals had used Malthus's pessimistic prognostications of the excessive increase of life over increases in production to argue for birth control. Furthermore, it is no coincidence that George Drysdale's *Elements of Social Science*, published anonymously in the 1850s by the secular press, in addition to advocating birth control adopted a humane and relatively sensible attitude towards masturbation. This important book accepted much of Malthus's analysis but also provided trenchant criticism.

> The great error in Mr Malthus's reasoning was that he, like most moralists of his and our own age, was unaware of the frightful evils and fearful natural sin of sexual abstinence. This ignorance of the necessity of sexual intercourse to the health and virtue of both man and woman, is the most fundamental error in medical and moral philosophy.[20]

Drysdale's book advocated contraception both within and outside of marriage and preferred free relationships to marriage. There were, then, available during Victorian times, alternative analyses of sexuality. In condemning the commonly held repressive view of sexuality we are not merely acting with hindsight.

At this time the advocacy of birth control was seen as an attack on the dominant morality. Another book, Charles Knowlton's birth-control pamphlet *The Fruits of Philosophy* was attacked in 1887. The Solicitor-General (Sir Hardinge Griffin) prosecuted Charles Bradlaugh and Annie Besant for its publication. Oscar Wilde was to be prosecuted by Sir Frank Lockwood, the Solicitor-General in 1895. Three years later George Bedbrough was prosecuted because he:

> unlawfully, wickedly, maliciously, scandalously did publish, sell and utter, a certain lewd, wicked, bawdy, scandalous and obscene libel, in the form of a book entitled *Studies in the Psychology of Sex, Volume I, Sexual Inversion* by Havelock Ellis ...[21]

According to John Sweeney, the plain-clothes man who arrested him said that the book was prosecuted because, at that time, Scotland Yard was:

> convinced that we should at one blow kill a growing evil in the shape of a vigorous campaign of free love and anarchism.[22]

From the viewpoint of official Victorian morality, movements that threatened sexual morality were as dangerous as, and were often associated with, political radicalism. The major movement in art also came under censure. Indeed there was sufficient overlap between the different kinds of radicalism to justify viewing them as part of a movement. Annie Besant (birth controller and socialist), Oscar Wilde (dramatist, sensualist and author of 'The Soul of Man under Socialism'), George Bernard Shaw (playwright and Fabian), Edward Carpenter (bohemian socialist and homosexual theorist), all straddled at least two of these movements. But those who had shown most abiding concern with sensuality were the artists. And they suffered directly because of this.

For the Victorian middle classes the criteria of excellence in art were utalitarian.

> Everlasting it seemed were those questions; would it be useful, would it be instructive, would it be moral? The authors stressed them, the readers stressed them.[23]

Such a view of art had little interest in the articulation of an understanding of the mysteries of life as it was *lived*, neither did it demand that the depths of human feelings should be explored or human sensibilities be extended and perfected by artistic endeavour. The pre-Raphaelite belief that in painting and poetry one should return to nature and away from convention was seen as an attack on the correct way of approaching art. In the 1850s, the *Contemporary Review* condemned Rossetti's poetry for its sensuality. In 1866 a cousin of the brotherhood, Swinburne, was also fiercely attacked. His poems and ballads, which contained tributes to Baudelaire and Villon, were condemned by the *Athenaeum*, the *London Review* and the *Saturday Review*. When the author was described as the 'libidinous laureate of a pack of satyrs', John Addington Symonds, another writer, was castigated in the *Contemporary Review* for the 'total denial of any moral restraint on any human impulse'.[24]

The last writer referred to was a homosexual, although he had to keep this information quiet. He wrote a number of books on homosexuality and was an unnamed collaborator on Havelock Ellis's book on sexual inversion. In these works he argued for the ennobling qualities of homosexual love and passion. Edward Carpenter, who lived with the same man for thirty years, in his *Love's Coming of Age* argued that relationships between men and women were so distorted by the institutionalised chauvinism and the related double standard that it was unlikely that there could be any truly integrated reciprocal relationship between them. If the comradely relationships between men were supplemented with mutual sexual experience then such relationships could perhaps be achieved. Such views were dangerous.

The Labrouchere amendment and the Wilde trials

In 1895 Oscar Wilde was found guilty of 'gross indecency with men' under the offence created by the Labouchere Amendment to the 1885 Criminal Law Amendment Act. Before examining this trial we wish to make a few remarks about this important amendment. There had been no separate homosexual offences; homosexual sodomy was prosecutable but only as one form of buggery. Such prosecutions were difficult because the act usually took place in private and was a 'crime without a victim'.[25] Convictions usually depended upon information provided for reasons of self-interest or with political intent or if there were minors involved. There was evident concern over homosexual activity in Britain at the time. In the 'transvestite' Boulton and Park case of 1870, the two named were prosecuted unsuccessfully, by the Attorney-General and the Solicitor-General. There was extensive homosexual prostitution in London, often involving soldiers, which of course hardly fitted into the equalitarian model of homosexual relations suggested earlier. In 1881 Britain was defeated in the first Boer

War. In early 1885 the national symbol, General Gordon, was killed in the Sudan. Britain's imperialist position was beginning to be threatened. Gladstone's government was blamed and it had been further discredited in 1884 when a 'sodomitical' scandal in Ireland involved many prominent men and members of the government. In 1885 this was replaced by Salisbury's Conservative caretaking government. A month later the Criminal Law Amendment Act was passed. One of the many amendments proposed by Labouchere included the following:

> Any male person who in public or private, commits or is a party to the commission of, or procures or attempts to procure the commission by any male person of, any act of gross indecency with another male person, shall be guilty of a misdemeanour, and, being convicted thereof, shall be liable, at the discretion of the Court, to be imprisoned for any term not exceeding one year with or without hard labour.

This clause was inserted with the approval of the government, for which Sir Henry James, the Attorney-General, moved that the penalty should be increased to two years. This was accepted and the Act became law. There seems little doubt that the government knew what it was doing and one can only speculate upon its intentions. It seems likely that Britain's concern over Germany's industrial and military might and the seeming prevalence of homosexuality in high places were seen as related for, after all, Lecky in his widely read *History of European Morals* (1866) had pointed to homosexuality to explain the collapse of previous empires. If Britain's military and industrial might were being threatened by internal weakness then perhaps attacking homosexuality might stop the rot.

It is very evident that Oscar Wilde's trials, some ten years later, were conducted in such a spirit. The nature of the questions put to Wilde, the severity of the sentence, the press comments and the repercussions of the trial all point to this.[26] The first court action was a libel suit brought by Wilde against Lord Queensberry for giving him a card saying 'To Oscar Wilde, posing as a Sodomite' (Queensberry's spelling). Wilde was questioned about an undergraduate magazine *The Chamelon* to which he had contributed, and about his book *The Picture of Dorian Gray*. He was condemned for his refusal to recognise the applicability of moral judgements to works of art, and attention was also drawn to Wilde's violation of Victorian conventions concerning the treatment of social inferiors. Eventually the libel action was dropped because it became likely that Queensberry's defence counsel would bring forth incriminating evidence. Immediately after the Trial, Wilde was charged, with an Alfred Taylor, with committing a number of offences including 'gross indecency with men'. At this, the second trial, the jury could not agree. A verdict reached, perhaps in part, because of a fine speech by Wilde on platonic love.

Such speeches were sufficient only to postpone conviction, for Wilde was tried again. This time a successful prosecution was led by the Solicitor-General, Sir Frank Lockwood. Wilde's plays were taken off. His books were withdrawn from circulation. Beardsley had to withdraw from the *Yellow Book* and this itself soon after ceased publication. But it was in the press that one finds the clearest statements about the significance of the Trials. The editor of the *London Evening News* wrote on the day of Wilde's conviction:

> ... Never has the lesson of a wasted life come home to us more dramatically and opportunely. England has tolerated the man Wilde and others of his kind too long. Before he broke the law of this country and outraged human decency he was a social pest, a centre of intellectual corruption. He was one of the high priests of a school which attacks all the wholesome, manly, simple ideals of English life, and sets up false gods of decadent culture and intellectual debauchery. The man himself was a perfect type of his class, a gross sensualist veneered with the affectation of artistic feeling too delicate for the appreciation of common clay. To him and such as him we owe the spread of moral degeneration amongst young men with abilities sufficient to make them a credit to their country. At the feet of Wilde they have learned to gain notoriety by blatant conceit, by despising the emotions of healthy humanity and the achievements of wholesome talent.[27]

The reaction against the literati was linked with the tendency of the middle class to explain the breakdown in the effective social consensus as being due to moral crisis, to anomie. And Britain in the 1890s was still volatile. There was no knowing what the working class was going to do. Unionism was growing, organisations such as the Social Democratic Federation seemed influential, the Independent Labour Party was increasingly evident. Britain's fears about Germany were not being allayed. The employers started organising for a counter-offensive and many battles were fought in the courts over union rights. Under these circumstances social conflict was publicly redefined as moral degeneration while, of course, effective action was being contemplated to cope with the reality.

Imperialism and the proletarian family

The recognition that effective action over Britain's declining world position would require positive action by the state came after Britain's involvement in the second Boer War.[28] The revelations by General Maurice of the low standard of recruits and the *Report of the Interdepartmental Committee on Physical Deterioration* (1904) made the health of the working classes a priority.[29] Naturally, attention was directed towards Germany where Bismarck had attempted to get 'the worker as a loyal and obedient ally' by a programme of social security legislation that also improved his health.[30] In addition to improving the health of the 'productive' working class, efforts were required to eliminate the degenerate unemployable class, the casual poor (so evident in London).

Newpapers, tracts and government reports all argued that a major goal of social policy should be the production of healthy, loyal and obedient workers and soldiers. The 'moral' disciplinary significance of Christianity for the working class was already recognised, now the importance of the family for health was stressed. Social security legislation was passed which strengthened the family, the Old Age Pensions Act 1908 and the National Insurance Act 1911.

Such social priorities necessarily undermined the double standard applied to sexual release by the rich. This required that a plentiful supply of 'lower-class female flesh' should be available and this was less and less tenable. The decline of Malthusian pessimism and its replacement with social Darwinism and the related concern over the cruelty of the race, the necessity to incorporate an increasingly *politically* organised working class into the national 'community' and the women's movement all played their part in this change. Legislation from the Offences Against the Person Act 1861, through the Criminal Law Amendment Act 1886 and up to the Punishment of Incest Act 1908 tended to stress the importance of the family and also the dignity of the individual since the issues of 'consent' and violation of bodily space were treated as grave. Such legislative concern expressed the expansion of the moral community. On the other hand there was harsher treatment of homosexuality, both in the 1885 Act, and also by the extension of legislation passed for other purposes, for example prosecution of importuning under the Vagrancy Act 1898 section 1(1) (*b*). These Acts were passed because, as elsewhere when the family becomes a universal interpretative image for the whole of society, homosexuality is repressed as dangerous because it questions the role categories (biologically male) — masculine — husband, and (biologically female) — feminine — wife.[31]

Parallel to the strengthening of the family was a desire to eliminate the degenerates. Failure to work was not explained by the structure of the market but rather by individual culpability or inadequacy. Crime and all forms of deviance were similarly explained. Deviance was viewed as both a cause and effect of racial degeneracy. Alcoholism and venereal diseases communicated by prostitution were thought to be particular culprits. Beveridge, 'the Father of the Welfare State', suggested that the essential criterion for citizenship was the ability to perform productive work. If 'through general defects' people could not do that they should be placed within public institutions. There they would be adequately maintained but denied the franchise, civil freedom and parenthood. Legislation informed by this view was subsequently passed. The Mental Deficiency Act 1913 prohibited sexual relations with the mentally defective not so much to protect them as to stop them breeding. It also included provisions for institutionalising prostitutes and alcoholics.[32]

From health in marriage to the 'glorious unfolding'

Although there were opponents to this mental deficiency legislation, many liberal thinkers shared its view of the world. The acceptance of the capitalist system and the identification of Britain's welfare with its imperial strength characterised such thinkers as Havelock Ellis and Marie Stopes. Ellis in 1922 published an essay entitled 'The Individual and the Race', and Marie Stopes used Saleeby's term the 'racial instinct' to describe sexual desire. Further, at her trial Marie Stopes justified setting up birth-control clinics among the working-classes as a way of eliminating inferior racial stock.[33]

But Maries Stopes's thinking marked a transitional phase. Although it is true that she was concerned about 'degeneracy', that was not the major thrust of her work. By the aftermath of the successfully fought First World War the changes in the employment market virtually eliminated the spectre of the degenerate poor. Her significance lies in her formulation and promulgation of an ideal of 'married love', wherein the union of two 'like' souls becomes the foundation of marriage. In order to understand this ideal one must trace its development and also explain why it became accepted. In the late nineteenth century Coventry Patmore, the poet and writer, was already combining a religious mysticism with a belief that sex and marriage should be integrated. 'In vulgar minds the idea of passion is inseparable from that of disorder' he complained in 'Rod, Root and Flower' (1895) and in 'Principle in Art' (1879),

> the best use of the supremely useful intercourse of man and woman
> is not the begetting of children, but the increase of contracted personal
> consciousness.

Bramwell Booth, son of General Booth, and Josephine Butler saw marriage in a similar way.[34] Marie Stopes believed that she had received a direct revelation from God about the mystic unity of marriage. This was the content of her 'A Gospel to All Peoples' which she sent to the Lambeth Conference in 1920. It was rejected then, but an almost identical view was proposed at the 1958 Conference.[35] Marie Stopes believed that marriage was the place where sensuality and spirituality could and should be united. But she was not advocating sexual liberation in the sense of free unions.

> All of the deepest and highest forces within us impel us to evolve an even nobler and tenderer form of life-long monogamy as our social ideal. ... The beautiful sense for love in the hearts of the young should be encouraged, and they should have access to the knowledge of how to cultivate it, instead of being diverted by the clamour for 'freedom' to destroy it.[36]

It was not till the late 'thirties that these views became incorporated into the public morality. That they were by then can be deduced from an examination of a publication such as *The Modern Women's Home Doctor,* obviously designed for middle-class homes. In this book the third section 'The Happy Marriage: Sex and Love' comprises over a tenth of the book and includes the passage:

> Of the fundamental importance of the mutual adjustment of the sexual instinct in marriage there can be no doubt. Failure will spell years of unhappiness, and may lead to nervous ailments, to infidelity, prostitution and disease.[37]

The reasons for the change in the attitudes towards sensuality and marriage must again be related to the necessity of incorporating the working class within some national 'community'. The attempts to strengthen the working-class family had attacked the double standard but this mainly affected middle- and upper-class males. Working-class sensuality had always defied to a greater or lesser extent the attempt to cast it within the categories used by the more politically powerful classes. Moral education had been resisted, and in the nineteenth century, as can be seen by consulting ballads and music hall songs, ideals of love relationships (with or without marriage) were constantly being upheld.[38] The working class would only accept marriage if sex was *positively* related to this institution. And Marie Stopes in her preface to *Married Love* recognised the importance of this.

> More than ever today are happy homes needed. It is my hope that this book may serve the state by adding to their numbers. ... The only secure basis for the present-day state is the welding of units in marriage;

but there is rottenness and a danger at the foundations of the state if many of its marriages are unhappy.[39]

It was no longer conceivable that a public figure, such as the Headmaster of Eton, would make the following statement, made by the incumbent of that post, the Reverend E. Lyttleton, in 1902.

A thoroughly conventional man in good society would sooner that his son should consort with prostitutes than that he should marry a respectable girl of distinctly lower social station than his own: indeed, it is not going too far to say that his son should seduce such a girl, provided there were no scandal, than marry her.[40]

While the forties, with war and the concern over an allegedly declining birth rate, engendered by the *Report* of the Royal Commission on Population (1949), the spread of this gospel to all classes was not so evident. But it was in the fifties, with affluence and more babies that the ideal of marriage, stressing a sexually satisfying relationship gained currency, particularly since sex was discussed more openly in that and the subsequent decades. This ideal had two important functions: it represented a criterion for normality applicable to all social classes and it also constituted an important discipline on the working population. If the social criterion for responsible adulthood is being a provider for the family and if the family itself provides man with a private world where he has dignity and control then disciplined production and disciplined consumption have powerful allies. Studies such as Lockwood, Goldthorpe, Bechhofer and Platt's *The Affluent Worker* demonstrate the present importance of such an ideal.[41] Now marriage combines the functions of producing healthy, loyal, obedient and dedicated workers with asserting certain allegedly shared styles of life and ideals. Moreover, with a move to 'consumer' capitalism the family becomes the essential consumption unit and a certain licensed hedonism becomes acceptable. There is not the same need for such an obviously sexually repressive culture.

Sexual deviance and consumer capitalism

In the fifties the idealisation of marriage and of heterosexual relations in general (romance) led to homosexual activities being viewed as the archetypes of sexual deviance. The alleged promiscuity of homosexuals made them seem irresponsible sensualists and the way their actions call into question the naturalness of male–masculine and female–feminine definitions made them particularly dangerous. But on the other hand the general stress on

sexuality made it possible to accept relations based on sex rather than repro-
duction and thus it was possible to conceive of 'homosexual relationships'
between men, whilst still not approving of them. In 1956 the Wolfenden
Report expressed this view when it argued that although homosexuality was
sinful and pathological, providing public decency was not outraged, it
should not be considered a crime. Eleven years later the Sexual Offences
Act 1967 was passed, with the support of most of the official bodies of the
Christian churches in England. This Act expressed clearly the abiding desire
to contain sexual activity within marriage combined with a pragmatic
recognition that since homosexual activity will not be eliminated its expression should be regulated and limited, particularly by the privacy clause and
by the age of consent being five years higher than for heterosexual exercise.
The continuing police harassment of homosexuals can be seen by examining
the criminal statistics before and after the Act.

Year	1965	1969
Indictable offences known to the police	4,659	4,662
Indictable offences cleared up by the police.	3,975	3,034
Indictable offences proceeded against by the police.	1,702	2,060
Prosecutions of males, 17–21, for buggery, attempted buggery, indecent assault and importuning.	209	200

Most of these prosecutions are for activities that are alleged to have taken
place in and around public toilets. Although charges are usually laid because
of 'outrages to public decency' it is very rare for complaints to be made by
members of the public. It is the police who discover these offenders by acting
as *agent provocateurs*. It was stated unequivocally in 1968 when on

> Giving evidence against a man charged with indecent assault and im-
> portuning for an immoral purpose in Southsea, a Sergeant of the Hamp-
> shire Constabulary boldy told the court, 'I was behaving as an *agent
> provocateur* which was part of my duty. This is what is commonly
> done in this city, and has been so for many years.'[42]

The judiciary, particularly in recent years, have been far from unanimous in condemning such police practices.[43] The police have wide discretion in the kind of charges that they can bring, some being indictable and some not indictable, for almost identical actions. There is vagueness about what constitutes an offence and there is a great deal of overlap between the different charges that can be brought. This is important since a man who is innocent may be pressurised to plead guilty to a lesser charge and less scandal. The discrepancy between the indictable offences known, cleared and actually prosecuted as such certainly seems to imply that charges were either tried summarily or changed to nonindictable offences such as 'breach of local and other regulations'.[44] Homosexuals still have no *right* to meet each other in intimate surroundings. They are liable to be convicted for actions for which heterosexuals cannot be prosecuted; importuning only refers, with deliberate vagueness, to self-advertisement in or near public conveniences. The fear of social stigmatisation and lack of social facilities has the ironic consequence that it pushes these men towards impersonal contacts where they are liable to more harassment under vague laws and then further stigmatisation.[45]

Conclusion

In this essay we have tried to relate the development of the capitalist mode of production, and the related needs to control and integrate the working class into bourgeois culture, to the changes in sexual morality which lead to an idealisation of marriage and a desire to limit sexual activity to its confines. At the same time we have tried to trace the history of the legislation against homosexual activities as a manageable index of general sexual attitudes. In so doing we have, we hope, made clear that sexual liberation cannot occur while the relationships that human beings have with one another are limited and distorted by the needs of capitalism.

Notes

[1] Marx, K. *Capital* (Progress Moscow), vol. 1.

[2] MacIntosh, M., 'The Homosexual Role', *Social Problems* vol. XVI, no.2 (Fall 1968).

[3] Contrast this with '[Religious ideas] are in themselves ... the most powerful plastic elements of national character, and contain a law of development and a compelling force entirely their own.' Weber, M. *The Protestant Ethic and the Spirit of Capitalism* tr. Parsons, Talcott (Allen & Unwin, London 1930), pp.277–8.

[4] I have relied in this discussion on the following sources: Taylor, Gordon Rattray *Sex in History* new edition (Thames & Hudson, London 1959); May, G. *Social Control of Sexual Expression* (Allen & Unwin, London 1930); Bailey, D. S. *Homosexuality and the Western Christian Tradition* (London, Longmans 1955) and Hyde, H. Montgomery *The Other Love* (Mayflower, London 1972).

[5] MacIntosh, op. cit.

[6] Anon. *Satan's Harvest Home: or the Present State of Whorecraft, Adultery, Fornication, Procuring, Pimping, Sodomy ... And Other Satanic Works, daily propagated in this Good Protestant Kingdom* (London 1749), pp.49, 51, 56–8.

[7] Hyde, op. cit., pp.54–72, 127–30.

[8] Bunyan, J. *The Pilgrim's Progress* (Penguin, Harmondsworth 1970), pp.41, 104.

[9] Weber, op. cit., p.263.

[10] Calverton, V. F. *Sex Expression in Literature* (Boni & Liveright, New York 1926), pp.58–9.

[11] Thompson, E. P. *The Making of the English Working Class* (Gollancz, London 1963), ch.11.

[12] Henriques, F. *Modern Sexuality* (Panther, London 1969), ch.6, 'Victorian Sexual Morality', p.219.

[13] Acton, W. *The Functions and Disorders of Reproductive Organs in Childhood, Youth, Adult Age and Advanced Life* (1875), p.143. Quoted in Petrie, G. A. *A Singular Iniquity* (Macmillan, London 1971), p.82.

[14] Petrie, op. cit., p.117.

[15] Henriques, op. cit., p.210.

[16] Marcus, S. *The Other Victorians* (Corgi, London 1969), p.135.

[17] Petrie, op. cit.

[18] Szasz, T. *The Manufacture of Madness* (Dell, New York 1970), p.189.

[19] Young, W. *Eros Denied: Sex in Western Society* (Grove, New York 1966), p.204.

[20] A Doctor of Medicine *Elements of Social Science* (Standring, London), p.345. We are grateful to Mr. Reginald Steele for bringing this book to our notice.

[21] Calder-Marshall, A., 'Havelock Ellis & Company' *Encounter*.

[22] Ibid., p.15.

[23] Calverton, op. cit., p.232.

[24] Pearsall, R. *The Worm in the Bud: The World of Victorian Sexuality* (Penguin, Harmondsworth 1971), p.457. Fuller, Jean Overton *Swinburne: A Critical Biography* (Chatto & Windus, London 1968), p.153.

[25] Schur, E. *Crimes without Victims* (Prentice-Hall, Englewood Cliffs 1965).

26 See Julian, P. *Oscar Wilde* (Paladin, London 1971), Millet, K. *Sexual Politics* (Hart-Davis, London 1971), pp.152–6, and Williams, R. *Culture and Society 1780–1950* (Penguin, Harmondsworth 1966), pp.169–75.

27 Hyde, H. Montgomery *The Trials of Oscar Wilde* (William Hodge, London 1948), p.12.

28 Semmel, B. *Imperialism and Social Reform* (Allen & Unwin, London 1960).

29 Stedman-Jones, G. *Outcast London* (Clarendon Press, Oxford 1971).

30 Rimlinger, G. V. *Welfare Policy & Industrialisation in Europe, America and Russia* (Wiley, New York 1971), p.116.

31 Pearce, F., 'How to be Immoral and Ill, Pathetic and Dangerous, all at the Same Time', in *Mass Media and Deviancy* ed. Young, J. and Cohen, S. (Constable, London 1973).

32 Jones, K. *Mental Health and Social Policy 1845–1959* (Routledge & Kegan Paul, London), ch.4.

33 Box, Muriel (ed.) *The Trial of Marie Stopes* (Femina Books, London 1967).

34 Pearsall, op. cit., p.190; Petrie, op. cit., p.247.

35 Briant, K. *Marie Stopes* (Hogarth, London 1962), p.125.

36 Stopes, M. *Married Love* (Putnam, London 1924), p.164.

37 *The Modern Woman's Home Doctor* (Odhams Press, London n.d. about Second World War).

38 Pearsall, op. cit., pp.80–8

39 Stopes, op. cit., p.xiv.

40 Henriques, op. cit., p.212.

41 Goldthorpe, J. H., Lockwood, D., Bechhofer, F., and Platt, J. *The Affluent Worker in the Class Structure* (Cambridge University Press, London 1969); Westergaard J., 'The Rediscovery of the Cash Nexus' in *The Socialist Register 1970* ed. Miliband, R., and Savile, J. (Merlin, London 1970).

42 De-La-Noy, M., 'First Catch Your Crime', *Man and Society* (Albany Trust, London p.10).

43 Humphreys, L. *Tearoom Trade* (Duckworh, London 1970), p.64; MacLean, D., 'Informers and *Agents Provocateurs*', *Criminal Law Review* (1969).

44 See Thomas's horrifying comments on negotiating pleas.

The system has great advantages for the police and indeed for the public. A conviction may be obtained for a lesser charge where the police think that their case for the grave charge might not stand up in court. For example, their evidence might not be sufficiently cogent; witnesses might be unreliable, there might be inadequate identification and so on. The guilty plea will thus enable the police to 'clear their books' and allow manpower activity to be concentrated elsewhere. The taxpayer would also be saved the cost of an expensive trial.

Thomas, P., 'An Exploration of Plea Bargaining', *Criminal Law Review* (1969), p.70.
[45] See also Pearce, op. cit.

We are grateful to Tony Marden, Jerry Palmer, Stef Pixner and Lesley Wilsher for their comments on the ideas expressed in this article.

The Family and the Social Management of Intolerable Dilemmas[1]

Roy BAILEY

One of the most widely held views among social workers and psychiatrists is that there is a growing incidence of mental illness. What the actual figures are and to what extent these represent the 'real' incidence of mental disorder may not be readily to hand or agreed upon, but few would deny that mental illness, particularly schizophrenia, is among our major medicosocial problems. During the sixties volumes of literature from various academic and medical viewpoints appeared to propose and contest alternative modes of comprehension of the 'problem', even to deny its existence as a 'real' phenomenon at all. In Britain various associations and institutions exist to sponsor and undertake research into causes, consequences and therapy—medical and social—of schizophrenia and its differential distribution among the population by class and/or habitation.[2]

The primary intention of this short essay is not to consider the alternative theses propounded and offer support for one or another, but rather to discuss the general social conditions which are related to the phenomenon in an immediate and crucial fashion. Such a question necessarily makes certain assumptions about the nature of the condition itself. As with all analysis the kind of question or problem one poses at the outset limits the 'choice' of frameworks one can utilise. In so far as I am concerned with the relationship between schizophrenia and social structure then the analytical framework for understanding schizophrenia itself will be a social one. To this extent and for this purpose I intend to accept the propositions which claim that schizophrenia should be viewed as a social process rather than a biological one.

This essay is therefore concerned with the general question of the nature of the social conditions in which the phenomenon occurs. The specific orientation will be to consider the social conditions within which so-called schizophrenogenic family structures develop and an individual comes to 'suffer schizophrenia'. By 'schizophrenogenic family structures' I am referring to those networks of family relationships which have been characterised by contradictions, dilemmas, antagonisms, anxieties, double-binds, knots or whatever in terms of the meanings for the individuals involved.

That such family networks can be characterised in this way has been amply demonstrated by those investigators who have contributed, through their work on schizophrenia, to a shift of attention away from the individual schizophrenic or the personality characteristics and social attributes of parents, towards an interest centring on the whole family as a unit for study and conceptualisation. Particular attention is paid to the patterns of interaction and communication among members of the family. I refer to the work of Gregory Bateson, Theodore Lidz, Lyman Wynne and, from nearer home, Ronald Laing and David Cooper.

What I intend to argue and hope to show is that such family charac-teristics are not peculiar to families that have one of their number officially labelled schizophrenic, or institutionalised as schizophrenic. Rather I will argue that far from such family structures being 'abnormal' or 'deviant' or 'pathological', in short not like other 'healthy' families, these very family characteristics are, in highly complex and structurally differentiated societies, the 'norm'. Schizophrenia as an 'illness' will now be conceived as being the result of an inability to 'live with' these normal conditions. Such a model of the family as an objective structure and a subjective network of meanings now prompts the following questions: (*a*) under what conditions do actors fail to cope or deal with the 'normal' antagonisms, contradictions and conflicts of everyday family life, and (*b*) and no less important, what are the conditions that are enjoyed by others that do enable them to cope and deal with the same contradictions, etc?

In other words, much of the work on schizophrenia that has taken the position that one must look at the network of family relationships to under-stand the individual actor who is labelled schizophrenic does by implication (and possibly unintentionally) suggest that such families are different from the norm, in the sense that 'normal families' do not exhibit similar networks of relationships. Clearly, families who have such a 'patient' are different from families who do not, but the difference might lie in characteristics other than those which suggest themselves at first sight. I hope finally to suggest a framework for confronting the latter problems.

A useful starting point for the discussion is an article by Berger and Kellner, 'Marriage and the Construction of Reality'.[3] In that paper the authors argue that marriage and the family form the institutionalised setting in which 'the individual can take a slice of reality and fashion it into his world'.[4]

The paper is concerned to inquire into the character of marriage and the family 'as a nomos-building instrumentality, that is ... a social arrangement that creates for the individual the sort of order in which he can experience his life as making sense'.[5] (One wonders merely as an aside, whether these sentences would read quite so smoothly if one substituted for 'he' and 'his', 'she' and 'hers'? This is a diversion at this point, however, although I shall return to it later.)

Marriage and the family are presented as an institutionalised protection against 'anomie'. The article is fascinating as an essay in the sociology of knowledge, taking Weber, Mead and Schutz as its main theoretical perspectives. Its most general sociological proposition is that

> The plausibility and stability of the world, as socially defined, is dependent upon the strength and continuity of significant relationships in which conversation about this world can be continually carried on.[6]

The authors claim that it is in marriage and family life that this process is most evident, and that the family occupies a privileged status in this process of stabilisation: 'marriage is a crucial nomic instrumentality in our society'.[7]

The emergence of a 'private sphere' of social life and existence, a segregation from the controls of public and secondary institutions are the preconditions for the family to perform such crucial functions. The authors argue that public and secondary institutions confront individuals as all-powerful, as alien, as incomprehensible, as an arena within which one must do one's best to survive and manipulate, and it is in the family that one acquires the crucial equipment or weapons to do so. The family provides the skills with which one sustains oneself through life. These crucially important attributes are not technological dexterities or professional qualifications but rather emotional and personality supports and props. Marriage partners build for themselves their own private sphere (within the boundaries of society) and while this partnership is at first precarious, children eventually render it less so. The family provides the last remaining sphere of social life in which actors can enjoy a fully shared world of meaning, a world of meaning that is transparent, not opaque, comprehended as being of their own making, not existing over and against them, given and to which they must adjust.

> The process we have been inquiring into is ... one in which reality is crystallised, narrowed and stabilised. Ambivalences are converted into certainties. Typifications of self and others become settled. Most generally, possibilities become facticities. What is more this process of transformation remains most of the time, unapprehended by those who are both its authors and its objects.[8]

One is tempted to ask whether the fact that most people do not apprehend

75

this kind of sociological proposition has anything to do with the fact that this kind of sociological proposition does not apprehend most people?

At a more explicitly macrosocial level there is a clear affinity between this paper and the work of Parsons and Bales, *Family, Socialisation and Interaction Process*.[9] Clearly the process of structural differentiation associated with industrialisation is the overriding societal development within which the nuclear family emerges, performing, it is argued, crucial and vital functions, not now so much on a macrosociological level but rather on a psychological level.

> ... the functions of the family in a highly differentiated society are not to be interpreted as functions on behalf of the society, but on behalf of personality.[10]

Families are '... "factories" which produce human personalities'.[11] Furthermore, and this is important in the context of the Berger and Kellner paper, the family also performs vital functions for the adult personality:

> ... the basic and irreducible functions of the family are two: first, the primary socialisation of children so that they can truly become members of the society into which they have been born; second, the stabilisation of adult personalities of the population of the society.[12]

In terms of networks of meanings, these functions are performed by the family precisely because the family is a kind of 'play area' where individuals can design, create, modify, etc. 'their world' and not upset any of the 'important social, economic and political applecarts'.[13]

The nuclear family, for Parsons and Bales and Berger and Kellner, is an arena which provides the setting for the development of the 'psychologically balanced individual'. Such people have not merely adjusted to reality, for Berger and Kellner they have socially constructed their own reality.

Finally, both Parsons and Bales and Berger and Kellner refer to evidence of rising or high divorce rates and refute propositions which suggest these rates indicate a decline in the importance of the family. Berger and Kellner claim that the rates reinforce their case in that a divorce is a statement that a particular marriage and family did not, as they put it 'come up to scratch'. It may well be that an increase in divorce rates is an index of the failure of *particular* marriages and families to meet with the expectations of the partners, and thus is evidence of an existing value and ideology attached to marriage and family. *It may also be an index, however, that the very conditions in which the nuclear family emerged, to perform the functions suggested by the authors, are simultaneously the same conditions which make it impossible for that nuclear family to perform those functions.*

An unstated yet clear implication of the paper by Berger and Kellner is the assumption that actors, when conceived of as members of a family, are stripped of all connection (except as observers) with the wider social world. Somehow it is thought legitimate and valid to regard the variety of roles and structures that actors are engaged in as not being interpenetrative. Yet, I suggest, oneself as an employee or employer, the associated tensions, securities and insecurities, one's income, one's property, or lack of it, being a white-collar worker, a skilled, semi-skilled or unskilled manual worker, being unemployed and on the dole, Christian or atheist, Conservative or Communist, one's degree of education and so on, all affect and are affected by one's family life, not just marginally but centrally.

The proposition that marriage and the family as an institution protects one against the stresses, strains, satisfactions and frustrations of one's experience of 'public' institutions, I suggest, is not valid. What kind of meaningful and stabilising world, what slice of reality is taken and made their own, by the chronic poor, the slum dweller or the homeless? In other words the wider economy intimately affects the private sphere. This surely needs no labouring. Modern technology, it has been argued, renders man little more than an object of rational production. The worker is distinct from husband, father, son and citizen and as such was conceptualised and expressed in the idea of 'scientific management'. The 'heuristic' device of distinguishing social roles has become viewed as a social reality and the totality of human personality ignored. The family and the home may be a private sphere in the sense that when you shut the front door most other people cannot actually see you, but their existence and the nature of your relationships with them are not shut out. Indeed, people you have never met or even seen, as well as those you have, penetrate the most intimate and 'private' areas of your life, not least, just *where* you may live it!

The changing economic, legal and social roles of women have affected their identities as mothers, wives and/or workers. The problems couched in terms of 'the generation gap' without doubt affect and threaten the idea of a meaningful and stabilising family life. It may be highly debatable whether these problems are best understood using such concepts as the 'generation gap'; it is not doubted that problems exist and are experienced by parents and children alike.[14] The conflicts and contradictions of contemporary life have been developed by authors for some time. In particular, Richard Titmuss discussed this issue in an excellent paper, 'Industrialisation and the Family', first published in Great Britain in 1958. In it he developed, among other things, 'the differences in the norms of behaviour expected of the worker in the factory and of the same worker in his home and in the community'.[15]

He points to dominant expectations of individuals outside the factory in terms of attitudes, behaviour and social relationships and shows how markedly different, even contradictory, they are, to what is expected of them within the culture of the factory. The analysis was developed in terms of 'stability', 'status and rewards' and 'initiative', contrasting conditions and expectations at work and at home.

> Take, for example, the concept of stability, which is so heavily stressed as an expected characteristic of 'healthy' family life. A 'good' parent is one who, by taking deliberate thought for tomorrow, provides a stable background and a regular coherent rhythm in which his children can grow and mature as successful individuals. He is expected to plan for their future, to strive to make them more successful than he has been, and to contrive a stable and economically secure base from which they may climb up the educational ladder. ...[16]

For the manual worker and indeed many white-collar workers, however, stability has very little to do with their world.

> The dominating characteristic of industrial conditions in the West during the past few decades has been, from the point of view of the worker, irregularity and impermanence. Unemployment, short-time working, the decay of skills as a result of technical change, the rationalisation of production have all spelled, in the workers' psychology, irregularity and uncertainty.[17]

What Titmuss did in that paper was to argue, quite convincingly, that there exists along many dimensions of our lives straight-forward contradictions between the conditions, expectations and self-identifications appropriate in one context and the conditions, expectations and self-identities appropriate in another. Little in the ensuing twelve or fourteen years has happened to suggest that such contradictions are any the less recognisable today.

It has not been possible here to do more than suggest how the distinction between private and public spheres of life is simply an analytical illusion which blurs more than it reveals. What I have attempted to indicate is that the structural changes associated with industrialisation do not just leave the nuclear family as an emergent institution performing crucial functions within a protected arena, but that the very differentiated structures, each with their own 'rules' of conduct are experienced and carried by people as a social structure of self, a structure characterised by conflict, antagonism and contradiction. These structures thus penetrate family life and shatter any notion of a discreet and private social milieu.

In different contexts one projects an image of oneself different from an image projected in association with another social context. Sometimes these identities are complimentary but increasingly they are antagonistic. One does not necessarily *experience* these antagonisms as personal dilemmas, contradictions or hypocrisies since one might be able to prevent these social milieux from 'meeting' as it were. When they do, or threaten to, then either mild embarrassment, acute discomfort or sheer intolerability results. Then one experiences the contradictions, etc., of social life. This experience, moreover, does not have to result simply from the face-to-face encounters of separate milieux. Such encounters can take place 'in our heads', for example:

> The problem lay buried, unspoken, for many years in the minds of American women. It was a strange stirring, a sense of dissatisfaction, a yearning that women suffered in the middle of the twentieth century in the United States. Each suburban housewife struggled with it alone. As she made the beds, shopped for groceries, matched the slipcovers, ate peanut-butter sandwiches with her children, chauffeured Cub Scouts and Brownies, lay beside her husband at night—she was afraid to ask even of herself the silent question—'Is this all?'[18]

This is how Betty Friedan opens chapter 1 of *The Feminine Mystique*. I suggest that this is not simply an American woman's dilemma.

Who among us has experienced the embarrassment occasioned by the meeting of our parents with our peers? Who among us has felt constrained to apologise for dad's jokes or political opinions to our personal friends on the one hand and, on the other, defend our rights to have whomever we like as friends. How humiliating it is to be treated as 'our little boy' in front of the new girlfriend with whom one has been energetically projecting the 'self-as-lover-and-sophisticated-man-of-the-world image' for weeks past? How many of us suffer Portnoy's complaint? Alexander Portnoy is not merely a figment of Philip Roth's imagination![19] You may not think these illustrations very important, but I am sure each of us has experienced the general point at issue.

I should like to suggest that it is in the family that such separate self-identities are potentially experienced as most problematic. There does exist within the family a pervasive ideology that one should 'be honest', 'share problems', 'talk out intimate dilemmas' and, perhaps strongest of all, a sense of obligation 'after all they've done'. At the same time we know how impossible it is to act in this way. Sons and daughters are many things other than sons and daughters; yet in these particular relationships they are busily projecting themselves as they think their parents would like them to be.

79

At the same time mother and father are also many other things yet they too are trying to project themselves as they think their children would like them to be. Brother likewise to sister, husband to wife and vice versa. Each in a way is making an effort to 'shore up', as it were, the other's definitions. Yet the other too is making an effort to shore up one's own definitions and projections. Everyone is thus striving to validate the shoringup projections of everyone else.

What I have tried to argue so far, possibly too briefly, is that the family, far from being a 'nomos-building instrumentality', is a highly differentiated and antagonistic social network and an arena where the social relationships are, to say the least, extremely precarious and tenuous.[20]

The problem now becomes, as I suggested at the outset, how do some actors 'cope' with these dilemmas and contradictions and others not? Under what conditions do such dilemmas become intolerable and under what conditions does one tolerate them?

I suggest that we might confront these questions by taking Elizabeth Bott's ideas as developed in her book *Family and Social Networks*. In this study, Bott introduces the concepts of close and loose social networks. By social networks, she is indicating the '... immediate social environment of families, that is ... their actual external relationships with friends, neighbours, relatives, clubs, shops, places of work and so forth'.[21] These relationships 'assumed the form of a network rather than the form of an organised group',[22] in which '... only some, not all, of the component individuals have social relationships with one another'.[23]

Bott further develops this concept by introducing the notion of the 'connectedness' of these networks.

> By connectedness I mean the extent to which the people known by a family know and meet one another independently of the family. I use the word *closeknit* to describe a network in which there are many relationships among the component units, and the word *looseknit* to describe a network in which there are few such relationships.[24]

This research argued that performance of conjugal roles, in terms of discrete and separate husband/wife activities, on the one hand, or highly fused and shared activities on the other, was clearly affected by the nature of the husband's and wife's social networks (as defined above).

> Those ... that had a high degree of segregation in the role-relationship of husband and wife had a closeknit social network.[25]

At the same time, those partners who shared the household tasks, who had joint role relationships in this respect, had relatively looseknit social networks. Bott explains the relationship of network systems and conjugal role performance in terms of the emotional investment, satisfaction and support provided by networks and family. The actors who enjoyed closeknit networks received considerable emotional support, etc., from them, and hence did not invest to the same extent in the family partnerships as did others who, through lack of supports, etc., from looseknit networks, sought a higher degree of involvement and assistance from the marriage partnership.

In terms of the problem stated above, I should like to put forward the following proposition: *The degree to which an individual actor, within the family, is able to cope with the normal dilemmas and contradictions of family life varies directly with the connectedness of his or her social network of relationships.* In other words, individuals, through a lack of close involvement with extra-familial relationships, which provide security and support, find themselves having to seek that security within the family. The precarious and tenuous nature of the social relationships of the family, for reasons suggested above, are thus experienced far more intensely and immediately since this is the *only* arena in which this individual can get the supports he or she needs. The family network as I have described it is thus more likely to be experienced by this actor as intensely threatening and anxiety provoking. On the other hand, individuals who enjoy closeknit social networks have a greater 'distance', as it were, from the family and hence a greater autonomy. They are much more able, I suggest, to cope with the conflicting demands, etc., of family relationships. Indeed, they may not even experience the family network as problematic at all.[26] One might even go on to suggest here that such actors are highly unlikely to comprehend the difficulties and dilemmas experienced by another member of the family. As Laing and others have said there is possibly but a short step between incomprehensibility and the introduction of such observations as 'odd', 'peculiar', 'strange' and 'mad'!

Finally, it seems to me that one further and important dimension of this analysis remains to be developed: namely the structure and distribution of power. It is possible, for analytical purposes, to conceptualise power at two levels. One may talk of the structure of power in a society, its general source and distribution within the community at large, and indicate the importance of such a structure for conditions and actions of those who make up that structure. At the same time one may talk of power, its production and distribution as a function of interpersonal associations—associations conceptualised as exchange processes. Both levels of power are related and relevant to any analysis of social action.[27] As I indicated earlier in this paper, general economic conditions, for example, exercise overwhelming constraints or opportunities on both the material and qualitative dimensions of family life. At this point, however, I wish to concentrate on the interpersonal level of power, while acknowledging that a deeper and more adequate analysis would require a greater development of both levels.

Individuals admire and find attractive certain social and physical attributes, and also reject and disdain others. For most, if not all, the time they evaluate the social and physical world around them. What they value and admire is not necessarily in abundant supply, and such a structure of scarcity is of crucial importance in terms of human social relationships. For example, person A finds certain qualities attractive and at the same time 'offers', as it were, certain qualities that he possesses, to others. Person B possesses those qualities that A finds attractive and at the same time finds attractive and rewarding those possessed by person A. Other things being equal then, there is good reason to suppose that both A and B could enjoy a reciprocal and mutually rewarding relationship. Let us now introduce the idea of scarcity. The qualities that A displays are rare and not easily obtainable elsewhere, while the qualities of B are in relatively greater supply and thus obtainable from a wider range of accessible people. In such a situation persons A and B are, in terms of interpersonal power, in an asymmetrical relationship. Since B cannot obtain the qualities desired from any other sources he must be careful, if he wishes to continue to enjoy the availability of those valued qualities, not to offend A. The latter, however, can obtain the qualities B is offering from C, D or E, and this gives him a greater independence from B. Not only must B not offend A, he must most likely contribute more to the relationship than A, say by being more ready to accede to the demands of A as to how they spend their time together.[28]

To return to my original thesis. An actor, by virtue of a lack of a closeknit social network, seeks emotional support and assistance in the family since he obtains them nowhere else. If, at the same time, other members of the family enjoy closeknit social networks then they do not depend on the family to the same extent. In terms of the above concepts of exchange and power then, the family member who is looking for support is at a distinct disadvantage in his relations with other family members. Not only does he experience most intensely the tensions and dilemmas of the family but he also lacks power, in interpersonal terms, to effect any control over what is already a difficult situation. This in turn only further aggravates the situation and functions to increase the sense of intolerability of family life. Intolerable, yet for this individual indispensable. In such circumstances it is not outrageous to suggest that this particular actor, if anyone, within the family is strategically located in that structure to enter a schizophrenic career.

In summary then, I have tried to argue that family life in highly differentiated social structures is characterised by tenuous and precarious social relationships which are deeply affected by wider social processes. This characterisation, it has been suggested, is the normal condition of family life and not a deviation or a pathological case. This structure is very akin to what are currently classified as schizophrenogenic structures. The development of a mental and social process called schizophrenia is suggested to result from the inability of actors to 'cope' with such a structure. This inability or ability is said to be in direct relationship to conditions described as close and looseknit social networks enjoyed by the participants and the distribution of power within the family. Power is conceptualised not just in formal economic and legal terms but also, with critical importance, in terms of interpersonal exchange.

Notes

[1] This essay is based on a paper originally prepared and delivered at a Symposium of the National Deviancy Conference in January 1971.

[2] The list of publications on this subject is of considerable length. The following is indicative only: Laing, R. D. *The Divided Self* (Tavistock, London 1960/Penguin, Harmondsworth 1965); Laing, R. D. and Esterson, A. *Sanity, Madness and the Family* (Tavistock, London 1964/Penguin, Harmondsworth 1970); Lidz, T., *et al. Schizophrenia and the Family* (International Universities Press, New York 1965); Jackson, D. D. (ed.) *The Etiology of Schizophrenia* (Basic Books, New York 1960); Szasz, Thomas Stephen *The Myth of Mental Illness: Foundations of a Theory of Personal Conduct* (Secker & Warburg, 1962); Handel, Gerald (ed.) *The Psychosocial Interior of the Family* (George Allen & Unwin, London 1969); Szasz, T. S. *The Manufacture of Madness* (New York 1970); Goffman, E. *Stigma* (New York 1961) and *Asylums* (New York 1961); Cooper, David Graham *Psychiatry and Anti-Psychiatry* (Tavistock, London 1967).

[3] Berger, B. and Kellner, H. *Diogenes* vol. XLVI (1964).

[4] Berger and Kellner, op. cit., pp.7–8.

[5] Berger and Kellner, op. cit., p.1.

[6] Berger and Kellner, op. cit., p.4.

[7] Berger and Kellner, op. cit., p.5.

[8] Berger and Kellner, op. cit., p.17.

[9] Parsons, T. and Bales, R. F. *Family, Socialisation and Interaction Process* (Routledge & Kegan Paul, London 1964).

[10] Parsons and Bales, op. cit., p.16.

[11] Parsons and Bales, op. cit., p.16.

[12] Parsons and Bales, op. cit., pp.16–17.

[13] Berger and Kellner, op. cit., p.17.

[14] For a critical discussion of this issue see Allen, S. 'Some Theoretical Problems in the Study of Youth', *Sociological Review*, vol. XVI (1968), pp.319–29.

15 Titmuss, R. M. *Essays on the Welfare State* (Allen and Unwin, London 1960), ch.6, p.111.

16 Titmuss, op. cit., p.111.

17 Titmuss, op. cit., p.112.

18 Friedan, B. *The Feminine Mystique* (Penguin, Harmondsworth 1965).

19 Roth, Philip *Portnoy's Complaint* (Jonathan Cape, London 1969). This novel is an excellent portrait, *inter alia*, of the tensions and anxieties of socialisation in a family setting.

20 Berger and Kellner, op. cit., p.16. The authors do recognise 'the difficulty and precariousness of the world-building enterprise'. Nevertheless this feature is not developed by them, concentrating as they do on the 'stabilising' effect of marriage and family life.

21 Bott, E. *Family and Social Networks* (Tavistock, London 1968), p.58. Whatever the criticisms of this particular research, they do not I think detract from the utility of the concepts I wish to utilise in this essay.

22 Bott, op. cit., p.58.

23 Bott, op. cit., p.58.

24 Bott, op. cit., p.59.

25 Bott, op. cit., p.59.

26 Lockwood, D., 'Social Integration and System Integration' in *Explorations in Social Change* ed. Zollschan, G. K. and Hirsch, W. (Routledge & Kegan Paul, London 1964).

Lockwood's essay is significant for my argument in that the distinction made between social integration and system integration can be applied to my analysis of family life. The contradictions which, I am arguing, are characteristic of all families in highly differentiated societies do not, of necessity, lead to interpersonal conflict and anxiety. Thus families not apparently schizophrenogenic in terms of the meanings and expectations of their participants may still be characterised as a structure of contradictions, for example, between husband and wife, children and parents. The nature of the family social networks in this respect is seen as a crucial 'intervening variable' affecting the *experience* and *meaning* of family life for its members.

27 For a discussion of these two concepts of power see Bachrach, P., and Baratz, M. S., 'Two Faces of Power' in their book *Power and Poverty, Theory and Practice* (Oxford University Press, London 1970).

28 Blau, Peter M. *Exchange and Power in Social Life* (Wiley, New York 1964).

Moralists in the Moron Market

Iain MANSON and Jerry PALMER

> Filthy literature is the great moron maker. It is creating criminals
> faster than jails can be built.
>
> *J. Edgar Hoover*

Etymologically, the word 'pornography' means the representation ('graphos')
of explicitly sexual behaviour, specifically the behaviour of prostitutes
('porne'—a whore). This analysis omits the essential: these depictions are
thought to influence behaviour. In reality, the pornography debate is not
about the nature of representations, despite the occasional intervention of
maverick critics like David Holbrook and George Steiner, but about the
social effects of the consumption of pornography, in other words about
personal sexual behaviour. According to Steiner, pornography is bad
because it intrudes upon our privacy. According to Commissioner Keating,
the author of a minority report to the Presidential Commission on Obscenity
and Pornography (hereinafter the Johnson Report) it is bad because it
causes sexual delinquency.[1]

Traditionally, if pornography has not been seen as a 'raging menace',[2]
it has been seen as a kind of safety valve. According to Polsky,[3] the most
often-quoted sociologist on the subject, pornography is the functional
equivalent of prostitution: both are required to allow for the expression of
the 'naturally anarchic' sexual desires that are present in every man and for
which there is no outlet within the framework of the family. Equally, the
stigmatization that falls upon prostitutes and pornographers has the function
of demarcating the boundaries of the sexually permissible: the fact of deviance
is used, with admirable economy, to emphasis the norm.

Polsky uses this argument to maintain that the distinction between hard-
and soft-core pornography is specious. In his view, since pornography is
that which is used to channel off what are defined as 'anti social' sexual
desires, in this case masturbatory fantasies, anything that facilitates these
fantasies is by definition pornographic. The difficulty with this definition
is that the most unlikely objects can in fact be imbued with sexual connotations—we are particularly impressed with the idea that police handcuffs
can be a sexual stimulus.[4] Polsky does not in fact pursue his argument to
its logical conclusion, namely that anything is potentially pornographic if
one feels inclined to make it so; indeed he cannot, for this *reductio ad*

absurdum reveals the argument's weakness. In fact, the mere use of something as a sexual stimulus is not sufficient for it to be labelled pornographic: the use has to be stigmatised by a social group with the power to make the stigmatisation stick. Pornography, in fact, has to be negotiated.[5]

Polsky's analysis corresponds to a situation in which the consumption of pornography, however imprecisely it is defined, is a minority activity. Over the last decade, there has been a vast expansion in the market for sexually explicit depictions and a massive change in the social definition of what sexual behaviour is considered acceptable: in England these changes are usually lumped together under the heading 'the permissive society'.

Our intention in this article is to describe the changes that have occurred in the erotic market and to outline the debate that has arisen as a result.

In general terms the production of pornography is organised in the oligarchic fashion found in many other industries. Berl Kutchinsky's remarks on the Danish industry are pertinent to the situation in Britain and the USA:

> ... the pornography business in Denmark ... has been developing in the direction of an ordinary modern industry, with mass production, disappearance of smaller companies, competition between the larger ones and appeal to foreign markets.[6]

Although production of all forms of pornography is legal in Denmark, the remarks still apply to the American and British situations in so far as the bulk of pornography produced in these countries is of the 'soft-core' variety, that is, material which is on the fringes of legality, and therefore, for the most part, not subject to prosecution. Prosecutions do take place, and there are allegations that pornography shops can only stock material liable to prosecution by bribing the police, but the vast majority of all the so-called pornography sold in Britain and the USA falls into the 'just legal' category; indeed this is the bed-rock of the pornography industry in these two countries.

The Johnson Report reproduces in detail the characteristics of 'hard-core' and 'soft-core' pornography that are utilised by the trade:

> The characteristics of hard-core materials are as follows:
> 1) The sexual activity depicted is certain. That is, photographs of human sexual intercourse (including bestiality) leave nothing to the imagination. The viewer has no doubt that the activity depicted is real, not simulated intercourse.
> 2) The photographic depiction of the sexual activity focuses upon the sexual contact of the genitals. The male genital organ is shown erect,

rather than in the flaccid state depicted in 'borderline' materials.
3) Intromission, or penetration, whether oral, vaginal or anal, is clearly shown, with particular emphasis on oral-genital contact.
4) The materials are not sold openly, but are distributed in an under-the-counter manner.

The market definition of the soft-core is reported thus:

a) Photographic focus on female genitalia or upon flaccid male genitalia;
b) Apposition of genitalia (in any combination) with no intromission and the penis in a flaccid state;
c) Implied fellation or cunnilingus (no matter how strong the implication);
d) Sexual intercourse which could be simulated because penetration is not shown; and
e) Sexual intercourse which is apparently real but does not focus on the genitalia. This category is doubtless the most 'border line'.[7]

The conclusion of this section of the technical report is that:

... the hard-core classification does not include the vast majority of magazines sold openly in self-labelled adult bookstores in the United States. In addition, the frontiers are constantly being challenged. Individual photographs of 'hard-core' activity are now found in books and magazines containing related text and non-hard-core photographs. The legal status of this technique is as yet unresolved.[8]

This market definition is equally applicable to Britain. In most of the book stores that we have visited the majority of the material available is 'soft-core', aimed at the heterosexual male. This includes 'strip-tease' pictures, straight 'nudie' pictures, books and magazines of the *Playboy* variety, and movie versions of the same. Most of them are domestic products, but there is usually a large selection of similar American imports.

The general content and layout of American magazines is more sophisticated; there is usually a text, and trouble is usually taken to make the text and the photographs relate to each other (in contradistinction to their British counterparts, as we shall show). The photographic work is usually of a higher standard than in the domestic product, and they tend, in general, to be rather more 'borderline'. Consequently they tend to be rather more expensive.

There is no doubt that this difference in levels of technical sophistication is due to the size and organisation of the American industry. For example, we have come across imported American catalogues for 'bizarre films'. These contain stills from the various films and brief textual descriptions. they serve the dual function of soft-core magazines and mail-order catalogue for 'the real thing'. This level of marketing sophistication is not reached in Britain; in general fullscale production of the type outlined by Kutchinsky has yet to get under way in Britain. The British market has without doubt rationalised itself and increased its production over the last few years to meet an expanded demand, but whereas the American industry has modified its products, and differentiated them in accordance with modern business practice, to appeal to an extended market, British production has tended to remain more traditional, in this as in other fields. For example, American 'soft-core' magazines have, in the last few years, emulated in many ways the successful girlie magazines like *Playboy*: pictures are well printed on good-quality paper, colour pictures are frequently used and texts are carefully related to the pictures. Although not attempting feature articles (this is not the market they are aiming at) the technical standard is approaching that of expensive 'respectable' publications. (In Denmark this is also true of 'hard-core' series such as those put out by the Colour Climax Corporation.) The American format has developed into a 'photo-reader' style that consists of full, half- and quarter-page size photographs linked by an accompanying text.

British production has also improved its technical quality, but the results are still more amateurish, especially in the borderline areas. Such magazines as do meet the professional standards of the USA are produced by wholesalers who work well within the safety-limit of current acceptability—for instance, publications such as *Probe* and *Exciting Cinema*, both produced by Goldstar. The more borderline the material, the lower the technical standard: texts which bear no relation to the photographs are commonplace, as are series of photographs which are obviously the prints of virtually everything shot during the session. Given that a modern camera rewinds in about a second, this leads to pages of photographs with very little difference between them. Typically these publications are marketed under titles such as *Bum Biters, Lesbian Love vols 1, 2 and 3, Bound to Please, The Bizarre World of Spanky Lane*, etc. The British pornographer has made little concession to demands for improved quality. The dominant attitude seems to be 'take what you're given and think yourself lucky'. This is possible because current police activity (seizure of whole editions of *Men Only* and *Club International*, which are both *Playboy*-format magazines) ensures that the business remains marginal to the entertainment industry and the consumer market in general. It is safe to predict that if the general trend towards liberalisation of the last decade continues, the pornography business will be forced to become more 'product-oriented'.

Photo-readers constitute one of the two main growth areas within the British pornography industry. The other is sex education publications. Of these there are two main types: 'love positions' and 'sex ed.' The love-position magazines and books are normally composed of pictures of simulated intercourse in various positions—*The 69 Positions of Love*—or various settings—*Sex in a Motor Car*. Most of these are well within the 'soft-core' category, not showing genitals at all, and it is these that have the largest sales—in some cases up to 50,000 copies.

The 'sex ed.' magazine market has grown immensely over the past four years. By far the most popular of these magazines are those using the format invented by *Forum* four years ago: 50–80 page, pocket size, consisting of feature articles, readers' letters and some illustrations. *Forum* remains the most serious of these magazines, but in the last four years it has been copied by several publications which can have no real claim to being serious sex education publications. Typically these contain overtly titillating material dealing with heterosexual and all forms of deviant sexual behaviour. Articles on such topics as 'A Question of Size—Does it Really Matter?', 'Randon on Rubber', 'The Feminine Fascination for the Dildo' are the stock in hand of these publications, the rest of the content being readers' letters. The standard is excruciatingly low; even the articles claiming to be instructive and written by people with (claimed) qualifications such as BSc MILT (C) produce gems like 'Once a girl lets her love juices out, she loses her zest for further copulation ... that is presuming that one orgasm was sufficient to satate [sic] her libido'.[9]

We have no exact figures for the production costs of such magazine, but they must be remarkably low. Most of the pictures are pirated from other magazines, catalogues etc. Much of the text is in the form of correspondence (some of which is probably genuine) and the cost of commissioning an article is minimal: £20–30/£50–75. Their retail price is between 50 p and £1.40, and the wholesale discount allowed on them averages out at about 25 percent, depending upon the size of the order. With a circulation of around 50,000 (the largest reported was 130,000) the profit level must be high.

The most enterprising of these magazines has stretched its market even further by introducing a quarterly edition and a monthly digest of readers' letters. This is published midmonth, which combined with the end-of-month publication of the regular magazine makes effectively a fortnighlty publication with quarterly extras. This is clearly a highly profitable sector of the trade, but it is open to prosecution. The same magazine has thirteen offences awaiting trial, one for each of its first thirteen editions.

It has proved impossible to obtain reliable figures on the overall profitabilty of the English market. We have read of and have been given by people in the trade estimates ranging from £5 million through 'several hundreds of millions of pounds'. However, as these estimates do not specify what they include, they are of little use. One thing is certain, however: those at the higher end of the scale are grossly exaggerated; the profits of the entire book-publishing business in Great Britain do not add up to 'several hundreds of millions'. There is no doubt that money is being made in the pornography trade in Great Britain, and it is being done by the normal business expedient of undercutting competitors and expanding the market. Those that are making the money tend to be the wholesalers/publishers. Although the number of retail outlets has increased over the past few years (probably doubled) these tend to be owner-occupied. The increase in their numbers can be seen as nothing more sinister than taking up the slack in a newly expanded market. Not all of these shops is successful: indeed, the business is fairly risky for the single retailer. His success depends upon many factors, not the least of which is the area in which the shop is located. We have come across several shops that have folded because of a miscalculation in the market potential of a given (usually suburban or provincial) area. The most successful areas tend to be in the centre of large conurbations. Here the profits are greater, but the market is also the most monopolised. The average retailer in an out-of-town shop makes a comfortable living, but very few make fortunes. Such fortunes as are made are by the limited number of wholesaler/publishers, and the reason for their success is their semi-legal status that ensures a relatively low degree of competition in what has become a fairly large market.

What does Anglo-Saxon society think of pornography? The sheer profitability of the industry reveals what one section of the population thinks, and campaigns demanding an end to this 'epidemic of filth' demonstrate the existence of another end to the spectrum. But John Citizen, caught between cries of horror and squeals of delight, has yet to opt definitively: the silent majority has lived up to its name.

There are indications, no more, of majority opinion. A survey conducted by the Johnson Commission found that a majority of the US population believed that adults should be allowed access to whatever sexual depictions they wanted, but that young people should not be so privileged. They also found that around two-thirds of those who favoured lifting restrictions did so with the proviso that they would change their ideas if it could be clearly demonstrated that the consumption of pornography was socially harmful. Only 2 percent of the sample surveyed spontaneously mentioned pornography as a 'serious problem', and the majority placed it relatively low as a priority problem among the thirteen topics spontaneously volunteered.[10]

In England a recent survey[11] revealed contradictory attitudes among the population. On the one hand, between 80 and 90 percent agreed that adults should be allowed access to whatever depictions they wanted provided it was not harmful; on the other hand a substantial majority—67 percent—felt that 'something should be done by the government about dirty books on sale in Britain'. What this probably reveals is that if you ask loaded questions, you will on the whole get loaded answers: put in terms of the freedom of the mature individual, naturally a majority will favour lifting restrictions; similarly, put in terms of 'dirty books', naturally a majority will favour restrictions—but what do they think 'dirty books' means: *Playboy*? What one can conclude safely is that people hold contradictory attitudes, and that the general area of debate is agreed to centre on questions of the freedom of the adult individual and of social harm, which is a relatively liberal way of approaching the matter, as we shall show.

Anecdotal evidence of English attitudes confirms their contradictory nature. We are particularly fond of this report in the national tabloid, the *Daily Mirror*:

> Mr Tom Yardley absconded from his old people's home in Cheshire to celebrate his 100th birthday with a six-day trip to London. 'One afternoon I went to the pictures and saw a French film,' said Tom. 'It was full of nudes, so I walked out in disgust after three hours.'[12]

The most remarkable aspect of the current attitudes towards pornography is that, as far as one can tell, most people, like Tom Yardley, are not concerned about hard-core pornography. According to the Technical Reports of the Johnson Commission

> Most elements in society are not concerned with hardcore pornography. What the general public is concerned about is that currently available representations of the erotic *may* lead to more realistic kinds of representation and ultimately to what you ... call hard-core pornography.[13]

There can be no doubt that this statement is true: the current debate is conducted more or less entirely in terms of the soft-core materials readily available. In part this is because, in Britain at least, the hard core is relatively little seen, in part because under British law it is still far from difficult to obtain convictions for hard-core pornography.

No doubt there is a general public level to the debate, the opinions held by the man in the street. But as we have shown, relatively little is known about those opinions. What is known is the opinions of the moral campaigners who have entered the debate.

We argue that the moral campaigns can be classified into two sets, whose approaches are remarkably distinct from each other. We propose to label them 'conservative' and 'liberal'. The first set consists of Citizens for Decent Literature (in the USA), whose views are best known through the minority report to the Johnson Commission by their national organiser, Charles Keating, Jnr, the National Viewers and Listeners Association (national secretary, Mrs Mary Whitehouse) in England and Lord Longford's Study Group on Pornography. The list is far from exhaustive, but these groups are the best known and most influential.

The liberal set is best represented by the majority of the Johnson Commission, by the Working Party on Obscenity of the Arts Council of Great Britain, and the influential Danish criminologist Berl Kutchinsky. who contributed to the Johnson Report.[14]

The conservatives

As far as the conservatives are concerned pornography is an absolute evil in itself, by definition:

> As the Apostle Paul put it ... in his letter to the Christians in Rome: 'To be carnally minded is death, but to be spiritually minded is life and peace'. It follows that recognising the harm pornography inflicts, and the evil that it is, does not depend on statistical research, or any other external 'evidence', but on the experience of its corrupting power in our own lives. No one can say he is immune to this corruption.[15]

And in case one imagines this is a peculiarly English view, Commissioner Keating says the same: pornography is wrong because 'the Judeo-Christian ethic ... does condemn the pursuit of pleasure for its own sake.' [16]

Having asserted that the harmfulness of pornography needs no demonstration, conservative campaigners then proceed to attempt such a demonstration. Sometimes this assertion takes the form of statements along the lines 'VD is increasing, abortions are increasing, illegitimacy is increasing'. The most remarkable instance of this particular view came from Paul Danlies, founder and organiser of the short-lived English Nationwide Save-our-Youth Campaign:

> People cannot understand why youth mature much earlier than they ever have before. You've got to realise that this is no accident. This has been made possible by filth and pornography, where you're indoctrinating a way of life. Normally, twenty or thirty years ago, children didn't think about sex, they grew up normally.[17]

On other occasions proof of the harm of pornography is more anecdotal. Mrs Whitehouse recounts an incident in her autobiography as just such proof.[18] While she was a teacher, the mother of one of her pupils came to her and said that here daughter had been so aroused by a sexy passage in a TV play that she had run away with her boyfriend. It is difficult to take this story at face value. Mrs Whitehouse got the story from the mother who would obviously have a vested interest in the explanation offered, since it makes her personally blameless; second, even if there were a relationship between the sexy passage and the girl's departure, it is hardly likely to be the only or even the dominant reason why she left home. One can see the situation quite clearly: on the one hand the girl was, in Mrs Whitehouse's words 'lively and headstrong, always 'after' the boys ...'; on the other she was faced with a mother who had very different ideas on the subject: 'I don't let her out, because she's too young to be going off with the lads.' In this conflict-ridden situation, where a breaking-point will more or less inevitably be reached sooner or later, anything, the slightest touch, will apparently *cause* a radical change of behaviour. In reality it is not the cause but the last straw.

As proof of the harm of pornography the story is not very convincing. What is shocking is that both the mother and, apparently, Mrs Whitehouse believe that the film was directly responsible for the girl's actions. This evidence of insensitivity actually tells us more about the girl's reasons for leaving home than Mrs Whitehouse's interpretation.

In Mrs Whitehouse's representation of the incident, the girl's behaviour is pathological: it is as if she had been injected with a strong dose of pornography and had acted under an uncontrollable sitmulus. The comparison of pornography to a drug is in fact commonplace among conservative moralists. Professor Anderson, a member of the Longford study group, compared it to heroin: the first dose has little effects; the second you enjoy immensely; with the third you are hooked.[19] He also compared pornograhy with environmental pollution, a comparison taken up by the Festival of Light, who organised their first national rally in London under the slogan 'moral pollution needs a solution'.

Such comparisons are apparently trivial, mere heuristic devices, analogies intended to make abstract arguments more readily understandable. But underlying them is a coherently organised view of what society is: society is, they argue, fundamentally an organic unity, held together by adherence to a common set of values, in the same way as the human body is an organic unity which holds together because it functions according to a set of biologically definable norms. Therefore, anything which disrupts the 'body politic' (a metaphor taken literally) can be dismissed as 'a disease', a 'foreign body' that is 'corrupting' an other wise healthy organism.[20] This view is given clear expression in a speech to Mrs Whitehouse's NVALA conference in 1965:

> [Dr Claxton] said that anything that was mental and physical poison should be excluded, anything that degraded the human person and sapped social energy. Dr Claxton said a healthy society was one which was free from the forces that made people ill. The (radio and TV) programmes he wanted were those that promoted health and social energy ...[21]

Dr Claxton was an officer of NVALA, until his retirement Assistant Principal Secretary to the British Medical Association, a member of the Council of Reference of the Festival of Light, and responsible for a memorandum to the Longford study group.

The set of values that the conservative moralists see as the foundation of our society is Christianity. Christian values receive their social articulation through a set of institutions (the Church, the education system, the law) and if the values are to be respected and adhered to, the institutions that articulate them must also be the object of respect. It is for this reason that conservative moralists can insist that their real concern is less for four-letter words and sexy pictures than the breakdown of social discipline: according to Mrs Whitehouse there is 'a developing trend in BBC programmes to undercut authority that is undermining the morals of the British people. ... Sex and four-letter words are just the tip of the iceberg. It is the constant attack on morals and authority that concerns us'.[22] And again: 'Dirty books and sleazy films are as much a danger to Britain as enemy agents. ... Those who try to persuade us that these things are simply a matter of taste do not understand the weapons of ideological warfare'.[23]

We stated at the beginning of this article that changes in the market had led to a shift in the debate. This is not true of the conservatives, for the arguments we have selected here from ongoing campaigns are in essence no different from the views advanced long before the current expansion of the market by their equivalents:

> The publication and distribution of salacious materials is a peculiarly vicious evil; the destruction of moral character caused by it among young people cannot be overestimated. The circulation of periodicals containing such materials plays an important part in the development of crime among the youth of our community. (J. Edgar Hoover, 1956.)[24]

The conservative premise is that pornography is an evil in itself, whose harmful nature needs no demonstration. Liberals make greater demands upon empirical observation: the Arts Council of Great Britain concluded that it was not for the state to prevent any citizen from reading or viewing anything he chose unless there was 'incontrovertible evidence' that this process was injurious to society as a whole.

Thus the disagreements between liberals and conservatives turn, on the surface, on whether the consumption of pornography is socially harmful or not. Beneath this, however, lies a disagreement on the nature of social harm.

For the conservative, pornography is socially harmful because it challenges established values with regard to sexuality—and therefore everything that challenges these values is (potentially at least) pornography. Mrs White-house's pet hatred for many years was Dr Alex Comfort, whose book *The Anxiety Makers* is a swingeing attack on the medical profession's views on sexual behaviour; she once accused him of 'pandering to the lowest in human nature'.[25] In general, sex education other than traditional moral propaganda is viewed by conservatives with extreme suspicion, if not down-right hostility: they are disgusted that young people should be told how to make love without at the same time being told not to. For the liberal there is a distinct dividing line between information and titillation: sex education, sociology, etc., come on one side of it, and pornography on the other. Second, the liberal sees no particular harm in disagreements over values, and cannot see that as such it constitutes social harm. His definition is stricter:

> Just as obscenity may involve a variety of contents and judgements, so also may 'antisocial' behaviour and moral character. A declining concern with established religion, new questions as to the wisdom and morality of war, changes in attitudes towards races and minorities, and conflicts regarding the responsibility of the state to the individual and the individual to the state may all be considered to represent changes in the moral fibre of the nation. To some, these phenomena are considered to be signs of corroding moral decay; to others, signs of change and progress. It was impossible during the brief life of the Commission to obtain significant data on the effects of the exposure to pornography on nonsexual moral attitudes. Consequently the Commission has focused on that type of antisocial behaviour which tends to be more directly related to sex. This includes premarital intercouse, sex crimes, illegitimacy, and similar items.[26]

Underlying the liberal conception of what constitutes social harm, there is of course a conception of what constitutes social normality. Whereas for the conservative society is a monolithic institution, for the liberal it is pluralistic: man is free to do whatever he likes provided his actions are not incompatible with the liberty of others, and the compatibility of his actions is decided by the state (the democratically elected legislature), which he implicitly contracts to obey. It is against the background of these fundamentals that the liberal view of limited conflict is comprehensible: limited conflict both ensures the survival of the fittest opinions and prevents grievances from festering. Therefore, the liberal's notion of social harm is fundamentally a legal one. Liberals think of social harm as a crime and therefore their insistence on statistical investigation of correlations between the consumption of erotica and the incidence of sex crimes makes perfect sense. But, of course, it only makes sense if one accepts the liberals' premises.

There has in fact been remarkably little investigation of the effects of pornography. The Longford study group, true to its conservative premises, did not study it at all: their 'evidence' consists of a dozen anecdotes told them by people who dropped into their office while their investigation was in progress. The serious work consists of the research commissioned for the Johnson Report, and research on the situation in Copenhagen by Kutchinsky and Ben-Veniste, both quoted in the Johnson Report.

This research presents two major conclusions. First, the consumption of erotica leads to sexual arousal in the majority of cases, and perhaps to some increase in sexual activity in the 24 hours following consumption. It is hardly a surprising conclusion: And it must be admitted that the sight of an attractive member of the opposite sex walking down the street—or even of one's wife hanging out the washing—might equally well produce the same results. Furthermore, as the Arts Council of Great Britain report argued, sexual activity is not a crime and 'it is surely an affront both to legal and to common sense that incitement to a non-crime should be punishable as crime'.[27]

Sexual activity becomes a crime when it is pursued without the consent of the others involved. The second conclusion of the American and Danish research is that there is no significant correlation between the incidence of sexual crime and the consumption of erotica. This is not to say that the consumption of erotica never contributes to the growth of a deviant career, but that it is highly unlikely to make any significant contribution. Furthermore, the research concludes, the consumption of erotica *may* actually help to decrease the incidence of sexual crime: one survey in America concluded that adolescent sex offenders had enjoyed less exposure to erotica than was normal among people of the same background who had not committed sex offences. And the Danish experience of the legalisation of pornography was found by Kutchinsky and Ben-Veniste to correlate chronologically with a real decrease in the incidence of some categories of sexual offences. These authors carefully did not attribute a causal relationship, but it is difficult to avoid the conclusion that there is some connection.[28]

Liberals conclude that the obscenity laws should be abolished. However, they maintain, with the conservatives, that children should be 'protected' from pornography. There is in fact remarkable agreement between the two camps on this subject, for both agree that children may well be either 'traumatised' or 'corrupted' by pornography. By 'traumatised' (which is never used in its clinical sense in moral propaganda) they mean so shocked that sex is refused, or found unpleasant or difficult; by 'corrupted' they mean so attracted that sex is not only not refused, but found so pleasant that it is actively sought. The child who reads pornography (and in this context that might mean anything from sadomasochistic photographs to Honeybunch Kaminski cartoons) is put in a double-bind: if he/she refuses sex, he/she has been traumatised; if he/she seeks it, he/she has been corrupted!

Conservative concern over the effects of pornography on children is merely an extension of their general fear of dislocation of the consensus. Liberal concern is more specific. Their pluralist vision is dependent (implicitly or explicitly) upon the notion of socialisation: it is only the mature individual who is capable of dealing with stimuli as powerful as those provided by erotica. But how does the individual acquire this maturity? How is he/she socialised into the capacity to respond to these stimuli in a way that is acceptable to adult society? The liberal answer is sex education, which does not exclude the use of erotica:

> Failure to talk openly and directly about sex has several consequences. It overemphasises sex, gives it a magical, non-natural quality, making it more attractive and fascinating. It diverts the expression of sexual interest out of more legitimate channels, into less legitimate channels. Such failure makes teaching children and adolescents to become fully and adequately functioning sexual adults a more difficult task. And it clogs legitimate channels for transmitting sexual information and forces people to use clandestine and unreliable sources. ... Gradual and age-appropriate exposure to erotic stimuli may lead to the development of socially appropriate defense mechanisms like sublimation, repression, postponement and self-control. Although the analogy may be somewhat far-fetched, it seems possible that graded exposure immunizes in somewhat the same fashion that exposure to bacteria and viruses builds resistance. If this analogy has merit, total lack of exposure would render the child who is totally exposed as helpless as the animal raised in a totally sterile environment who later encounters the invariably contaminated real world.[29]

Clearly liberals do not see anything particularly worthwhile in pornography.

Their view is that people who are regular consumers are sexually inadequate,[30] but they do not see this consumption as constituting a social threat. In the words of the Johnson Commission it is a 'nuisance' rather than an 'evil'. Bernard Levin, who gave a classic version of the liberal case in a televised debate in England on the Longford Report, argued that it was a by-product, undesirable but not threatening, of society's changing definitions of the permissible.

Towards a radical alternative

The limitations of a short article preclude a full discussion of alternative views, for which we refer the reader to our *Dirty Old Man on the Last Tube*. Briefly, we would argue that the liberal view of socialisation is merely a more subtle way of containing social change than the conservative monolith: the same aim, different methods. We would contend—and there is some empirical evidence to support this contention[31]—that children have values of their own that inform the manner in which they acquire new information, about sex as much as about anything else, and therefore they are as capable as adults of 'dealing with' new stimuli. The difficulty (for adults) is that their ways of dealing with them may be very different from adult ways, for one of the central values that children recognise is the pursuit of pleasure. The pursuit of pleasure is also recognised in the value system of the adult world, but only if one has *earned* the right to it: as Jock Young has put it, 'Pleasure can only be legitimately purchased by the credit card of work' according to the formal value system of our society.[32] Children, by contrast, recognise pleasure as an inalienable right. The other relevant values that they recognise centre around their integration into their peer and reference group. These values are likely to bring them into conflict with the adult world since they stress their independence from it.

Underlying this apparently purely empirical view is a theory of personality development. Put in its most schematic form, we accept the view put forward by the 'symbolic interactionist' school of social psychology, which emphasises the individual's capacity of constructing, in active partnership with the group that he perceives as relevant to his life, a world that is his own, oriented around projects and values in whose development he actively participates. This applies as much to his psychosexual development as to any other aspect of personality development.[33]

This perspective contrasts markedly with the traditional view of sex as a biologically rooted instinct which has direct control of personality. If an instinct theory of sex is applied to the study of pornography, as it is (implicitly or explicitly) by both conservatives and liberals, the individual consumer

98

will appear the victim of an anarchic instinct aroused by an antisocial stimulus; concomitantly the pornographer is stigmatised for 'pandering to the lowest in human nature' for easy money. Conservatives and liberals agree on this description, but disagree on how much of a threat to society pornography constitutes.

If, on the other hand, a theory of psychosexual development such as we have referred to above is applied to the study of pornography, it will appear in a rather different light. In this perspective, people internalise conflicting socially created demands, and nowhere is this more true than in the area of sexuality. As an instance: men are brought up to be sexual predators; when they marry they are expected to exchange the skills of the jungle for those of the home—monogamous fidelity. The stresses and strains that result from such conflicts (there are genderspecific versions for women) engender a variety of solutions. The recourse to pornographic fantasy is one of them—a rational solution to an absurd situation.

Notes

[1] Steiner, George, 'Night Words', in *Language and Silence: Essays 1958–1966* (Faber & Faber, London 1967), pp.97ff; *Report of the US Presidential Commission on Obscenity and Pornography*, (Bantam Books, New York 1970), 'Individual Report by Commissioner Keating', *passim*.

[2] Gagnon, John H., and Simon, William, 'Pornography—Raging Menace or Paper Tiger?', in *Deviance: Studies in the Process of Stigmatization and Societal Reaction*, ed. S. Dinitz, Dyners and Clarke (Oxford University Press, New York 1969).

[3] Polsky, Ned *Hustlers, Beats and Others* (Penguin, Harmondsworth 1971), pp.184–200; cf. Brikson, K., 'Notes on the Sociology of Deviance', *Social Problems* vol. IX (Spring 1962), pp.262–88.

[4] We use this as a single example of the theme of bondage, commonplace in contemporary pornography.

[5] Cf. our *Dirty Old Man on the Last Tube* (Davis-Poynter, London 1973), ch.2.

[6] Kutchinsky, Berl, 'Pornography in Denmark', in *Technical Reports of the Presidential Commission on Obscenity and Pornography*, (US Government Printing Office, Washington DC, n.d., vol. III, p.267.

[7] Ibid., pp.181–2.

[8] Ibid.

[9] Andereisz, Godfrey J., 'The Jockeying Cult', *Search Quarterly Edition* vol. III (London, 1972), pp.18–22.

[10] *Technical Reports of the Presidential Commission,* quoted in Burns, Alan *To Deprave and Corrupt* (Davis-Poynter, London 1972), p. 190.

[11] *Evening Standard,* 6 October 1972, p.17.

[12] Quoted in *Films and Filming,* September 1972.

[13] *Technical Reports of the Presidential Commission on Obscenity and Pornography* vol. III, p.183 (n).

[14] Our two sets correspond to the two models outlined by Gagnon and Simon, op. cit.

[15] Muggeridge, Malcolm in *Pornography: The Longford Report* (Coronet Books, London 1972), p.215.

[16] *Report of the US Presidential Commission on Obscenity and Pornography,* p.582.

[17] In a lecture at Hornsey College of Art, London, November 1971.

[18] Whitehouse, Mary *Who Does She Think She Is?* (New English Library, London 1971), p.48.

[19] In a lecture at All Saints' Church, Blackheath, January 1972.

[20] This view of society is well known in sociology. It is an extreme version of the consensus model put forward by the Chicago School in its early days. Nowadays it is mostly to be found related to the study of deviancy, where it is usually known as the 'social pathology model' of deviancy; cf. e.g. Rosenquist, Carl M., 'The Moral Premises of Social Pathology', in *The Study of Social Problems,* ed. Rubington and Weinberg (Oxford University Press, New York 1971).

[21] Reported in the *Birmingham Post,* 10 May 1965.

[22] *Nottingham Guardian Journal,* 5 May 1967.

[23] *Scottish Daily Record,* 11 January 1971.

[24] 84th Congress of the USA, 2nd Session, 28 June 1956.

[25] *Birmingham Post,* 28 January 1964.

[26] *Report of the US Presidential Commission on Obscenity and Pornography,* p.4.

[27] Report of the Working Party of the Arts Council of Great Britain, published as *The Obscenity Laws* (Deutsch, London 1969), p.36.

[28] For a fuller analysis of the statistical evidence and its interpretations we refer the reader to our *Dirty Old Man on the Last Tube,* ch.5.

[29] *Report of the US Presidential Commission on Obscenity and Pornography,* pp.53 and 454.

[30] Cf. *The Dirty Old Man on the Last Tube,* ch.5.

[31] Notably in the work of Jean Piaget. Cf. especially *The Construction of Reality in the Child,* tr. Cook, M. (Basic Books, New York 1954); and *The Child's Conception of Physical Causality,* tr. N. Gabain (Littlefield, Adams & Co., Totowa, NJ 1960).

[32] Young, J. *The Drugtakers* (MacGibbon & Kee, London 1971), p.128.
[33] Cf. Simon and Gagnon, 'On Psychosexual Development', in *A Handbook of Socialisation: Research and Theory* ed. Goslin, D. (Rand McNally, New York 1969), pp.733–52.

Awareness of Homosexuality

Ken PLUMMER

In both England and America, homosexuality is a stigma symbol.[1] To be called a homosexual is to be degraded, rendered as morally dubious, or treated as different. To be publicly known as a homosexual is to invite your employer to sack you, your parents to reject you, the law to imprison you, the doctor to cure you, the moralist to denounce you, the public to mock you, the priest to pity you, the liberal to patronise you and the queerbasher to kill you. Further, given the currently fashionable theories of homosexuality which locate its origins in the parents, it is to court shame not just for yourself—but for your parents and loved ones too. Given such costs it is little wonder that most homosexuals elect to conceal their identity from public gaze.

Thus while the private incidence of homosexuality is high (around one in twenty),[2] the public awareness of it is low. While members of society are constantly rubbing shoulders with homosexuals in their family networks, their places of work and in their neighbourhoods, they normally remain unaware of this fact. Homosexuality thus becomes a well-guarded secret identity harboured by many members of society. In this article, I wish to explore the conditions under which this 'homosexual secret' is kept, the conditions under which it breaks down to become public knowledge, and the consequences to the homosexual of keeping such a secret.

Awareness contexts and homosexuality

My take-off point in this study is Glaser and Strauss's concept of 'awareness contexts', which can be used to describe the sum total of knowledge about identities held in any situation.[3] This includes knowledge of one's own identity, knowledge of the other's identity, and knowledge of the other's view of your identity. While such contexts may include many people, for simplicity I will limit my analysis to the simple dyad.

From this concept, a continuum of awareness about homosexual identities can be depicted. At one extreme is the closed context, where one partner does not know the homosexual identity of the other and where the homosexual knows this. At the other extreme is the open context, where the homosexual is aware that his partner knows his identity, where the partner does in fact know this identity, and where the homosexual also knows this.

Both partners establish a consensus about each other's actual, perceived and understood identities.[4] Both of these types are extremes, and in between a whole range of 'suspicion' contexts could be depicted,[5] where homosexuals suspect others know their identity when they do not, where others suspect people of being homosexual when they are not—and so on, through a range of possible permutations.

While each of these contexts could be described[6] statically, it is important to see their precarious and unfolding nature. A closed context may be supported by a number of structural conditions, but as soon as one of these begins to break down, the contexts may rapidly topple from being closed to being one of suspicion, or even openness. Further it is important to see the differing consequences of each kind of context: in a closed context, homosexuals may feel relatively secure and not have to work too hard to preserve their secret; in a suspicion context, homosexuals may feel very threatened and have to muster great skill to avoid full disclosure; in an open context, the mask is completely dropped and the homosexual need not worry at all about his 'secret'—though he may well have to cope with the problems of possessing a discredited indentity.[7] In what follows my main emphasis will be placed upon the movement from a closed context to a suspicion or open one, and upon the consequences of preventing the emerggence of open contexts.

Maintenance of closed awareness

I have suggested that members of society are generally unaware of having any contact with homosexuals.[8] When this is combined with the homosexual feeling secure that others do not know his real identity, there is a situation of closed awareness. At work for example, the homosexual may feel sure that his workmates do not suspect his homosexual identity, and they may not in fact suspect.[9] While always precarious, I suspect that closed awareness is a very common situation. Indeed, I would suggest that because of certain structural features surrounding homosexuality in England and America, it is relatively easy to maintain a situation of closed awareness. At least four broad factors contribute to this:

(a) Homosexuality is generally invisible. Unlike the physically handicapped, whose overt stigma makes them a highly visible group,[10] homosexuality is not usually open to public gaze.

(b) Homosexuality is generally irrelevant. For most people and in most situations, homosexuality remains outside of the 'domains of relevance'.[11] It is simply not given much thought.

(c) Sexuality is privatised. The major parts of the sexual life of Western man are restricted to certain 'back regions' and excluded from everyday routines. Sexual experiences are delegated to the realms of the private.

(d) Society is segregated. Much of the social life of complex society is characterised by extreme segregation, both of groups into subcultures and individuals into role segments. It becomes increasingly possible for an individual to 'slice' his life into parts—territorially, temporally and biographically. Only under a few limited circumstances—if any—need people be known in their totality.

Breakdown of closed awareness

While these four broad features may generally help to sustain a closed awareness context, many factors could contribute to its breakdown. Most generally, the breakdown becomes more likely whenever (i) homosexuality increases in visibility (b) homosexuality increases in relevance (c) sexuality becomes deprivatised and (d) social groups become less segregated. Each of these hypotheses is interconnected. In what follows, I wish to isolate a number of variables which contribute to such changes.

Making homosexuality visible[12]

Recognition of homosexuality depends upon both perception and action: somebody must identify a homosexual, and certain actions must be identifiable as homosexual. With the exception of being caught in the act there is nothing automatic and intrinsic about such recognition processes; they depend largely upon the mediation of certain patterns of socially constructed meanings. Given this, it becomes possible that some people who see themselves as homosexual will never become visible; and some people who are not homosexual will be identified as such.[13] A potentiality for miscarriage of justice becomes possible.

As Kitsuse discovered in his study of the reaction of American students to homosexuals some ten years ago, identification of homosexuals may be direct or indirect.[14] Directly, homosexuals may be recognised by discovery, denunciation or declaration; indirectly, homosexuals may be recognised through stereotypical symmetry and rumour. I will discuss each of these variables briefly in turn.

Discovery as direct visibility

By discovery here, I refer to the chance of being caught literally with one's trousers down. Sexual acts between the same sex are relatively clearly definable as homosexual—though there is always the chance that an 'account' of some form can neutralise away the apparently explicit homosexual meanings of the act. Schoolboys may say that 'it's only a phase, sir,' and teenage boy prostitutes may say they were only doing it for the money—and in both cases the homosexual act may be reinterpreted as 'not really homosexual'.[15] In general, however, being caught *in flagrante delicto* is sufficient to be tagged 'homosexual'.

Since homosexual acts, like heterosexual ones, generally take place away from easily offended eyes, such visibility is rare. At the same time, there are a number of public locales—parks and commons, cinemas, baths, public conveniences—where some homosexuals do meet to 'have sex'. Although, as I will argue later, they are generally shielded from public surveillance, activities in these locales are more likely to be rendered visible.[16]

Denunciation as direct visibility

For a variety of reasons, some homosexuals who offend society's norms may find themselves ushered into a public role of infamy from which there can be little return. With fanfares and trumpets, witch-hunts seek out homosexuals; the media announces them and the courts and prisons castigate them. A private identity becomes a public one, recognisable to all. Such denunciations may take place on a national level, as in the infamous English scandals of Wilde, Montagu, Harvey or Vassal, where a public figure becomes universally degraded and stigmatised.[17] Or they may take place on a much more local level, where, for example, local newspapers fill in the lurid details of local homosexuals who come before the courts. In both cases, individuals are ushered into deviant labels visible to society's members. Once again, given the proportional infrequency of public prosecutions of homosexuals, most homosexuals evade becoming visible in such a manner.

Declaration as direct visibility

Under a variety of situations, the homosexual may actually decide that it is expedient for him to voluntarily declare his homosexuality. Not all homosexuals, for example, are able to withstand the pressures of leading a double life with their parents and a few therefore find it necessary to inform parents of their sexual proclivities. Others, visiting psychiatrists, may again find it necessary to inform the analyst of their identity. Likewise the 'professional homosexual' who uses his public declaration to 'advance homosexual

106

causes', the soldier who declares his homosexuality in order to get out of the service and the Gay Liberation Front member who publicly wears his badge and holds hands in the street may all find it expedient to reveal their identities and in so doing break down the closed awareness entext.

One especially important reason why a homosexual should declare his sexuality, albeit discreetly, arises from his need to locate other homosexuals. There is a paradox here: to the extent that the homosexual succeeds in making himself invisible, so he will cut himself off from contact with other homosexuals—who are, after all, potential lovers. The more successful he is at 'saving face', the less successful he may be at 'finding a trick'.

Stereotypical symmetry as indirect visibility

Although there is evidence to suggest that only a limited section of the population hold rigid stereotypes of the homosexual,[18] and evidence to suggest that very few homosexuals actually match this stereotype,[19] the existence of homosexual stereotyping is beyond dispute. Such stereotypes provide 'cues' for some perceivers to interpret an individual who exhibit these 'cues' (whether homosexual or not) as homosexual. To assist the public in recognising homosexuals, several accounts exist in both the academic and non-academic press of 'points to watch for'. The *News of the World*, in England, advised its readers in 1964 to be cautious of 'the man who has never married; the fussy dresser; the office or factory crawler with a smarmy grin on his face; the man with an excessive interest in youth activites; the man who cannot resist pawing you as he talks'.[20] These men, the article suggests, are likely to be homosexual.

Another, much more comprehensive, list is provided by a religious crusader, David Wilkinson, in an article for *Teen Challenge* in America entitled 'Hope for Homosexuals'. He writes:

> ... there are many ways to tell whether or not a person is overtly homosexual. Listed are 25 ways to tell a homosexual.*

1 Demonstrations of pouting—petulance.
2 Short interest spans—shifting moods.
3 A taste for unconventional clothing.
4 Attraction to bright colours, tight clothing and special boots.
5 Attraction to ornaments and gadgets.
6 Swaying hips.
7 Striking unusual poses.
8 Flirting with the eyelids (fluttering).

9 Tripping gait and swaggering shoulders.
10 Certain types of chronic alcoholism.
11 Insane jealousy.
12 A tendency to lie and deceive.
13 Overly emotional.
14 Withdrawn—a tendency to want to be alone.
15 Delicate physique or overly muscular.
16 Broad hips.
17 Soft, pale skin.
18 A limp wrist.
19 Prettiness effected by make-up.
20 Special hair styles and artful combing.
21 Too much deodorant or toiletry.
22 Gushy, flowery conversation, i.e. 'wild', 'mad', etc.
23 Shrillness of voice, lisping or a tendency to falsetto.
24 A dislike for belts, garters, laced shoes, ties, hats, gloves.
25 A compulsion to move around, walk, hustle.

* Normal men may demonstrate a few of these tendencies, while homosexuals will usually demonstrate most of the listed characteristics.

Such lists are plentiful, and they are not restricted to the popular press. Clifford Allen, for example, writing in his *Textbook of Psychosexual Disorders* tells the serious student:

> It is not necessary to be homosexual to be able to detect inverts in casual social life. Although I am normal I have seen many homosexuals and am able to observe them in a crowd by minute gestures, tones of speech, and so on. Even on the wireless one can tell them by their speech which is either excessively soft and slightly slurred or else grating and harsh.[21]

Clearly, if an individual matches some of these stereotypical portraits, he stands a greater chance of being recognised as a homosexual—whether or not he in fact is. Such stereoptypes could have disastrous consequences for the effeminate-looking heterosexual.[22]

Rumour as indirect visibility

In the study of students' reactions towards homosexuals by John Kitsuse, the author discovered that many homosexuals were recognised through aid of rumours and gossip; and in Schofield's recent work involving over

300 young respondents, the most frequent answer to the question 'How did you get to know that X was a homosexual?' was simply that 'Others told me'. Such rumours may not be restricted to people; they may also be applied to places. Thus knowledge may become public about a homosexual bar or public convenience, or even a whole community, and all who frequent it become suspect. Students in one class at a Midlands Technical College informed me of a homosexual bar nearby, and warned that anyone who goes there must be a 'poof'. Such knowledge then, once public, places a strain on the homosexual, particularly at those points of entry to 'bars' and 'cottages' (public conveniences) where the public may see him and demand some kind of explanation. Of course this rarely happens but for the homosexual it may become a significant issue. One homosexual in Humphreys's study commented about his departures from public conveniences this way:[23]

> Sometimes when I come out of a tea-room, I look up to the sky just to make sure that some plane isn't flying around up there writing JOHN JONES IS A PERVERT.

Making homosexuality relevant

I suspect, though it is a matter for empirical inquiry, that most members of a society normally face situations in which homosexuality is absolutely irrelevant. Even when confronted with information about it, they ignore or deny its significance. As Wildeblood wrote:

> I had on several occasions discussed the problem of homosexuality with my mother and father, hoping to find some ways of telling them about myself. But it was impossible. Their attitude like that of so many people was not one of particular condemnation or of particular tolerance. It was simply that they had not given the matter much thought because they did not believe they knew any homosexuals.[24]

Generally, then, closed awareness can be easily maintained because homosexuality figures so low in most members' 'domains of relevance'. There are, however, some *people*, some *times* and some *situations* when homosexuality becomes an issue, and it is these that I wish to consider here.

People who make homosexuality relevant

Ironically, the most significant group to treat homosexuality as an issue are homosexuals themselves. Each situation that a homosexual enters may, amongst other things, be briefly assessed for potential homosexual partners and for potential discreditors. To the homosexual, the secret identity looms so significantly in his consciousness that most situations will be briefly interpreted through it. This may well mean that seeing everyone as potentially homosexual and being seen by everyone as a homosexual becomes an implicit assumption of much homosexual interaction. And if such an assumption is held, closed awareness breaks down to a suspicion awareness.

Homosexuals, however, are not the only group in society for whom homosexuality is a salient issue: there are also those whom Goffman calls the 'wise' ('persons who are normal but whose special situation has made them intimately privy to the secret life of the stigmatised individuals and sympathetic with it') and the 'knowing' who have knowledge and awareness of homosexual activity even if they do not support it.[25] Examples of the 'wise' may include the 'gay moll' (the 'straight' female who hangs around with male homosexuals and who enjoys their company) and the 'straight' friend who—through contact with homosexuals—becomes sensitised to the world view of the homosexual without being one. Examples of the 'knowing' include both agents of control (such as the police patrolling a local 'cottage'), and exploitative others who are able to prey upon the homosexual's vulnerability, (such as the blackmailer and the 'queer-basher'). All of these people then become aware of homosexuality as an issue and render situations of closed awareness highly vulnerable.

Times when homosexuality becomes relevant

Homosexuality may also become significant as an issue at certain critical times, particularly those that have been called times of 'moral panic'.[26] One such American incident is that of the 'Boys of Boise' reported by John Gerassi.[27] On Halloween night 1955, a witch-hunt hysteria began with the arrest of three men for homosexual offences in Boise, Idaho—a ('respectable') middle-class town with a population of about 30,000. Two days later the Idaho *Daily Statesman* published an incendiary story entitled 'Crush The Monster' clearly indicating that 'these arrests mark only the start of an investigation that has only 'scratched the surface'; and suggesting that the task of uncovering the homosexual underworld in Boise was 'too big and too sinister to be left alone to a private detective and an officer of the probate court'. About a hundred boys and several adults were said to be involved by this time. Police, community and press panicked and within weeks a list of 500 names of suspected homosexuals had been constructed; before the scadal ended in 1966, some 1,472 men had been questioned. All men became suspect in this highly charged atmosphere, where women would ring up the police and say: 'I've just seen so and so sitting by the high school practice field with a funny look on his face', and men had to avoid meeting other men alone for fear of being labelled homosexual. One male respondent told Gerassi in 1965:[28]

> ... after they arrested that pianist fellow and Larsen, both of whom were charged with indecent acts against adults, well, let me tell you, every bachelor became jittery. I was a buyer then, so I had to travel a great deal. Everywhere I went, people started making jokes. I used to wear my school ring on the third finger of my right hand. Well, I had to stop that. I remember talking to a guy in Denver, a buyer from Salt Lake, a guy I had gotten to know quite well. And all of a sudden, he starts kidding me about boys-y, and then he looks at my hand and says with the goddamest sarcastic smile, 'hey, I see you're wearing a ring these days ...'. Boy, I felt like punching him in the nose. He had seen that ring ever since we first met, three years before. Well, anyway that's the way it went. It got so bad that everytime I left Boise on business I was sure some dirty gossiper was spreading the word that I was going to see my boy friend who had left Boise not to get arrested.

Situations where homosexuality becomes relevant

Although in the past, homosexuality has been considered a taboo topic which cannot be raised in 'polite company', more recently it has become eligible for public discussion and debate—both jocular and serious. University unions debate homosexuality, women's magazines run feature articles on it, and the entertainment media constantly depict it. For the homosexual today, then, there is the increasing probability that he will be confronted with situations in which 'straight people' in his presence will be discussing homosexuality—the 'queer joke' which embarrasses, the discussion in which he must conceal his expertise and insight,[29] the gossip where 'cool' must be kept. In each of these situations, the homosexual may try to avoid the situation or else enter a state which could be characterised as 'stage fright'—a state where identity is severely at risk.[30]

Deprivatising sexuality

Seeing homosexuality as largely invisible and irrelevant is a specific example of a more generalised phenomenon: the privatised nature of sexuality.

Most sexuality lies well within the realms of privacy and concealment. Wayland Young, amongst others, has described how sexuality has developed within a shroud of excluded imagery language, actions and people: people are not provided with a language with which they can talk about sex, are inhibited by morals which prohibit sex from any form of public display, and are denied access to most forms of sexual imagery.[31] Under such circumstances it is easy for concealment of sexuality to occur. Nobody can see and nobody can ask.

For the homosexual, then, the fact that sexuality is rarely openly raised serves as an insulating factor, protecting his sexual identity from public gaze. Once again, however, there are situations in which the homosexual may find sexuality becoming an issue, and at such times his identity becomes tentatively vulnerable. The most apparent examples of this are the direct situations when sex is spoken about or when sex activity is actually expected, for there are, despite protestations to the contrary, a number of situations in our culture where sexual activity is actually prescribed. The most noticeable examples seem to come from the imperatives of male culture, where men together may be expected to talk sex and boast of their exploits. This may be particularly strong at adolescence: adolescent boys 'clearly talk about girls and sex a good deal of the time they are together'.[32] Likewise, sexual jokes, 'stag nights', work talk and gang chat may all raise sex as a matter of course, and simultaneously raise problems of identity for the homosexual. Is he, for example, to 'play along' with a group whistling at women and talking about sexual exploits, or is he to 'drop out' of the conversation or the group? In the first case, his fragrant lying may be a source of embarrassment while, in the latter, his silence will be suspicious. In either case, when sexuality is raised, his identity becomes a problem.

So far, I have spoken about sex as it relates to genital meanings: it clearly also has broader gender and social (for example, marital) ramifications. Here, sexuality is much less privatised. It is, after all, very much a matter of public knowledge whether one is a man or a woman, and whether one is married or not. There are times and situations when a man may be able to get away with not being masculine, and there are times too when a man may be granted celibacy or bachelorhood. But, in general, failure to publicly demonstrate that one is a *man* or that one is *normally married* will be regarded by others with suspicion: people will wonder, questions will be asked and gossip will spread. Ralph Turner, in his textbook on *Family Interaction* suggests that marriage is one of the cornerstones of our value system, providing an important basis for judgements of normalcy and masculinity. He writes of the:[33]

implication of personal competence and normality associated with the married state, and the suspicion that the unmarried may be disoriented, incompetent, maladjusted—in some sense personally inadequate. ... For the man there is ... reflection of his masculinity. If the man is not especially attractive, then his failure to marry is identified with weakness and possible impotence. If he is clearly attractive and holds on too long, the suspicion of homosexuality is often spread through gossip. The attractive man or woman with no discoverable personal deficiencies who fails to marry represents a continuing puzzle to those about him and is likely to be plagued constantly with questions or insinuations about why he or she has not married.

Desegregating society

It is a commonplace of social science that complex societies like England and America are characterised by differentiation and segmentation. Individuals may divide their lives temporally, territorially and biographically—living off the knowledge which they present in any situation to that which is strictly relevant for the purpose at hand, and avoiding being known in their totality. For the homosexual, this means that he may restrict the information that any group has about him merely by restricting his contact with that group. At work, he is known as the clerk; at church, he is the organist; in the street or on the bus, he is simply a stranger. Given the fleeting, impersonal and role-specific nature of most interaction in complex society, the homosexual need never be known as a homosexual in most groups. Closed awareness prevails.

Of course, in some parts of his world,[34] the homosexual may well seek to be known as a homosexual. He may establish relationships where his role is specifically that of a homosexual, and he may move into protective, home territories where his homosexuality is taken for granted. By virtue or one's presence in certain bars, toilets and other public places, one may be presumed to be a homosexual. Open awareness prevails. The gay bar may be seen as one important 'home territory in a back region',[35] a region invisible to the mainstream of daily activity where the regular participants enjoy a relative freedom of behaviour and a sense of intimacy and control. It is thus a place which permits many homosexuals the chance to drop the mask they wear during their working day and, in relative security and and anonymity, to 'let their hair down'. A number of factors serve to protect such places from public visibility. First, such bars are concealed from 'front regions'. They lie at the top of long flights of stairs, or below eye level in basements, in the most remote bars in hotels, ones that are least likely to be wandered into by chance, or behind a 'protective front room reeking with respectability'.[36] Very rarely are highly luminous signs displayed, and then they assert only that it is 'members only'—I know of no club which labels itself publicly as a homosexual club. The point of entry to such meeting places then is rarely left to chance factors: in clubs, it is almost impossible to enter without being at least aware of the homosexual nature of the setting.

A second factor in territorial defence is the management's policy of 'insulation'—in which a barrier is erected 'between the occupant of the territory and potential invaders'.[37] The most obvious technique of insulation is the policy of 'membership'—where membership cards are regularly checked at the door by a gatekeeper, with varying degrees of stringency according to the gatekeeper's familiarity with the patron, or the patron's 'tales'. In London, for example, Continental visitors will be allowed in at most clubs on sight of a passport, but a lone stranger may well find it impossible to penetrate without knowing an insider or being a member. The policy may be taken to extremes, and in some instances remote-speaking systems have been introduced into clubs in order to 'screen' visitors before even opening the door. One club gives all its members a key to the front door, which enables them—but only them—to come and go as they please.

Although barriers are set up to prevent territorial encroachment, there are occasions when 'outsiders' may find their way inside. This is much more likely to occur in the 'pub' sector of the gay-bar world, where techniques of insulation are not usually so well developed, and sometimes may well be acceptable to the *habitués*—in some bars the two worlds seem to exist side by side. But more generally, the *habitués* and management will need to employ further techniques of territorial defence. Thus the bartenders may well display aloofness and unfriendliness to 'strangers', as Cavan recounts:[38]

> There were only about sixteen people present when we entered, although they took up all the seats at the bar. I sat down at one of the small tables along the wall opposite from the bar, and [my husband] went to the bar to get our orders. The bartender was standing almost in front of him, more or less listening to the conversation between two patrons. It took the bartender almost five minutes to decide to take the order and another three or four minutes for him to make the drinks, which were very, very light.

The *habitués* themselves may well always try to make the 'outsiders' feel out of place, uncomfortable and embarrassed. This may arise simply through inattention, monopoly of the facilities available and so forth or it may take the form of outright 'offensive' behaviour. Indeed while many 'straights' entering a gay bar may well instantly feel threatened by the activity—'You

114

can spot the action straight away,' 'There's no mistaking what's going on,' 'Just takes a couple of minutes to tell',[39] there is some evidence that some gay bars are not immediately noticeable as such to an outsider: one contact in Westwood's research commented:[40]

> I once took a normal friend of mine there who said it might be the National Liberal Club. Everyone was so good mannered and quiet. He said he wouldn't have suspected a single one of the people there.

Thus, if it is true that the bar does not instantly offend—one technique of territorial defence is to make it offend. Therefore, homosexuals may deliberately exaggerate their feminity, or make direct passes at heterosexuals when they enter the establishment. The segregated nature of complex society, then, helps to separate some situations which sustain closed awareness from others where open awareness is prevalent. The homosexual may normally move between the two worlds in relative security.

While it is true that complex society is characterised by segregation, this insight must not be pressed too far. For homosexuals, like everybody, are clearly also likely to build up a small group of primary relationships— among friends and family—where affective bonds may be established and interaction patterns intensified. In situations, there may well arise what Simmel has called a 'strain towards totality', through which the knowledge about one's self that is presented to close friends is constantly broadened. Further, in such situations, there may arise a constant questioning by others in which the homosexual is asked to account for his sexuality, his marital status, his use of time and so forth. The business of establishing 'full' relationships is costly for the homosexual. For some homosexuals, this dilemma may be resolved by restricting their primary group contacts to other homosexuals with whom the problem of concealing sexual identity does not arise. Thus, the homosexual may leave home and his family, and maintain a simple working relationship with his colleagues at work, segregating his life into parts while keeping his full personal relationships for other homosexual friends. But for many others, such tactics are not readily available—it is not possible to leave the parental home and it would be a problem in itself to keep aloof from work colleagues. At these points, then, homosexuality may remain a constant potential threat to relationships.

The prevention of open awareness

It is clear from the above that although conditions of closed awareness are pervasive, they are also highly precarious. There are many situations in

115

which closed awareness may be sent hurtling into suspicion or openness; when the homosexual could render his closely guarded secret to the high costs of public exposure; when the smooth flow of routine interaction becomes ruptured. The homosexual cannot leave such exposure to chance, and builds up a repertoire of skills for concealing his discreditable identity and for passing as normal in a world of normals. I have no space here to discuss these passing strategies—information control, avoidance techniques, role distance etc.—or to consider their game-like features. These have been discussed elsewhere.[41] Instead I wish to highlight two important consequences of the homosexual's attempt to prevent the emergence of open contexts.

The homosexual as practical methodologist and dramaturgist

One consequence is that the homosexual develops a heightened self-awareness: the logistics of homosexual identity become a central part of his consciousness. As one fictional homosexual put it:[42]

> Is there ever a second—just a single second—when, no matter what you're doing or saying, or supposed to be keeping your mind on, you're not also thinking to yourself: you mustn't let it show. Whatever you do, or say, or whatever gesture you make, even in a casual, or of hand moment, you must never let it show. ... You try to dismiss it, try not to think of it at all. But always there seems to be some sort of isolated cell in your mind that keeps twitching away at it. Watch your step in front of Barbara. Watch your step in front of your clients. Watch your step in front of your family, ordinary normal friends. Watch your step when you're on the street. Watch your very step itself, the way you walk. It goes on and on ...

Or as Peter Wildeblood expressed it in *Against the Law*:[43]

> The strain of deceiving my family and my friends often became intolerable. It was necessary for me to watch every word I spoke and every gesture that I made in case I gave myself away. When jokes were made about queers I had to laugh with the rest, and when the talk was about women I had to invent conquests of my own. I hated myself at such moments but there seemed nothing else I could do. My whole life became a lie.

'Living a lie' and 'Watching one's step' become key features of much homosexual interaction, and as a consequence of this many homosexuals develop

116

a dramaturgical awareness—an awareness of the stage-like features of social life. The homosexual is forced to hide behind a mask:

> Society had handed me a mask to wear, a mask that shall never be lifted except in the presence of those who hide behind its protective shadows. Everywhere I go, at all times, and before all sections of society, I pretend.[44] I've learned to put up a show to fool the straight world.[45]

While sociologists have recently stressed the usefulness of analysing the world *as if* it were drama, they also suggest that there are some problematic situations and roles where people may actually view the world this way.[46] I suspect that homosexuals often view themselves as 'acting parts', 'presenting selves' and 'managing their identities'—that dramaturgy in fact becomes part of their consciousness. While it does not necessarily loom large in their daily round (for such skills may become internalised and routinised),[47] I suspect that homosexuals become very adept at stagecraft and that with this comes both a potential for self-depreciation and self-liberation. First, dramaturgy may mean estrangement and alienation. Hiding and posing, presenting first this mask then another, the homosexual comes to see his life as a series of plastic fronts lacking in authenticity and validity. Constantly denying his sexual identity, he becomes estranged from it. Constanly compelled to play other roles, he forgets who he is. Living a lie and shrouded in secrecy, his whole life may become denigrated and devalued.

But this need not be the case. For some homosexuals, dramaturgy may be a first step towards self-liberation. Here, the homosexual becomes what Garfinkle has called a 'practical methodologist'[48]—developing an uncommon sense knowledge of the ways in which social reality is daily produced as an ongoing accomplishment of its members. Through his constant encounters with situations that others may take for granted but which he finds problematic, the homosexual becomes aware of the fragile and negotiated order of everyday interaction and of the part he plays in sustaining such a reality.

From such an awareness, greater freedom and control over one's life become potentially possible. The world no longer has to be seen as 'natural' or 'God given', but can be seen as the social construction of men in historical situations.

Paradox of homosexual secrecy

A second consequence of preventing the emergence of open awareness is that stereoptypes and misunderstandings about homosexuality may be

117

daily confirmed and reinforced in society. As long as homosexuals remain largely invisible, they remain unable to contradict or alter the imagery used by other members of society about homosexuals. Thus, paradoxically, the desire for concealment exacerbates the homosexual's problems. For, while most members of society are daily rubbing shoulders with many homosexuals, they are hardly aware of this fact and remain dependent upon the often-mythical knowledge of both the scientific and lay media. Thus, condemned by society, the homosexual must hide; hiding he is unable to alter the sterotypes and condemnation. It is this which I have termed the paradox of homosexual secrecy.

Conclusion: social change and awareness contexts

In this article, I have analysed some conditions of closed awareness contexts, suggested ways they may break down, and discussed some of the consequences of preventing open awareness. Building upon this, it is possible to speculate about developments taking place in society which could bring about radical change in the prevalent closed awareness contexts.

'Out of the closets and into the streets'

Perhaps the most significant recent development is the emergence of the militant homophile organisations in America and to a lesser extent in England.[49] These organisations, of which the Gay Liberation Front is the most famous, explicitly attack the notions that homosexuality should be invisible and irrelevant and thus, for the first time in modern history, have produced homosexuals who are willing to go onto the streets, into the parks, and onto the media as 'full frontal homosexuals'. Wearing 'gay is good' badges, holding hands and kissing in the street, carrying banners which declare 'Be blatent, not latent', shouting slogans like 'Say it loud, we're gay and proud', and gathering together in public places as homosexuals—all these incidents have helped to change the climate for at least many younger homosexuals, and some older ones too. Some homosexuals have clearly decided that the costs of concealing one's homosexuality is too high a price to pay for the avoidance of stigma.

But there is more to the liberation fronts than just visibility. They have also taken up the challenge of being publicly slandered, stereotyped and scapegoated. For example, in their eyes, the sickness theory of homosexuality has been a popular form of slander for many years—and nobody until recently has ever contested this as a homosexual. It is true, of course, that

118

for some time homosexuals have, among themselves, attacked such a rhetoric; but they have not been willing to do so publicly. Now, with the Gay Liberation Front, one hears in England of demands to withdraw 'slanderous' books and of protest marches against aversion therapy; while in America, those social scientists who propound the sickness theory of homosexuality are likely to be greeted by hostile homosexuals in their audience. Teal, for example, in his book *The Gay Militants* describes how the Gay Liberation Front interrupted the national convention of the American Psychiatric Association on 14 May 1970, where aversion therapy was being discussed, how they 'nonplussed a workshop on "family medicine" organised by the American Medical Association', and how uproar broke out at the 2nd Annual Behavioural Modification Conference of the same year when Dr Feldman (of Birmingham University, England) was publicly attacked for his film on aversion therapy.[50]

Homosexuals were not only visible, they were vociferous. This is certainly a dramatic change, with far-reaching consequences. Just ten years ago it would have been unthinkable for a homosexual to reveal himself publicly as such, unless of course he had been hounded into such revelations. But today there are many people publicly visible as homosexuals. Society has not yet accommodated to this new position: broadcasters still 'guarantee anonymity' to homosexual speakers, when the homosexual speaker wants his name to be used; priests who used to be able to condemn homosexuality with no fear of reprisal at public meetings, now find that such meetings will be attended by many homosexuals willing to stand up and be counted. Certainly, such changes have only so far affected a minority of homosexuals: but the change is such a startling new one, that it must still be regarded highly significant.

The rising tide of permissiveness

The emergence of the GLF is not the only indicator of change in the nature of homosexual awareness contexts. Another is the emergence of the so-called 'permissive society'.

Whatever doubts one may have about the notion of a 'permissive society' (and I have many), there are undeniable changes occurring in the amount of public discussion of sex taking place in this society. If GLF is helping to break down the invisibility of homosexuality, the permissive society is helping to render homosexuality as relevant and sexuality as deprivatised.

Thus, for example, as Sagaring has commented:

Few subjects for so long completely enshrouded in silence have so quickly becomes so widely discussed. It strains one's memory to recall that the word was literally banned from the pages of the *New York Times* in the early 1950s, only to make its appearance there a few years later in the headlines.[51]

Sagarin, relates this growth largely to the publication of the Kinsey Report— 'a veritable sexual atom bomb'—in 1948, and the concomitant growth of awareness of the extent of the homosexual phenomenon. Whatever the reasons may be, in the nineteen-seventies homosexuality is a publicly spoken about issue—in films, plays, books, television, public meetings and so forth, homosexuality if not accepted, is at least no longer quite so firmly banished from consciousness. It is now more relevant. And, of course, the increasing discssion about homosexuality is but an example of the more widespread consideration of sexual matters in general.

Towards open awareness

These factors—militant homosexuals and the 'permissive society'—are just two signs of change in the nature of homosexual awareness contexts. In the past, as I have suggested in the body of this article, homosexuals have had to become skilled at dramaturgical stagecraft while the underlying structures of society helped them to conceal their homosexuality by facilitating the existence of closed awareness. In the immediate future, one may suggest that things are about to change—that homosexuality will become increasingly visible, spoken about and an issue; and that sexuality will also become a more public experience. If this does happen, the interaction problems analysed in this article will become speedily outdated.

Notes

[1] In the arguments to be developed here, I am drawing from by observations of the *male* homosexual in *London*. I suspect that it also has relevance to female homosexuality and the American experience in a general way.

There is no study to date of the variations in the homosexual experience between England and America, although Hoffman, M. in *The Gay World* (Basic Books, London 1968), p.36, makes reference to a possible variation in sexual behaviour. I suspect—though it remains an empirical problem— that there are real differences. For example, America is probably more hostile to homosexuals—since psychiatry and organised religion seem more pervasive, police surveillance seems greater and in most states the law still condemns it. I suspect too that the longer history of homophile organisations and the existence of larger ethnic minorities gives a different flavour to American experience.

2 'One in twenty' is the most quoted 'guesstimate'. However, we do not (and probably never will) know the true incidence of homosexuality in society. See Gebhard, Paul H. *Incidence of Overt Homosexuality in the United States and Western Europe* (Working Paper for Hooker Report on Homosexuality) (Mimeographed, Indiana University, Bloomington, Indiana 1969).

3 Cf. Glaser, Barney G., and Strauss, Anselm L., 'Awareness Contexts and Social Interaction', *A.S.R.* 29 (1964) pp.669–79; and Glaser, Barney G., and Strauss, Anselm L., *Awareness of Dying* (Weidenfeld & Nicolson, London 1966).

4 I treat this in an elementary way. See the more sophisticated treatment by Scheff, T. J., 'On the Concepts of Identity and Social Relationship' in *Human Nature and Collective Behavior: Papers in Honor of Herbert Blumer*, ed. Shibutani, Tamotsu (Prentice-Hall, Englewood Cliffs NJ 1970).

5 In their original study of dying, Glaser and Strauss stressed a fourth kind of context: 'mutual pretence'. However, as Abrahamson points out, this confuses the cognitive with the behavioural. For clarity, therefore, I restrict my discussion to the open-suspicion-closed continuum only. See Abrahamson, Mark *Interpersonal Accommodation* (D. Van Nostrand Co., London 1966), ch.3. See also Haystead, Jennifer, 'Social Structure, Awareness Context and Processes of Choice', *Sociological Review* vol. XIX (1971), pp.79–94.

6 Glaser and Strauss suggest a six-point paradigm for the analysis of awareness contexts. In this article I deal with only three of these—conditions, change and consequences. Elsewhere I have considered 'tactics and counter-tactics'.

7 Cf. Goffman, Erving *Stigma: Notes on the Management of Spoiled Identity* (Penguin, Harmondsworth 1968), p.57.

8 In the Kitsuse survey of 700 students, 75 'had known a homosexual'. However, Schofield, ten years later and in England, found that 48 percent of his sample of 376 young adults from all classes had known at least one homosexual. Such contacts may have been transitory. See Kitsuse, J., 'Societal Reaction to Deviant Behaviour: Problems of Theory and Method', in *The Other Side: Perspectives on Deviance*, ed. Becker, Howard S. (Free Press, New York/Collier-Macmillan, London 1964), pp.87–101, and Schofield, Michael, *Follow-up Study to 'Sexual Behaviour of Young People'* (forthcoming).

9 For example, in one survey the author was concerned with, 1,832 male

respondents asked by postal questionnaire: 'Do your employers know that you are a homosexual?', 1,152 replied that their employers did not know, 233 replied that they did know and 447 were not sure. See also Westwood's comment on this: Westwood, Gordon, *A Minority: A Report on the Life of the Male Homosexual in Great Britain* (Longmans, London 1960), ch.9.

Both these studies, however, do not necessarily indicate closed awareness— as neither were concerned with discovering the perceptions of the employers.
[10] Cf. Davis, Fred, 'Deviance and Disavowal: The Management of Strained Interaction Amongst the Visibly Handicapped', *Social Problems* vol. IX (1961), pp.120–32, Lemert, Edwin M. *Social Pathology* (McGraw-Hill, New York/London 1951), ch.5 and 6, and Edgerton, Robert B. *The Cloak of Competence: Stigma in the Lives of the Mentally Retarded* (University of California Press, Berkeley 1967).
[11] Cf. Schutz, Alfred *On Phenomenology and Social Relations* (University of Chicago Press, Chicago 1970), especially ch.5.
[12] Cf. Merton, Robert K. *Social Theory and Social Structure* (Collier-Macmillan, London 1967), p.336. McCall, George J., and Simmons, J.L. *Identities and Interactions: An Examination of Human Associations in Everyday Life* (Free Press, New York/Collier-Macmillan, London 1966), ch.5.
[13] Cf. Becker, Howard S. *Outsiders: Studies in the Sociology of Deviance* (Free Press, New York/Collier-Macmillan, Lond 1963), p.20.
[14] Kitsuse, op. cit., p.92.
[15] On 'accounts' in general, see Lyman, Stanferd M., and Scott, Martin B., *A Sociology of the Absurd* (Appleton-Century-Crofts, New York 1970), ch.5. For the context of the two examples given see Westwood op. cit., p.37 and Reiss, Albert J., 'The Social Integration of Queers and Peers', in *The Other Side*, ed. Becker, H. S. (Free Press of Glencoe, 1964), pp.181 et seq.
[16] See the discussion by Laud Humphreys on the visibility of sexuality: Humphreys, Laud *Tearoom Trade: A Study of Homosexual Encounters in Public Places* (Duckworth, London 1970), pp.156 et seq.
[17] See the general discussion of this by Pearce, Frank, 'How to be immoral and Ill, Pathetic and Dangerous, All at the Same Time: An Analysis of the Mass Media Treatment of Homosexuality', in *Mass Media and Social Problems* ed. Cohen, S. and Young, J. (Constable, London 1973). See also: Wildeblood, Peter *Against the Law* (Weidenfeld & Nicolson, London 1955); Harvey, Ian *To Fall Like Lucifer* (Sidgwick & Jackson, London 1971); Hyde, Montgomery *The Other Love* (Heinemann, London 1970).
[18] There are only a few studies of stereotyping and homosexuality. See expecially Simmons, J.L., 'Public Stereotypes of Deviants', *Social Problems* vol. XIII (1965), pp.223–32 and Steffensmerer, Jarrell J. *Factors Affecting Reaction Towards Homosexuals* (Unpublished MA thesis, University of

Iowa 1970). Apart from these studies, most discussions of homosexual stereotyping remain crudely impressionistic. See for example, McCaffrey, J. A., 'Homosexuality, the Real, the Stereotype', in *The Homosexual Dialect*, ed. McCaffrey, J.A. (Prentice-Hall, Englewood Cliffs NJ 1972).

[19] Most accounts suggest that no more than 15 per cent of the homosexual population are recognisable as homosexuals. Pomeroy suggests that 15 per cent of men and 5 per cent of women may be recognisable. Sonenschein, after ethnographic fieldwork, concluded that 95 per cent are invisible. Westwood, who assessed the stereotypical traits of his respondents during his interviews, commented that only 13 per cent were recognisable as homosexuals (see Westwood op. cit., p.92). Magee also comments: 'At a very rough guess I would hazard that something like one-twentieth of homosexuals are to the heterosexual eyes recognisably homosexual'. See Magee, Bryan *One in Twenty* (Corgi Books, London 1969), p.40.

[20] 'Into the Twilight World', *News of the World*, 27 July 1964. See also 'How to Spot a Possible Homo', *Sunday Mirror*, 28 April 1963 and Wyden, Peter, and Wyden, Barbara, *Growing Up Straight: What Every Thoughtful Parent Should Know about Homosexualtiy* (Stein & Day, New York 1968).

[21] Allen, Clifford *A Textbook of Psychosexual Disorders* (Oxford University Press, London 1969), p.221.

[22] Albert Ellis has suggested how sometimes an effeminate-looking male or masculine-looking female may be handicapped in social relationships. See Ellis, Albert, 'Constitutional Factors in Homosexuality' in *Advances in Sex Research*, ed. Beigel, H. (Harper & Row, New York 1963), p.173.

[23] Humphreys, op. cit., p.82.

[24] Wildeblood, op. cit., p.32.

[25] Goffman, op. cit., p.41.

[26] Cf. Cohen, Stanley *Folk Devils and Moral Panics: The Creation of Mods and Rockers* (MacGibbon & Kee, London 1972).

[27] Gerassi, John *Boys of Boise: Furor, Vice and Folly in an American City* (Macmillan, New York 1966).

[28] Ibid., p.48.

[29] Cf. Matza, David *Becoming Deviant* (Prentice-Hall, Englewood Cliffs 1969), p.153.

[30] Cf. Lyman and Scott, op. cit., ch.6 and 7.

[31] Young, Wayland *Eros Denied* (Corgi, London 1968).

[32] Cf. Willmott, P. *Adolescent Boys of East London* (Penguin, Harmondsworth 1969), ch.3.

[33] Turner, Ralph H. *Family Interaction* (Wiley, London 1970), p.50.

[34] I have no space here to consider the full range of experiences in the 'homosexual world'. I discuss these in *Deviance, Reality and Sexuality: An Interactionist Approach to Sexual Deviance*, ed. Plummer, Ken (Routledge &

Kegan Paul, London, forthcoming). See also the classic statement by Hooker, E., 'The Homosexual Community', in *Sexual Deviance* ed. Gagnon, John H., and Simon, William (Harper & Row, New York/London 1967), pp.167–84. Also see Mileski, Maureen and Black, Donald J. 'The Social Organisation of Homosexuality', *Urban Life and Culture* vol. I (1972), pp.187–202. In this article I restrict my comments to 'gay bars'.

[35] On 'protective places', see Lofland, John *Deviance and Identity* (Prentice-Hall, Englewood Cliffs 1969), pp.62–9, 162–73. On 'territories', see Lyman and Scott, op. cit., ch.4. On 'region behaviour', see the work of Erving Goffman in general, especially *Behavior in Public Places: Notes on the Social Organization of Gatherings* (Free Press, New York/Collier-Macmillan, London 1963) and *Relations in Public* (Allen Lane The Penguin Press, London 1971). For its applicability to bars, see Cavan, Sherri *Liquor License: An Ethnography of Bar Behaviour* (Aldine, Chicago 1966).

[36] Donald Webster Cory and John P. LeRoy: *The Homosexual and his Society: A View from Within*, (Citadel Press, New York 1963) p.106.

[37] Cf. Lyman & Scott op. cit., p.103.

[38] Cavan, op. cit., p.229.

[39] Cavan, op. cit., p.222.

[40] Westwood, op. cit., p.71

[41] See Plummer, op. cit. General discussions about 'passing' which embrace insights on homosexual tactics and 'game moves' include Goffman, op. cit.; Lyman and Scott, op. cit.; McCall and Simmons, op. cit.; Humphreys, op. cit.; Garfinkle, Harold *Studies in Ethnomethodology* (Prentice-Hall, Englewood Cliffs 1967), ch.5.

[42] Jackson, Neville *No End to the Way* (Corgi Books, London 1967), p.160.

[43] Wildeblood, op. cit., p.32.

[44] Cory, Donald Webster *The Homosexual Outlook* (Peter Nevill Ltd, London 1953), p.11.

[45] Williams, Colin J., and Weinberg, Martin S. *Homosexuals and the Military: A Study of Less than Honourable Discharge* (Harper & Row, London 1971), p.145.

[46] Instead of being 'second-order constructs', they become 'first-order constructs'. On the problems of dramaturgy, see Messinger, Sheldon L., Sampson, Harold and Towne, Robert D., 'Life as Theatre: Some Notes on the Dramaturgic Approach to Social Reality', *Sociometry* vol. XXV (1962), pp.98–110.

[47] See the comments given to Carol Warren by a respondent on this. Reprinted in Douglas, Jack D. *American Social Order* (Collier-Macmillan, London 1971) pp.231–2 and Scott Robert A. and Douglas, Jack D. *Theoretical Perspectives on Deviance* (Basic Books, London 1932), p.77.

[48] Cf. Garfinkle, op. cit., ch.5 and Williams and Weinberg, op. cit., pp.142–5.

[49] On the homophile movement, a general statement has been provided by Sagarin, Edward *Odd Man In: Societies of Deviants in America* (Quadrangle Books, Chicago 1969). The most helpful statement on the Gay Liberation Front is Altman, Dennis *Homosexual: Liberation and Oppression* (Outerbridge & Dienstfrey, New York 1971).
[50] Teal, Donn *The Gay Militants* (Stein & Day, New York 1971).
[51] Sagarin, op. cit., pp.78–9.

Sad, Bad or Mad: Society's Confused Response to the Skid-Row Alcoholic

Peter ARCHARD

In a recent study, entitled *Stations of the Lost*,[1] Jacqueline Wiseman makes an important contribution to our understanding of skid-row alcoholics in so far as her theoretical orientation enables us to grasp simultaneously both the views of the alcoholics and those of the agents of social control. All too frequently, sociologists undertaking studies of deviant behaviour lay emphasis on the world of the deviant but fail to incorporate official definitions of the phenomena they are describing and explaining. Their analyses do not include any substantial account of policies, designed to eradicate or control social problems or of the ideological basis of such policies.[2] Changes in the moral, social and political character of institutions and agents of social control remain implicit or are taken for granted. Thus students of deviant behaviour are unwittingly pushed into committing a methodological and theoretical error in their claim to understand the social reality of particular deviant phenomena because any societal response to designated social problems is not considered problematic in itself. In effect, then, any portrayal of reality, at a sociological level, remains incomplete when only the activities of the deviant actors are accounted for.

The following analysis seeks to redress the bias inherent in a onesided view which is exclusively concerned with the experiences of the deviant by shifting attention away from the assumption that

> the crucial condition for the emergence of new cultural forms is the existence, in effective interaction with one another, of a number of actors with similar problems of adjustment.[3]

Instead, the analysis attempts to demonstrate that official explanations for the existence of homeless alcoholics in the inner-city areas of large conurbations, and the consequent strategies of control directed towards containment or eradication of the problem, have significant implications in extending and reshaping the phenomena. Changes in society's response to skid-row alcoholics have implications for the symbiotic relationship between habitual drunks and agencies of social control, expecially in view of the shifting definitions imputed to the deviant by organisations attempting to punish, cure or rehabilitate him.

The interest which the illicit consumption of marihuana, LSD, amphetamines and heroin evokes in industrial societies has resulted in a widespread popular awareness of the problems associated with their use. This awareness arises out of a number of related factors. First, illicit drug use is popularly equated with a youth culture which is held to reject the normative standards morality, deferred gratification, and work espoused in Western societies. Second, in an attempt at controlling both the use of illicit drugs and the subcultures associated with them, the expertise of medicine, psychiatry, and social science have been coopted to programmes of legislative and social control. Finally, in a process by which they both create and reflect the moral panic engendered by the phenomenon, the mass media magnify the issues involved and contribute to their awareness on a scale made possible only by modern electric technology and the mass circulation of newspapers.[4]

In contrast, the awareness of the general population to problems associated with alcoholism is markedly restricted. The skid-row alcoholic and the world he inhabits, especially, pass relatively unnoticed by the mass media. To the general population he is a less familiar object of widespread moral indignation than the marihuana smoker or heroin addict. The relative uninterest of the media in skid-row alcoholism is attributable to the fact that skid-row alcoholics are not part of an oppositional youth culture; they are involved for the most part in the consumption of a socially and legally approved drug, and they have constituted a problem at least since the development of the modern industrial city.

Most contemporary research surveys point out that the alcoholic on skid row is part of a wider population which includes the vagrant, the casual labourer and the itinerant navvy, the mentally ill, the physically disabled, and the old-age pensioner with no family ties. Stereotypically, the individual with a drink problem is middle-aged, has never married or his marriage broke down, has lost contact with all relatives, is occupationally unskilled, and has spent some time in the merchant navy, armed forces, or in heavy labouring and construction.[5] The public label him a meths drinker; law-enforcement officials view him as an offender; the medical profession defines him as suffering from a disease; social workers and sociologists speak of him as disaffiliated, undersocialised or anomic. When he is not in one of the institutions that aim to control or change his behaviour he is to be found in parks and open spaces, sharing a bottle of cider, cheap wine, or crude spirits.

The major difference between skid row in Britain and its counterpart across the Atlantic is that in Britain it is not ecologically concentrated—

128

the institutions associated with the subculture are spread over large areas of working-class districts in cities and major towns. In the United States, on the other hand, skid row is often located within a highly concentrated geographical area consisting almost exclusively of skidrow institutions such as flophouses, taverns, pawnshops, soup kitchens and missions. It is this physical concentration which is often regarded as crucial to the moral and cultural isolation of skid row. But Matza has correctly pointed out that we should beware of positing an exact relation between ecological and moral facts.[6] Though ecological segregation facilitates the development of a peculiar world, it may not always be a necessary condition for such development. In fact, although the institutions of skid row are relatively dispersed within British towns and cities they nevertheless constitute a continuous psychological and sociological territory for the alcoholic. Prisons, common lodging houses, reception centres, mental hospitals and rehabilitation hostels, parks and open spaces, derelict houses and main railway stations constitute the situations which the habitual drunk continuously moves through. He rarely leaves this complex public and institutional circuit.

The high visibility and vulnerability of alcoholics on the row in terms of personal demeanour and public behaviour serve both to dramatise their condition and elicit the type of moral indignation which highlights the social distance separating them from what is widely considered normal behaviour.

> Such persons tend to cause offence or annoyance to members of the public, if only by reason of their unkempt appearance and slovenly behaviour ... it is difficult to avoid coming into contact with them ... their uncontrolled urination gives rise to offence ... they are often agressive and the police are frequently called on for assistance in removing them. The position is aggravated by the fact the drinkers usually congregate in groups.[7]

Maximum moral opprobium is elicited by dramatising the condition of homeless alcoholics who consume socially unacceptable beverages such as crude or surgical spirits.

> Unwashed, evil-smelling, incapable of work, occasionally emerging from his psychotic drunken state ... his condition gives rise to contempt even amongst the worst of the alcoholics who only drink recognised alcoholic beverages.[8]

Beyond the gut response evoked by the stereotypical behaviour of the skid-row inebriate, moral indignation is often cast in the language of humanitarianism, expecially in the case of powerful groups who seek to change behaviour by the implementation of policies, legislation and recommendations. The alcoholic's identity is defined not so much by his manifest public behaviour as by his lack of conformity to widely accepted criteria of what moral entrepreneurs term normal.

> We use [the term 'skid-row alcoholic'] in the sense in which it is probably understood by most professional medical and social workers concerned with alcoholism, i.e. to describe the habitual drunken offender at the end of the road, separated from the normal social supports of family, possessions, settled employment and a permanent address, frequently sleeping rough, and whose only regular companions are people who share the same deprivations and the same problems.[9]

This focus on the individual's manifestations of a particular social problem reflects the central concerns of contemporary agencies wishing to cure and rehabilitate skid-row alcoholics. The existence of skid row as a social institution is accepted as given; the emphasis is placed on attempts to rescue individuals affected by it. Psychiatrists, social workers, hostel wardens and others professionally concerned with rehabilitation do not seek to alter the social reality through which the alcoholic makes meaningful his own experiences. Instead, clues to the client's problems are sought in his personal biography: his date of birth, family, educational and occupational background as antecedents to his problem drinking; his number of convictions for drunken offences, the incidence of hospitalisation and imprisonment, and the intensity of his drinking as consequences of his skid-row life-style.

However, the contemporary emphasis on concepts of medical cure and social rehabilitation, as emergent notions of a treatment ideology, mask a complexity of institutions and agencies of social control more traditionally associated with skid row. The police, courts and prison, together with the common lodging house, mission and soup kitchen, continue to perpetuate a societal response in which the criminal and moral character[10] of the deviant are the focus of interest. To these are being added the mental hospital, detoxification centre and therapeutic hostel. In essence, then, the complexity of this punishment and treatment matrix is the product of conceptual and practical confusion about whether the public drunk should be defined as morally weak, criminally deviant, mentally sick or socially inadequate. The twin factors of alcohol addiction and poverty combined with involvement in the skid-row life-style have produced in society's response a widening of the institutional network of control. The emergence of a more complex and extensive social-control matrix—and the confusion inherent in it—is succinctly summarised in a recent government report.

Whether one takes the view that habitual drunken offenders represent a penal, social, or medical problem or, as we believe, a combination of all these, the fact that the problem exists as an overt one requires some response from the community.[11]

In spite of this complexity, it is the emergent conceptions of cure and rehabilitation which represent a social movement attempting to become the dominant ideological and practical response to the problem of the habitual drunken offender. The transition, in practice, is an example of moral indignation by domininant interest groups anchoring their rationale in the language of humanitarianism. The report on habitual drunken offenders represents this transition:

> ... society should be concerned about the habitual drunken offender both in the sense of humane reaction to his plight and in the practical sense of commitment to more rational and effective methods of treating him.[12]

This statement is indicative of the main ideological thrust currently developing in the treatment of skid-row inebriates. The concern expressed by the report underpins a set of practical recommendations which defuse the moral and penal character of traditional responses to the alcoholic and place the onus of responsibility on agencies of sociomedical treatment. In practical terms the strategy is to replace the police station, magistrates' court and prison by the detoxification centre, rehabilitation hostel and community care. Yet this linear characterisation reflecting society's attempt to shift its definition and responsibility for the skid-row alcoholic from an overtly punitive to an overtly therapeutic response is too simplistic. For, in reality, the new moral entrepreneurs are confronted by an enduring historical legacy in society's reaction to the problem in the shape of institutions whose view of the habitual drunk is rooted in an ideology of punishment or moral and quasi-religious reform. The experiential world of the alcoholic is thus markedly expanding. The institutional revolving door[13] permits the individual to be at different times a prisoner, patient, social work client, potential convert to a virtuous Christian life or common-lodging-house inmate. At all times he remains a dosser: for the one irrefutable fact about the skid-row alcoholic in relation to all forms of social control is the intractable character of his recidivism.

The historical legacy already alluded to acts as a significant backcloth to an understanding of how contemporary efforts at containment and amelioration of the problem are being promoted by sociomedical agencies. The creation of skid row as an institution and an awareness of its attendant problems arose with the rapid development of industrial and urban life in Western societies, particularly during the nineteenth century. Historically, the generic roots of a skid-row life-style are to be found in feudal economic and social change. Vagrancy legislation, at the time, reflected a policy that sought to curtail the migratory habits of a populace affected by the wage-stabilisation policies which paralleled the break-up of feudalism and the depopulation caused by the black death.[14] The economic failure of pre-Elizabethan vagrancy statutes eventually resulted in a situation whereby

> ... the roads of England were crowded with masterless men and their families, who had lost their former employment through a variety of causes, had no means of livelihood, and had taken to a vagrant life.[15]

The economic changes brought about by England's Enclosure Acts and the urgent thrust westwards by American frontiersmen contributed significantly to a migratory population which eventually settled in expanding urban centres. The rise of the industrial city during the nineteenth century consolidated the residual elements of a mobile working class into institutions created by the old Poor Laws and a competitive *laissez-faire* socioeconomic system.

Habitual drunkenness, as one concrete expression of chronic poverty, became a major target for economic, but particularly moral, reform. The emergence of the 'dangerous classes' in Britain and skid row in America elicited a reaction which was articulated in a combination of moral and economic terms. The central concern of middle-class philanthropists and social reformers focused on the existence of poverty; their moral crusades were based on the premise that the eradication of poverty from the social and economic structure would lead to the amelioration of vices such as prostitution and drunkenness. But the link between poverty and the vice of habitual drunkenness was not one in which moral turpitude was invariably perceived as the effect of poverty. For reaction to public drunkenness involved a demand by moral crusaders that the inebriate seek the answer to his problems in reform and religious conversion at the individual level.

General Booth, founder of the Salvation Army, viewed the consumption of excessive alcohol as the fundamental cause of the moral weakness that permeated major sections of the British working class.

> Darkest England may be described as consisting of three circles, one within the other. The outer and widest circle is inhabited by the starving and homeless, but honest poor. The second by those who live by vice; and the third and innermost region at the centre is peopled by those who exist by crime. The whole of these three circles is sodden by drink.[16]

The Victorian preoccupation with the moral condition of the working class led to a reformism which avoided any fundamental questioning of the social structure within which the problem of drunkenness manifested itself. Although the existence of chronic poverty was debated, British philanthropic and charitable organisations primarily sought to attack the moral consequences of poverty. Under a number of legislative measures commencing with the Habitual Drunkards Act 1879 and culminating in the Inebriates Act 1918, the widespread problem of public drunkenness resulted in the establishment of special homes and reformatories for inebriates. The ethos permeating the reformatories consisted of first moral persuasion and, eventually, compulsory detention. They were mostly organised and run by religious and quasireligious charities. But by 1921 the authorities were forced to arrive at the conclusion 'that the treatment of the unwilling was too seldom successful to justify the continuance of compulsion, and it was consequently allowed to drop'.[17]

In the United States the rapid development and expansion of the economy at the turn of the century provided an economic rationale by which the emergence of skid row as a sociological entity could be explained. Unattached males, part of a larger migrant population moving the frontier westward, were recruited to the geographically mobile armies of lumberjacks, miners and railway gangs. But the seasonal and shortterm nature of the work forced men to return to the major cities during periods of slack employment or the winter months. The cities acted as recruitment centres for further employment. By the end of the nineteenth century, shelter facilities and large cheap hotels for single men were constructed near city centres.

> These facilities served to centralise the low-income, unattached male population, with the result that it became an associational group whose members had the opportunity for daily contact and for the development of a distinctive subculture.[18]

Selection to skid row was primarily defined functionally in terms of structural forces operating within the economy. In essence, skid-row communities were not then looked upon as socially pathological entities in the manner they are now defined by government agencies and medical and social-work professions.

Nevertheless, on both sides of the Atlantic the reformist zeal of the middle classes assailed the intemperance of the working class and grounded their crusading activities in the quality of life they perceived as inherent in 'darkest England' and America's skid rows. In England the Charity Organisation Society encouraged active cooperation between casual wards, refuges, and other institutions in their common aims of containment and reform for the increasing numbers of 'homeless poor, destitute wayfarers and incorrigible rogues'.[19] The Women's Christian Temperance Union in the United States advocated the improvement of the moral condition and the material situation of those less favourably situated in the economic and social structure. During the nineteenth century the movement based its programme on the slogan 'Drink is the curse of the working classes' and promoted total abstinence as the solution to the problem of poverty.[20]

One significant exception to the characteristic moral indignation of the American reformist middle-class was the unfolding of a political reaction by the itinerant working class to the working conditions they endured. The collective organisation of migrant workers into movements like the revolutionary and Marxist-based International Workers of the World, and the less radical International Brotherhood Welfare Association and the Migratory Workers Union[21] during the early part of the twentieth century shifted the focus of attention from the moral consequences of skid row to its economic causes. These organisations served the interests of specific occupational groups characterised by seasonal or day labour such as lumberjacks, longshoremen, and migratory farm workers in the Midwest wheat belt. The important common denominator which linked these groups was not only economic oppression but also the fact that their exclusively male culture, both at work and on the row, consolidated their class consciousness into a political understanding of their work situations.

Thus it was their working conditions rather than the living conditions prevailing on skid row which unified the members of the movement. Moreover, to the railway gangers and the longshoremen the meanings given to heavy drinking and drunkenness while they were young enough to be employed were defined in the context of their own work and cultural norms— not those of a reformist middle class. It was only with the advent of middle age, when employment became more difficult to obtain, that affiliation to skid-row institutions became more permanent for the migrant worker. At this stage chronic dependency on alcohol was the result of a process of socialization which began with heavy drinking in labour camps and working-class taverns and ended with street 'bottle gangs' on the row. There is little evidence, then, that the permanently unemployed chronic alcoholic on skid row played any central or sustained role in movements based on the emergence of a revolutionary class consciousness.

The demand for unattached males as part of the expanding economy slackened considerably during the 1920s. Rooney indicates that this decline in demand continued 'until in the public view they were considered unnecessary for the maintenance of the economy ... their predominant status changed from worker to outcast.'[22] The rise of welfare institutions attempting to cushion the worst manifestations of a competitive economic system were held reponsible for playing a relatively greater role in drawing men to skid row.[23] The perpetuation of skid row as an institution was now regarded as depending

> upon one important remaining function: providing a refuge for drop-outs from the working class who have psychic disabilities, a significant proportion of whom involve alcoholism. If present (economic) trends continue, the population of skid row will continue to decline and the proportion of psychically disabled skid-row men will increase. Consequently skid row may come to function as an open asylum.[24]

In effect, explanations for the continued existence of skid row shifted away from the political and economic rationale of the migrant workers and the missionary zeal of middle-class reformism. In its place emerged an ideology which emphasised a new interpretation of individual failure. The notion of individual culpability rested on two new premises: the medical conceptualisation of alcoholism as a disease and, in the case of skid-row alcoholics, the added social-work dimension of social inadequacy which was seen to typify men defined as weak and passive.

In the absence of a British equivalent to the American working-class movement, the population of vagrants and casual labourers in London and other major cities remained the exclusive concern of the middle classes. The rise of the trade-union and labour movement in the latter half of the nineteenth century did not encompass as a central concern the economic conditions of casual work and itinerant workers or the social conditions existing in common lodging houses and casual wards. The Victorian preoccupation with 'the drink question'—as the debate on the problem of habitual drunkenness was referred to by a dominant middle class—also gradually changed its moral standpoint. The premises on which medicine and social work base their efforts at cure and rehabilitation did not so much supplant as extend the perspectives imputed to public inebriates by moral-reform groups. In the context of a contemporary ideology, the vestiges of a Victorian attitude to the drink question remain through the work done with homeless single persons by the Salvation Army, the Church Army, missions, and Christian charitable organisations. But the emergence of professional experts in the field of alcoholism has merely helped to alter the current *modus operandi* of these organisations. Increasingly, they tend to combine their traditional missionary work with definitions of habitual drunkenness that seek answers in professional social work and psychiatry. The 'sciences', therefore, are made use of to fortify their moral standpoint. However, the uneasy relationship between a moral and a scientific view of problem drinking and alcoholism serves to weaken the position of interest groups that base their campaigns on notions of Christian virtue. For the claim to a scientific view of alcohol addiction on skid row properly belongs to medical and professional social-work groups. The growing strength of these secular professions in ensuring that deviant behaviour falls within the orbit of their own expertise has resulted in the relative demise of traditional moral crusades towards problems of drink and drunkenness.

The movement to redefine the skid-row alcoholic as a sociomedical case attempts, in addition to removing the moral stigma, to decriminalise his status. The criminal identity assigned to habitual drunken offenders on skid row by virtue of their perennial involvement with penal establishments is held to be incompatible with their sociomedical status. Vagrancy laws handed down from a pre-Elizabethan era and legislation proscribing public drunken behaviour ensure that punishment by imprisonment forms a central thread in the experience of the public intoxicant. The skid-row alcoholic is imprisoned for offences involving suspicion, begging alms, and being drunk and disorderly—offences commonly defined as misdemeanours. Occasionally, marginally more serious charges, such as demanding money with menaces, petty theft, and trespass, lead to longer sentences. But the most common official reason for imprisonment is the skid-row alcoholic's inability to pay fines imposed by the court for being drunk in a public place. His recidivism, coupled with short-term sentences in custody, ensure repetitious processing through the penal treadmill. The revolving door of bottle gang, police-station cell, court and prison reinforces the criminal identity[25] of the individual and further ensures his identification with the skid-row subculture.[26]

With the tentative acceptance of alcoholism as a disease imposed by medical opinion grew an awareness of the fundamental logical weakness of processing skid-row alcoholics through overtly punitive institutions. The contradiction inherent in imprisoning individuals for what came to be defined as an illness led to a relabelling of the skid-row inebriate by interest groups wishing to cure and rehabilitate rather than punish. However, both in the United States and in England the new conceptualisation of skid-row alcoholism for the most part remained academic. Legislation changed the status of the public intoxicant in theory only, since medical and rehabilitative facilities were rarely implemented. In some instances attempts to alter the essence of the revolving door while retaining its structure were reflected in the ambiguity of combining punishment and rehabilitation. In 1957 a Board of Commissioners reported that the recidivism statistics were the best evidence that existing procedures are failing to rehabilitate the alcoholic. The Board concluded their report forcefully:

There is no deceiving ourselves: many of the chronic repeaters are individuals who ... are getting drunk for the express purpose of getting arrested and sent to the workhouse as a place to sleep, eat, obtain medical care and clean clothing, and to contribute what little they can to work.[27]

Moral indignation was backed up with a recommendation by the Board that the vagrancy laws should be tightened. The imposition of indeterminate sentences of one day to one year in the House of Correction would improve opportunities for alcoholic assessment for those men native to the District of Columbia and, it was thought, would remove strain from police stations and courts. In addition it would make alien alcoholics leave town and deter other 'transient bums' from coming to Washington.[28]

But on both sides of the Atlantic the impetus to decriminalise the alcoholic on skid row gathered force although it has not succeeded in removing him from the institutional reality of prison, common lodging houses and reception centres. For example, in the United States the District of Columbia Alcoholic Rehabilitation Act (1967) claims to

come to direct grips with drunkenness and its relationship to the criminal system by unequivocally defining simple intoxication as a public-health responsibility. ... under the new law, drunkenness, *per se*, is no longer against the law. ... it is now viewed as an acute medical problem entitled to prompt treatment in lieu of or prior to criminal prosecution.[29]

In England the Criminal Justice Acts 1967 and 1972, by legislating for the provision of hostels and detoxification centres, attempt to remove responsibility for the habitual drunken offender from the courts and prison. This redefinition of the status of the police-case inebriate provides a further rationale by which the medical and social-work professions include him within the scope of their specialisms. However, as Cahn has pointed out,

alcoholism does not conform to the traditional model of a disease— its cause is not specific or unidimensional; there is no well-defined area of biological pathology; its natural history remains unclear; and there is still much uncertainty about its treatment.[30]

The confusion Cahn drew attention to was reflected in the United States Supreme Court decision in 1968 that chronic alcoholism could not be a valid defence to a charge of public drunkenness. The Supreme Court's decision not to follow those of the lower courts[31] was based on the argument that there were not enough solid facts to support the disease concept, and that causes of alcoholism and its treatment needed further investigation.[32]

Interest groups representing the medical profession reemphasised the need to define alcoholism as an illness that requires treatment by a medical practitioner instead of punishment in a jail. In spite of any legal persistence in viewing skid-row alcoholics as offenders and a reluctance to accept alcoholism as a sociomedical problem, two new types of social control agencies— detoxification centres and halfway houses—are being added to the institutional complex of skid row. In both cases these new practical efforts at treatment collude with the contemporary notion of individual culpability as an explanation of why men live on the row, since in the main their objective is to rescue individuals from what is defined as a pathological subculture.

Thus, in advance of the Supreme Court decision, the first detoxification programme for habitual drunks was established in St Louis in 1966. By 1970 some 25 centres had opened in the United States as a result of the St Louis community experience. The detoxification concept is based on a medically oriented facility embodying five main objectives: (a) it removes the criminal label and substitutes a civil procedure for the public drunk thereby avoiding the stigmatising effect of criminal procedures; (b) it provides 'more appropriate, humane and sanitary' shelter for the men than is typically found in the 'drunk tank' of a jail; (c) it makes expert medical help available to the men; (d) it reduces the burden on the criminal agencies resulting from the processing of large numbers of drunk arrests; (e) it introduces the potentiality of rehabilitative therapy or referral.[33] This last objective establishes a clear-cut departure from the traditional shortterm punitive concern of law-enforcement agencies. It is the crucial objective. Through it cure and rehabilitation become the long-term central concerns around which an integrated system of detoxification, assessment and aftercare is anchored.

Now, where detoxification centres have deflected the customary legal processing of the alcoholic the police still retain a vital role in ensuring that the intoxicant enters the initial stage of drying out. Theoretically, it is this stage which embarks the individual on the route towards physical and, eventually, psychological and social recuperation. But, since, by definition, the alcoholic continues to be regarded as a public nuisance, it becomes incumbent upon police intervention to ensure the referral of the public drunk for detoxification.[34] The ascription of a new role to the police on street patrol is spelled out in nonpunitive terms but, in fact, the vestiges of a punitive system often remain. In St Louis intoxicants are picked from the street but the procedure requires the arresting officer to enquire whether the arrested person wishes to be taken to the drying out centre. A refusal may lead to the invoking of traditional penal sanctions; the premature self-discharge from the centre may also lead to the processing of a summons to appear before a court. Similar discretionary sanctions are recommended

138

in the setting up of detoxification centres in England.[35] The paradox involved in the redefinition of the police role *vis-à-vis* their handling of the public inebriate is apparent. Nimmer reminds us that

> the police labour under the influence of traditional ways of handling the men, a general attitude that the police task is to handle violent crime and scepticism concerning the validity of treatment as an effective method of handling the drunk.[36]

Thus, despite new definitions of alcoholism promoted by the humanitarianism of professional experts, there remain the stereotypical images of the skid-row man held by the police. These images are based on the gut reaction aroused by having to handle men who are perceived as perennially out of work, living off welfare institutions and the state, and who publicly elicit offence by virtue of their unkempt appearance and uncontrolled behaviour. The abstract language of humanitarianism gives way to the situated language of gut reaction.[37] The central point about this differential reaction to the way a social problem is viewed is that social reality, for the deviant, is objectively represented by the everyday situations he encounters. His view of the arrest process is based on his own practical knowledge of how the police handle him, and not on any quasi-treatment role imputed to the police by policy-making groups.

The skid-row alcoholic's social distance from the normative expectations held by a dominant middle class adds a social dimension to the medical definition of his affliction. This dimension is reflected in a recent government report:

> Social deprivation can perhaps be regarded as the most important of the three elements [crime, alcoholism and social deprivation] from the point of view of treatment, and our recommendations lay stress on this and other social supports as crucial needs.[38]

Problems of social deprivation are met by advocating the treating of skid-row alocholics in therapeutic hostels. The conception of the therapeutic community as a means of social rehabilitation and eventual re-entry into the community further crystallises society's redefinition of the problem. It reinforces the process of decriminalisation and removes the stigma associated with a moral view of habitual drunkenness. Halfway houses fulfil the dual purposes of noncustodial treatment and aftercare and serve as an extension to casework initiated by hospital-based social workers. Resocialising the skid-row alcoholic into the community through sobriety, steady employment and social stability are the ideal goals which therapeutic hostels strive for.[39]

But therapeutic communities are seen as an essential extension, rather than an alternative, to the services of the psychiatrist. Sociomedical treatment becomes meaningful only within the framework of hospitals and detoxification centres cooperating with 'facilities in the community such as supportive hostels capable of providing the props necessary to social stability'.[40]

Finally, in an attempt to propel the emergent ideology of treatment to its logical limits, the traditional institutions of skid row are encompassed within the scope of a sociomedical strategy. Agencies which provide 'handouts', shelters and common lodging houses, are redefined as

> a necessary element in the overall treatment system, primarily as milieux in which the potential client can be reached and an attempt made to motivate him to receive treatment in more therapeutically oriented facilities.[41]

Moreover, the vital link between the public drunk and detoxification centres becomes the responsibility of the police who are invoked to think of their role in the treatment process as positive and constructive. If drying-out centres are not available and penal establishments continue to process habitual drunks, then courts are urged to make greater use of their powers to remand individuals for social and medical investigation and prisons are recommended to increase their awareness of the problems of alcoholism through medical and welfare services.[42]

Medicine and social work, then, are expanding and reshaping the world of skid row. Novel strategies of control have been added to those historically associated with problems of drunkenness and destitution. The missions and penal establishments are being supplemented by mental hospitals, detoxification centres and community-based hostels. Notions of individual pathology are now invoked to explain the continued presence of men on the row since the objective is not to seek solutions to the *a priori* question of why skid row exists in the first place. In essence, the rhetoric of modern medicine and professional social work assumes the dominant rationale by which society attempts to control both the institutions of skid row and skid-row alcoholism. Traditional moral indignation is transformed into the language of contemporary humanitarianism.

Notes

[1] Wiseman, J.P. *Stations of the Lost: The Treatment of Skid Row Alcoholics* (Prentice-Hall, Englewood Cliffs 1971).
[2] The potential for a simultaneous understanding of how both deviants and

social control agencies define interactive situations is too often neglected. See, for example, Spradley, J.P. *You Owe Yourself a Drunk: An Ethnography of Urban Nomads* (Little Brown and Co., Boston 1970), p.264, n.4.

[3] Cohen, A.K. *Delinquent Boys: The Culture of the Gang* (Free Press, New York 1955), p.59.

[4] Young, J. *The Drugtakers: The Social Meaning of Drug Use* (MacGibbon & Kee, London 1971), pp.178–83.

[5] There are numerous surveys on skid-row men. For a comprehensive bibliography see Bahr, Howard M. (ed.) *Disaffiliated Man: Essays and Bibliography on Skid Row, Vagrancy, and Outsiders* (University of Toronto Press, Toronto 1970).

[6] Matza, D. *Becoming Deviant* (Prentice-Hall, Englewood Cliffs 1969), p.26.

[7] London County Council *Report on Crude Spirit Drinking* (unpublished, 1965), p.5.

[8] Ibid., p.2.

[9] Home Office Working Party Report, *Habitual Drunken Offenders* (HMSO, London 1970), p.5.

[10] Contemporary welfare agencies on skid-row are almost exclusively organised by voluntary charities. Most of them are based on Christian moral principles. In Britain, statutory social services organised by local and central government do not, on the whole, concern themselves with the skid-row man.

[11] Home Office Working Party Report, op. cit., p.192.

[12] Ibid., pp.192–3.

[13] The term 'revolving door' is traditionally applied to the circuit of skid-row, police cell, court and prison that the alcoholic is continuously processed through. However, the addition of new agencies concerned with treatment does not pull men out of this process—the circuit is merely being widened.

[14] Foote, C. 'Vagrancy-Type Law and its Administration', *University of Pennsylvania Law Review* vol. CIV (1956), p.615.

[15] Ibid., p.616.

[16] Booth, General W. *In Darkest England and the Way Out* (Salvation Army, London 1890), p.24.

[17] Levy, H. *Drink: An Economic and Social Study* (Routledge & Kegan Paul, London 1951), p.156.

[18] Rooney, J. F. 'Societal Forces and the Unattached Male: An Historical Review', in Bahr op. cit., p.16.

[19] Report of a Special Committee of the Charity Organisation Society, *The Homeless Poor of London* (Spottiswoode and Co., London 1891).

[20] Gusfield, J. R. 'Social Structure and Moral Reform: A Study of the Women's Christian Temperance Union', *American Journal of Sociology*, no. 61 (November 1955), p.225.

[21] Rooney, op. cit., pp.30–3, and Wallace, S. E. *Skid Row as a Way of Life*, (Harper and Row, New York 1965), pp.79–80.

[22] Rooney, op. cit., p.21.

[23] Ibid., p.28.

[24] Ibid., pp.33–4.

[25] The notion of the skid-row alcoholic internalising a criminal identity arises out of an outsider's view of the alcoholic's experiences with law-enforcement agencies. In fact the skid-row alcoholic does not perceive himself as criminal, in spite of his familiarity with courts and prisons.

[26] The prison experiences of the alcoholic are held by some writers to be crucial to socialisation into the total skid-row way of life. See, for example, Spradley, op. cit.

[27] Washington Area Council on Alcoholism, Prison, Probation, and Parole in the District of Columbia (Excerpts on Alcoholism) (unpublished, 1957), pp.103–4.

[28] Ibid., p.105.

[29] Tatham, R. J. 'Detoxification Centre: A Public Health Alternative for the "Drunk Tank"', *Federal Probation* (December 1969), p.48.

[30] Cahn, S. *The Treatment of Alcoholics* (Oxford University Press, London 1970), pp.6–7.

[31] In March 1966 the US Court of Appeals for the District of Columbia handed down a decision which held that alcoholism should be met by treatment and not punishment. US Court of Appeals for the District of Columbia, no. 19365, DeWitt Easter, Appellant *v.* District of Columbia, Appellee, 31 March 1966.

[32] Saylor, L. F., 'Public Health Report: The Court's Decision on Alcoholism', *California Medicine* vol. CIX (September 1968), p.263.

[33] Nimmer, R. T., 'St Louis Diagnostic and Detoxification Centre: An Experiment in Non-Criminal Processing of Public Intoxicants', *Washington University Law Quarterly* no. 1, (Winter 1970), pp.5–6.

[34] On some American skid-rows, recovered alcoholics and police in civilian clothing are employed to pick up drunks for referral to the detoxification centre.

[35] Home Office Working Party Report, op. cit., pp.190–1.

[36] Nimmer, op. cit., p.25.

[37] Young, op. cit., pp.99–100, 177.

[38] Home Office Working Party Report, op. cit., p.3.

[39] The enormously high relapse rate of skid-row alcoholics would seriously undermine the *raison d'être* for therapeutic hostels and their staff if they upheld these goals as real. Consequently their aims are lowered to fit with the realities of a high recidivism rate. Three months' sobriety is considered a good performance for the client.

40 Home Office Working Party Report, op. cit., p.183.
41 Ibid., p.187.
42 Ibid., pp.188–9.

Drug Use: The Mystification of Accounts

John AULD

It is now little more than a truism to state that the prevalent conception of the illegal drugtaker in our society is that of a person who is sick using drugs that are pathogenic. Despite the evidence that a substantial and growing number of people are users of illegal drugs, and despite the frequently voiced claims that this activity is normal and, in the case of marihuana smoking for example, even preferable to indulgence in the legally endorsed drugs such as alcohol and tobacco, it is a conception which seems curiously resistant to attack. There still exists a widespread belief that people 'resort' to illegal drugs for purposes of 'escape', either because they have nothing better to do or because they are suffering from some form of mental disturbance. Similarly, the effects of these drugs are themselves described in negative terms: not only are drug users as individuals seen only as becoming *more* disturbed, *more* lacking in inclination to 'do' anything (witness the much-cited 'amotivational syndrome'); they also continue to be regarded as a dangerous social liability.

Only last September, for example, at the annual conference of the British Pharmaceutical Society, the suggestion was made by Dr Frank Fish of Strathclyde University that some otherwise unexplained road accidents may have been caused by drivers 'high' on drugs. Although the purported evidence for this claim was just 'one accident in which a student drove straight into a wall instead of turning at a junction', the press was quick to report it not just as fact, but as an alarmingly widespread occurrence. 'Drugs caused crashes', read a headline in the *Daily Telegraph* of 16 September 1972. Similar reports appeared elsewhere: 'Menace of drivers 'high' on drugs' warned the *Liverpool Daily Post*; while the *Daily Mail* was more specific: 'Cannabis may cause mystery crashes'.

Now in one sense there is an obvious wisdom in this. It may well be the case that the links between cannabis and either crime and insanity or the 'horrors' of heroin addiction are now seen by many informed opponents of drugtaking as having become rather too tenuous for them to be effectively called upon as justification for the continued illegality of the drug. If this is so, then an association between the drug and a form of behaviour which is as unambiguously anti-social as 'dangerous driving' provides a fairly effective substitute.

In more general terms, it is now well accepted that the social reaction to deviant behaviour can only be understood in terms of the kind of information that is received about it.[1] Correspondingly, much attention has recently been given to the part played by the mass media in structuring and disseminating such information.[2] In the field of illegal drugtaking, discussion of the sources and character of the public perceptions of the phenomenon has focused predominantly upon the questions of whether and why the media report it; what reasons they (along with other control agents such as police, doctors and politicians) invoke as justification for its legal and moral status *as* deviant; and how the information which they contain is patterned by its impact upon the actual behaviour of drugtakers.[3]

Yet an insufficiently explored source of the stereotyped ideas held by society about deviants consists in the kinds of explanations which they *themselves* provide for their behaviour when called to account by the upholders of public morality. Here as elsewhere, the seminal work of C. Wright Mills on vocabularies of motive gives an obvious lead.[4] Although the problem of imputing motives from the statements provided by deviants has been the subject of much discussion in recent years,[5] the central insight contributed by Mills remains unchallenged: namely that people typically formulate and cite motives for their behaviour which they consider will be regarded as acceptable by those who constitute their audience. If no such motives are available, then the behaviour itself may not occur. Thus, although drugtakers, for example, may claim that their activity is both normal and desirable when, as in the case of the underground press, they are addressing an audience which they believe to share such views and when they are in no immediate danger of running foul of the law, they may claim quite the opposite in situations such as arrest or court appearance where they are under strong pressure to conform to a more conventional interpretation of their behaviour.

We reserve a special place for the repentant sinner. Just as the greatest abuse and indignation tends to be levelled at those individuals who, having enjoyed all the benefits entailed in membership of a group, forsake it for another, so the greatest welcome is typically extended to those who publicly announce their return from the company of the wicked. In itself, though, mere return under conditions of hardship or duress is not enough, and in this sense the Biblical return of the prodigal son is an inadequate parable for modern times. Since modern societies face greater problems of preventing their members from straying from the narrow path of virtue, the fate of those who do stray must be seen as correspondingly more dire. Only thus can the fiction be sustained that their return is really voluntary and that

146

their punishment has little more than epiphenomenal significance. Deviance, in other words, must be seen to be unpleasurable.

If, therefore, the arguments of third parties appear unable to stem the gathering tide of betrayal—as has occurred in the case of drugtaking—one alternative strategy is to call upon the deviant himself to proclaim the folly of his ways and describe the unpleasantness of his experiences. Public testimonies in the 'I was a teenage drug pusher' vein constitute perhaps the most powerful ideological weapon of all, for they strengthen a faith in the desirability of the rewards to be obtained by conformity at the same time as they imply a rejection of whatever might be achieved through deviance. Moreover, they have the virtue of being based upon first-hand experience, something valued by deviant and non-deviant alike.

To the extent that these testimonies are made public by the media, they may decisively affect the character of public debate about the deviance in question. If, in the case of drug use, the majority of drug users featured in the media appear to endorse conventional views of their activity, then clearly there will be little pressure to change these. In the remainder of this article, therefore, I propose to consider three different types of statement involving drug use which receive regular expression through the columns of the national and local press: first, those which embody the efforts of drug users themselves to provide adequate accounts[6] for their behaviour in situations of actual confrontation with the official agents of social control; second, those which represent the attempt of other deviants to claim diminished responsibility for their actions by citing the effects of drugs; and finally, those which represent the more general attempt to explain or make sense of instances of highly abnormal behaviour when other modes of explanation are either unavailable or unappealing. I shall argue that all three types of statement, though in different ways, assist in the maintenance of the prevailing stereotype of drug use as pathological, and that, at a perhaps more sinister level, they derive their cogency from a continuing ignorance about the real causes and effects of use of the drugs concerned which the individuals expressing them have a vested interest in maintaining.

The documentation for my argument takes the form of reports concerning instances of the suspected or actual use of illicit drugs which appeared in the national and local press during 1971 and early 1972. In all but one case these are concerned with either marihuana or LSD—the two drugs which continue to attract most widespread public concern, despite the continuing ambiguity about the reasons for their designation as 'dangerous'.[7] Lest misleading imputations of responsibility and blame be inferred from this procedure, it should be emphasised at the outset that I have no evidence which would suggest that the individuals featured in such reports are to be held accountable for the uses to which their statements are put by the press. Instead,

I rely tacitly upon the now commonplace principle that decisions concerning both whether and how to report any such statement will be made in the context of the peculiar set of news values of the newspaper concerned. Although analysis of these is highly problematic and well beyond the scope of the present discussion, there are clearly often cases in which the heading of a report alone reveals something of the degree to which they approximate to what must be judged to be the aims and interests of social control.[8]

Accounts of drug users under arrest

A major contribution to the maintenance of the traditional equation of drug use with pathology is provided by the accounts of drug users themselves at the time of or following their apprehension by the agents of social control. This can be readily understood. Faced with the prospect of a heavy fine or even a jail sentence, it is only sensible for the drug user who is 'busted' to explain his activity in terms consistent with the dominant public rhetoric regarding the causes and likely effects of drug use. As Jock Young puts it:

> If the individual found in possession of marihuana actually finds himself in the courts he will find himself in a difficult position, namely that if he tells the truth and says he smokes marihuana because he likes it, and because he believes that it does no harm and that therefore the law is wrong, he will receive a severe sentence. Whereas if he plays their game and conforms to their stereotype, namely that he had got into bad company, that somebody (the pusher) offered to sell him the stuff, so he thought he would try it out, that he knows he was foolish and won't do it again, the court will let him off lightly. He is not then in their eyes the true deviant. He is not the dangerous individual whom the police and the courts are really after.[9]

At one level, to plead leniency in such terms has merely an instrumental function, representing an attempt by the defendant on a drugs charge to 'get off lightly'. At the same time, however, it betokens a willingness, however reluctant and even perhaps unwitting, to assist the apparatus of social control in its efforts to explain and defend the continued ban on use of drugs such as marihuana in terms which are accessible to the layman. In effect, it involves cooperating in the maintenance of mystification.

First, so far as the issue of *causation* is concerned, there is of course a strong tendency for the defendant to assign the responsibility for his actions to external agents by citing the importance of either curiosity or compulsion. The former element usually locates responsibility with the mass media, the

148

latter with the pusher, thereby reaffirming popular beliefs about the decisive part played by these in the aetiology of drugtaking. Both, however, refer to external agencies: that is, they locate responsibility with factors which say little about the characteristics of the individual's situation prior to deviation. The alternative explanation is equally positivistic, but nevertheless apparently favoured by many drugtakers when officially called upon to account for their violation of the law. The following are some examples: 'I was depressed said cannabis man' (*Camden & St. Pancras Chronicle*, 23 April 1971); 'Fed-up youth had cannabis' (*Havering & Romford Express* 17 March 1971); '"Worried" student smoked pot' (*Surrey & Hants News* 7 April 1971).

Similar statements are contained in a report entitled 'Drugs Charge: Four Accused' which appeared in the *Leyton Express & Independent* of 12 February 1971. Charged with possession of cannabis, one of the defendants claimed that 'he was a bit tense', while another said 'I was in a bit of a mess, and found it an escape, something to crawl into.'

The dominant theme represents a clear reaffirmation of the traditional medical view of the drug user as someone suffering from personality disorder who somehow 'can't cope' with his problems and needs drugs as a substitute. The drug, in this case marihuana, becomes regarded as providing either an artificial crutch for tackling one's difficulties, or a means of escaping from them altogether. In either case the arrested marihuana user unequivocally defines himself as 'sick' in the terms of both conventional psychiatry and the common sense.

In the light of such a perspective, one might expect the deviation away from normality and the process of regaining it to be described as basically unpleasurable. This indeed appears to be the case. If one turns from statements concerning the cause of drugtaking to statements concerning its effects, it seems clear that arrested drug offenders are usually eager to conform to the orthodox belief that deviance is inherently unpleasurable. The two most common strategies in this regard are to either (*a*) claim that they got more than they bargained for—that the effects of the drug, in other words, were unpleasant or even horrific—and that, consequently, they will not risk trying it again; or (*b*) claim that they experienced nothing at all, with a similar promise to abstain in the future.

The following are examples of the first type of account: 'Drug boys tell of "terror trip"' (*Southend Evening Echo* 28 April 1971); 'LSD "more dangerous" than he thought' (*Ilford & Redbridge Pictorial* 3 March 1971); 'Youth didn't enjoy first experience of cannabis' (*Peterborough Standard* 1 March 1971); 'Drugs charge man says: "cannabis is dangerous"' (*The Gloucester Citizen* 8 January 1971). One of the defendants in this latter case testified as follows: 'I discovered I could not work because of its effect. I now realise how harmful it is. I think it is dangerous stuff and I have learned my lesson.' The other claimed: '... it made me lazy. It was having a terrible effect on me.

149

... I found it detrimental to my health.'

An alternative to describing the effects of the drug in such negative terms is to deny the experience of such effects altogether. In this case the defendant tacitly suggests either that he did not really deviate at all, since he did not obtain the kind of gratification which is generally assumed to provide both motivation and rationale for the deviant act, or that through apprehension and labelling unmitigated by the experience of such gratification he has to some extent paid the penalty for deviance already. For example, one report headed 'Drug experiment disappointment' (*Peterborough Evening Telegraph* 1 January 1971) states that 'A Peterborough youth who experimented with cannabis was disappointed, his solicitor told city magistrates yesterday.... He had only taken the drug because "everbody else was".' Another report headed 'I grew pot, says drugs case man' (*Southend Evening Echo* 17 February 1971) paradoxically records that the defendant was alleged to have told police officers, '... I had a puff of what was supposed to be a cannabis cigarette, but it didn't do anything for me.'

Assertions about the tactical nature of such accounts must, however, be qualified by making the necessary distinction between their probable effect upon those who hear them and the degree of their genuine reflection of the personal characteristics and social circumstances of those who make them. Although the claims of drug offenders that the drug experience was unpleasant or even horrific may have the effect of substantiating and thus [ustifying the prevailing orthodoxy regarding illicit drugs, it cannot be doubted that in many cases they are voiced by individuals whose psychological characteristics or social milieu precisely render them liable to a drug-induced experience of a kind likely to attract the attention of social control agents. As Howard Becker has pointed out, the individual who takes a drug such as marihuana or LSD in an uncontrolled setting, without subcultural support, is highly prone to an unpleasant experience deriving from the belief that he is 'going crazy'.[10] Such an individual will find considerable difficulty in marshalling the powers of self-control necessary to escape detection by agents of law enforcement should occasion necessitate this. He may even, as Becker suggests, seek help from control agents in the belief that he *is* crazy. Writing about the extent to which the stereotypes held by the police about LSD users are a product of this kind of selective perception, Richard Blum *et al.* have suggested that

> ... the wildness atrributed to the hallucinogens reflects an interaction effect between the drug, the kinds of people who use it and become exposed to the police, and the kind of behaviour users were exhibiting at the time of arrest. In other words, the police come in contact with a highly selected sample of users.[11]

There is a further aspect to this, inasmuch as one of the most characteristic elements of the accounts provided by drug offenders is the degree of emphasis upon the fact that apprehension coincided with the individual's first and only acquaintance with the drug. At one level such assertions are tactically necessary if the protestations concerning the 'disappointing' or 'horrific' character of the drug experience are to appear credible, if only for the commonsense reason that the repetition of an activity renders claims about its unpleasantness somewhat suspect.[12] At another level, however, they may contain more than a germ of empirical truth. Again, as Becker points out,[13] it is quite common for the individual to dislike his first experience of marihuana or LSD, particularly if he takes the drug in an uncontrolled setting without taking adequate precautions to ensure that its effects can be interpreted favourably.

The possible outcome in such a situation is vividly illustrated by the following report in the *Southend Evening Echo* of 14 April 1971:

> *LSD boy's 'trip' ends on top of a car.* A teenager danced on the roof of a car after taking LSD, a court was told. And when police arrived he was lying on the grass calling: 'Please help me, I'm dying'. [In court, the defendant said] 'It was a terrifying experience, and I would not like to try it again.'

A similar qualification is in order with regard to the assertions made by some drug offenders that they experienced no effects from the drug concerned at all. To the extent that, at least in the case of marihuana use, the effects of the drug have to be identified before they can be enjoyed and are thus subject to a complex process of learning, such assertions may in some cases be true.

Nevertheless, few of those who are arrested and appear in court on drugs charges, and whose accounts are reported in the press, are likely to be representative of the totality of drug users. For every LSD user who acts out a bad trip in public, there will be hundreds of others enjoying the effects of the drug in supportive company behind closed doors. In the same way, therefore, that a misleading picture of the conventional criminal is likely to emerge if one concentrates solely upon those criminals who have failed to adequately cover their traces and have consequently been apprehended, so will a false portrayal of the typical drug user be the inevitable outcome of an over emphasis upon the protestations of the atypical drug user who finds himself in court. The important point remains that it is the latter type of drug user, atypical and unrepresentative though he may be, who with the help of the press and the other media defines the reality of drugtaking for a significant proportion of both control agents and members of the public. Equally important, he makes available a socially acceptable theory of drugtaking to his fellow drugtakers. Although it is difficult to imagine that these in turn will not be exposed to other sources of information about drugs (such as that contained, for example, in the underground press) it would be equally difficult to gainsay their claims to the contrary. In this sense, then, the relationship between accounts, motives and action is a highly intricate, dialectical one: stated summarily, the presentation of the atypical experiences of some drug users as typical may be acted upon by other drug users as if they are typical. The circle of mystification thus easily becomes closed.

Donald Cressey has noted such a possibility in his discussion of so-called compulsive crimes such as kleptomania and pyromania:

> ... a person might in some situations identify himself as a kleptomaniac, since that construct is now popular in our culture, and a full commitment to such an identification includes the use of motives which, in turn, release the energy to perform a so-called compulsive act.[14]

In the case of drug use, the situation is complicated by the fact that accounts of the kind described may also 'release the energy' to 'go crazy' while under the influence of the drug concerned. It is to this possibility that I shall now turn.

Accounts of deviants claiming diminished responsibility through drug use

A second type of contribution to the maintenance and continued credibility of the equation of drug use with pathology is to be found in the attempts of individuals arrested on charges of deviant behaviour *other than* the use or possession of drugs to plead diminished responsibility for their actions by appealing to the effects of drug intoxication. The range of deviant behaviour for which such effects are invoked as a mitigating device appears to be fairly wide, as the following reports bear witness:

Theft

> Stole money at dance during drug trip' (*Hereford Evening News* 18 March 1971).

> *Girls on LSD used stolen cheques to get clothes.* Two Maidstone girls who were 'tripping' on the drug LSD came to Gravesend and passed stolen cheques for more than £60 worth of goods.... 'We were tripping

from the effects of LSD at the time', Hoad (one of the girls) said in a statement to the police. 'I saw a cheques welcome sign and that triggered it off.' In her statement Laverick (the other defendant) said ... 'I only signed the cheques because I didn't realize what was happening.' (*Gravesend Reporter* 5 March 1971.)

Drugs 'the cause of pub theft'

Cannabis was responsible for a burglary committed by four young men, Gloucester quarter sessions were told yesterday. 'This might serve as a salutary warning to those who are advocating the spread of soft drugs', said Mr Brendan Shiner prosecuting. Mr Shiner said the men broke into the Green Dragon Inn at Cockleford, Gloucestershire, and stole cigarettes because they were under the influence of cannabis.... McDowell (one of the defendants) told police: 'We had been smoking cannabis. This probably played a large part in what followed as I feel we wouldn't have done it if we hadn't been smoking. Normally, I wouldn't have the nerve even to think about it, let alone do it'. Milne (another defendant) said: 'I would never have thought of doing such a thing if I had not been under the influence of drugs.'... Mr Jonathan Woods, defending all three, said they were all amazed at what they have done (*Western Daily Press* 28 April 1971).

Assault

Attacker was on LSD

Edward Clayfield, aged 20, told Thornbury magistrates yesterday that he was on an LSD trip when he attacked a schoolboy on a bus. ... Clayfield, who said that LSD made him aggressive, admitted assault (*Western Daily Press*, 3 March 1971).

Homicide

Manson girl: LSD made me kill (*Evening Standard* 19 February 1971). *I killed family on LSD trip, says man* (*Evening Standard* 24 November 1971).

Rape

Rape bid case told of drugged smoke

A man told police he smoked a drugged cigarette before an incident involving a 21-year-old woman. ... According to Mr Northcote (the presecutor) Anthony Lawrence (the defendant) 'told police it began when he visited a pub, where he met someone who gave him a drugged cigarette'. He got into his car, lit the cigarette and drove off. He felt terrible, his eyes were 'going all funny' and his head started swimming around. He got out of the car and a girl passed. He remembered walking alongside her and then everything went blank. Whatever she said in her evidence he would accept (*Shropshire Star* 7 January 1971).

Transvestism

Drugs made me do it—says youth who dressed in women's clothing. This was the explanation given to the police by Thomas Michael Lynam, Cranbury Avenue, when he was seen leaving the rear of a building dressed in women's clothes, knee-length boots and wearing a blond wig. ... Lynam told the police that since coming out of Borstal he had been taking amphetamines to give him confidence, and 'had the urge to take ladies' clothing' when he was 'coming out of withdrawal' from the drugs. 'I am not a "queer"', he said, 'and I get on quite well with girls.' (*Southern Evening Echo* 3 February 1971)

Perhaps the most noticeable characteristic of the accounts contained in such reports is their doubtful credibility. It is difficult to accept, for example, that an individual can successfully negotiate the necessary sequence of actions leading up to a crime and then to credit his claim that at the moment of actually committing the crime he 'didn't realise what was hap-happening' or that suddenly 'everything went blank'.[15] The law, too, is suspicious of such claims, and does contain certain safeguards against their easy acceptance.[16] However, if the individual can successfully claim a *complete* loss of responsibility, the original charge against him may be waived in favour of one of drug intoxication alone.[17] There are at least two factors which are likely to assist him in this. First, in the case of LSD, for example, the law has to contend with two important difficulties, in so far as the drug is odourless, colourless and cannot be detected in the human body once its effects make themselves apparent, and is usually of such a composition that it may with some legitimacy be claimed to have been taken in mistake for something else. This latter difficulty is particularly significant, for it raises the possibility of the individual successfully denying what Peter McHugh[18] describes as the element of conventionality ('it might have been otherwise') as well as that of theoreticity ('he knew what he was doing') and thus evading the charge of deviance altogether.

Second, there is the contribution of widespread ignorance and its counterpart, romanticisation. Unlike most other psychotropic drugs, and despite the continuing pleas for more research, little is known at the public level about the effects of psychedelic drugs such as marihuana and LSD except that they are highly unpredictable and may well give rise to insanity. This enables them to serve as the basis for denials of responsibility for deviance even in cases where explanations in terms of the effects of other drugs might seem more appropriate. Thus the report headed 'Attacker was on LSD' which was cited above, for example, continues with the following paragraph: 'He had taken half a tablet of LSD, plus some antidepressant drugs prescribed by his doctor, then gone out to drink five or six pints of cider.' Yet both the defendant and the newspaper which reported his offence clearly favour an explanation exclusively in terms of the effects of LSD.

Now in one sense this may appear contradictory, since it might be thought that the psychedelics—as their designation implies, and as many of their advocates claim—function to 'expand the mind' and to heighten perception rather than dull it. Indeed, drawing attention to what he believes to be the fallacy of the claim that cannabis provokes behaviour for which the individual cannot be considered responsible, Michael Schofield has written that

> Although this claim is sometimes made, the truth is that cannabis will not produce a 'black-out' similar to the loss of memory under the influence of alcohol. It is difficult to believe the reports about individuals who have taken so much cannabis that they do not remember what they have done. People under the influence of cannabis may act unconventionally and antisocially, but they know what they are doing and cannot escape responsibility for their behaviour.[19]

This may be so. Yet for Schofield to inform his readers of 'the truth' that people who use cannabis know what they are doing is not the same as suggesting that it is a truth shared by those concerned with controlling the activity. In practice there are at least two factors which help to ensure that any perceptual enhancement continues to be viewed as perceptual distortion: first, one must consider the mystifying terminology employed by many drug users themselves. As Reich has pointed out, 'The term "getting stoned" is confusing: it implies losing consciousness rather than a higher awareness.'[20] Similarly, the notion of 'blowing one's mind', although having favourable connotations within the drug subculture itself, is likely to mean something quite different to those outside it. Second, there are the mystifications and exaggerated claims expressed by control agents, a characteristic example of which is the following statement made by a police superintendent before an audience of Liverpool schoolchildren: 'In plain language this cannabis sends you absolutely round the bend, and make no bones about that.'[21] Though this effect may be unanticipated by drug users and control agents alike, both types of mystification contribute to the maintenance of popular misunderstandings about the effects of these drugs, making it likely that claims about their pathogenic characteristics will continue to be honoured.

This gives rise to one last point. For to the extent that such misunderstandings, and the kinds of alarmist statement to which they give rise, remain current, there continues to be a danger that individuals who do have serious mental absormalities will remain undetected. As Richard Blum has observed:

> The person who is hallucinating and then takes hallucinogens can blame his disorder on the drugs.... As long as he doesn't stop using drugs, the disturbed person can believe that he *could* stop hallucinating if he wanted to—that is, if only he stopped drug use. By making the drug responsible, he joins his explanation to the popular one. By adding his voice to the popular conception he also aids his social adjustment, for his accounting for himself then conforms to a 'normal' explanation. This accounting also provides 'evidence' in support of a popular theory of drug effects.[22]

The impenetrable quality of such a theory thus becomes almost assured. There is, moreover, an important rejoinder to this; in so far as some of the hallucinogenic drugs, notably LSD, are of such a composition that their consumption is of very low visibility and may even, as I have already suggested, occur by accident, Blum's proviso 'as long as he doesn't stop using drugs' may in practice be superfluous. It is possible, in other words, for the disturbed individual to claim that his behaviour is due to the effects of drugs when in fact he has not taken any drug at all. But whatever the case, there is good reason for supposing—as observers of the beats and the hippie phenomenon have suggested[23]—that the widespread use of psychedelic drugs has contributed to a significant blurring of the traditional distinction between normality and mental illness. At the very least, there is an implied qualification here of Thomas Scheff's ideas about the likely consequences of 'residual rulebreaking'.[24]

Having said this, it must be admitted that some of the claims put forward by deviants to the effect that they 'didn't know what they were doing' while under the influence of marihuana or LSD may be genuine, even if seemingly implausible. To exclude such a possiblity would clearly be inconsistent with the remarks made in the last section. However, this is almost impossible to ascertain in any given instance, and in any case does little to alter the impact of such claims upon those who hear or read about them. This, as I have suggested, includes other drug users, some of whom may—

in the absence of moral directives to the contrary—conform to what they believe is a prevalent response to the drug. These apart, many of those who require confirmation of their beliefs about the harmful nature of such drugs are likely to act upon the assumption that such claims are in fact genuine.

Accounts of control agents and the 'law-abiding public'

Awareness of the postulated effects of drugs such as LSD and marihuana is of course not totally confined to those who, however misguidedly, believe that appealing to them will condone their deviant actions, and it would indeed be surprising if the tendency to explain instances of criminal or deviant behaviour in terms of the effects of drug intoxication were not also shared by control agents and members of the ordinary public. To the extent that this is the case, it may be argued that the combined attempts of apprehended deviants and defenders of the ban on these drugs to emphasise the pathogenic effects of their use have succeeded in creating a situation where *almost any form* of behaviour, provided it is sufficiently abnormal, unexpected or bizarre, is a candidate for explanation in terms of the effects of drug intoxication. A key element involved here is the process of sensitisation: as Stanley Cohen has pointed out, 'any item of news thrust into the individual's consciousness has the effect of increasing the awareness of items of a similar nature which he might otherwise have ignored.'[25]

One important effect of this is to obscure any understanding or appreciation of deeper motivations for such behaviour. Indeed, attributions of the effects of drug use seem particularly likely to occur where such motives are unappealing to the observer. There is a clear analogy here with the historical function performed by the concept of mental illness; in the same way that, as Szasz has argued, the label of mental illness has been used 'to straddle and evade the conflict of interests between the patient and his social environment',[26] explanations of behaviour in terms of the effects of drug use frequently perform the function of concealing its real social meaning. In such cases drug use provides both a convenient scapegoat and a potent ideological weapon.[27]

A good example of this occurred during the presentation of the 1970 Miss World Contest, which was fairly effectively disrupted by members of Women's Liberation. Faced with the problem of maintaining order and explaining how, as he put it, anyone could wish to interrupt such a beautiful event, Bob Hope, the star guest of the show, concluded that they 'must be on some kinda dope'.[28] For many of the millions of people watching the event on their television screens, the political significance of the demonstration was thereby presumably negated and their worst fears about the

157

antisocial effects of illegal drugs confirmed. A similar attempt to simultaneously explain away a politically problematic event and sustain the prevailing stigma associated with the drug concerned was evidenced more recently by the suggestion that the My Lai massacre was caused by the acute toxic effects of marihuana upon the GIs involved, although this particular theory seems now to have fallen largely into disrepute.

Such explanations nevertheless perform a useful function in glossing over the complexities of real-life situations and neutralising political dissent. It is not difficult, for example, to attribute dissent or non-conformity to the effects of drug use, and the association is frequently made. Since illicit drugtaking is fairly widespread among those groups expressing such dissent, moreover, it is an association difficult to throw off. The police are not unaware of this, and according to the provisions of the Misuse of Drugs Act, which has confirmed their power to stop, search and detain anyone whom they suspect of being in unlawful possession of drugs, have almost complete freedom to intervene in the activity of deviant groups.

Appeals to the effects of illicit drugs are not inspired by political considerations alone, however. In the case of behaviour for which the motives would otherwise remain almost totally inexplicable, such drugs become even more likely candidates for explanation. Thus the *Guardian* of 17 March 1971, for example, ran an article headed 'Drug doubts on naked runner', which read as follows:

A man found dead after running nude on the Berkshire Downs may have been under the influence of drugs, an inquest was told yesterday. Dr Richard Cowdell, who conducted the post mortem, said: 'People who have taken a drug like LSD can act in this manner'. But traces of LSD and cannabis were hard to detect and he found none in the body of Michael Cattermole, aged 25, although Cattermole had a drug record.

For some people, indeed, so apparently mundane a phenomenon as the pop festival may defy explanation in terms other than drug use, as the following letter to the *Daily Telegraph* of 24 August 1970 eloquently suggested:

How has it come about that the present young generation have such a fanatical devotion to music?. ... The answer is *drugs*. At the pop (or pot) festivals it appears that young people can drug themselves to the eyeballs without fear of interference from police and parents. Under the influence of these drugs the yells, the moans and howls of the groups sound like the choirs of angels, the muddy grounds become elysian fields, and the filth and squalor are transformed into things of wonder and joy.

158

Sometimes, on the other hand, the effects of illicit drugs may be invoked to explain behaviour which, although highly abnormal or deviant to the observer, may in fact be motivated by what in different circumstances might be deemed perfectly rational consideration. That the individual himself may deny such motives—as is the case in the following report—is immaterial:

> *Drug probe after young girl strips.*
> Police have started a drug probe after a young girl stripped naked on stage at a town's dance hall. They have questioned a number of girls who were at the disco dance at the Top Rank, Reading. They have also taken a statement from a 16-year-old schoolgirl. The girl has told detectives she was at the dance but can remember nothing. ... The trouble started when a girl stripped on stage at the hall after a joke got out of hand. Disc jockey Phil Miller, aged 18, offered £5 to the first girl to take her clothes off, then boys threw money on the stage and a rush of girls started stripping. (*Evening News* 16 January 1971.)

Thus economic motives are curiously overlooked in favour of a confirmation of the perhaps less problematic notion that anyone who takes their clothes off in public must be 'high' on drugs. The kind of misrepresentation which such *ad hoc* appeals to the effects of drugs can result in is further illustrated by the way in which the press recently reported a rather gruesome incident in which a woman and her child were found dead, with their bodies badly mutilated. Although the story featured on the front page of both principal London evening papers of February 8 1972, in the newsworthiness stakes the report in the *Evening News* could hardly be surpassed, beginning as it did with the lurid headline:

> *London killing: hunt for drug-crazed hikers.*
> 'Two drug-crazed hitch-hikers were being hunted by Murder Squad detectives today after the mutilated bodies of a young mother and her two-year-old son were found in a South London flat. ... A police officer said: '... It was the sort of fiendish thing you would have to be pretty far gone to do. It looks like the act of a drug-crazed man.'

The unsubstantiated opinion expressed in this last sentence thus becomes translated into the factual assertion contained in the headline, and the strategy of the subsequent police manhunt is shaped accordingly. As the report further states: 'Hitch-hikers were being searched for drugs and early today a number had been taken to police stations for further questioning.'[29] In the event, however, the stereotype proved a poor guide to the facts of the case: for tucked away in the inside pages of both the *Times* and the

Guardian four days later were brief announcements of the fact that the woman's brother in-law had been charged with the offence. In neither paper was there any mention of drugs, and one may presume that they played little part in the proceedings. But few people are likely to have occasion to become aware that there is any discrepancy between the stereotype and the reality it attempts to portray, and the press is unlikely to assist them in the task.[30]

If such a discrepancy exits, it seems important to ask what the effects of its maintenance by press reports of the kind described might be. Some of these, of course, have been outlined already. But two further possibilities should at least be noted: first, for the deviant or potential criminal who is aware of this discrepancy, the unspoken message becomes: 'If you have it in mind to kill somebody, make sure that you so mutilate his body that the police think they are looking for a "drug-crazed hitchhiker", and if through ill-fortune you are caught, claim that you took LSD, preferably in mistake for something else, and can remember nothing.'[31] Second, as far as control agents are concerned, the rationale of drugs control is justified and, to the extent that deviants do not decide to act in the manner just described, rendered more effective. It seems at least arguable that the more difficulty the police have in controlling the spread of illicit drugs through the apprehension of individual drug users, the more likely are they to resort to the strategy of exploiting the existing state of ignorance and fear concerning their effects for purposes of deterrence. This presumably operates in terms of both encouraging the potential and otherwise law-abiding drug user to fear that he might suddenly turn into a murderer or a madman if he does indulge, and justifying the beliefs of those who already disapprove of drug use on the grounds of its harmful effects.

Constructed in this way, stereotyped explanations of abnormal or bizarre behaviour in terms of the effects of drug use assume a coherence and a systematic quality which militates against the easy acceptance of notions that the activity is *anything but* pathological. It is perhaps not surprising, therefore, (although there are clearly other reasons for this as well) that drug users, in the attempt to emphasise the normality of their behaviour, should have adopted a considerably more agressive stance towards the wider society than most other types of deviants. What, in short, they have to confront is a widespread tendency on the part of society at large to use their activity as a basis for explaining behaviour which may, ultimately, be unexplainable. This last example will perhaps give some indication of the fanciful suggestions which the exploitation of this tendency may give rise to:

Club told of perils of drugtaking.
Det.-Con. Collier (member of the Lancashire Drug Squad, talking to

Oldham Business and Professional Women's Club) death with the problems of the 'mind-bending' drug LSD.... And he put forward his own theory which could explain the mystery of the deserted ship the *Marie Celeste*. 'It could have been that all the men had eaten infected rye bread—a source of LSD—and jumped overboard, because they thought they were fish or something. It produces such fantastic hallucinations,' he said. (*Oldham Chronicle* 24 July 1971.)

Prospects for change

It is difficult to see how the types of mystification which I have described might most effectively be combated, for in practice there is little incentive for those whose actions are caught up in them to attempt this. This is certainly the case so far as publicly stated explanations of the causes and effects of illicit drug use are concerned. If for the sake of simplicity one restricts one's attention to the basic dyadic relationship between the individual who finds himself in court on a drugs charge and the magistrate whose task it is to implement the penal sanctions which the law prescribes for the activity, it seems clear that strong constraints operate to ensure that neither party will be likely to challenge orthodox conceptions about these. The magistrate, for his part, is exceedingly unlikely to act in a manner which might indicate a departure from such conceptions, if only because doing so would cast doubt not only upon his relationship to the law and to others charged with its maintenance, but also upon the available justifications for the sanctions which the law prescribes. Moreover, as at least one study of the attitudes and policies of control agents has indicated,[32] magistrates seem strongly inclined to favour positivistic explanations for deviant behaviour even in cases where the body of available information suggesting a more voluntaristic perspective may be considerable.

Similarly, the drug user himself—or his legal representative—has little to gain from suggesting that he takes drugs because he wants to, that he enjoys their effects and considers them to be harmless. Whilst it is virtually impossible to correlate the prevalence of such claims with the severity of sentences obtained, common sense and subcultural lore agree that they can scarcely be expected to earn the indulgence of the court. At first glance this may appear paradoxical, since it might be thought that the kind of drug user who is most vulnerable to police action—epitomised by the stereotype of the unkempt, long-haired hippie—has relatively little to lose by proclaiming the virtues of marihuana of LSD. His very life-style and behaviour bear witness, after all, to a certain estrangment from 'straight' society. Yet such an argument would ignore the most basic economics of the situation in a context where the most common penalty for a first offence involving drugs is the imposition of a fine.[33] Precisely because of such estrangement and the kind of social stigmatisation that is likely to accompany it, such a person is likely either to hold a relatively low paid job or to be living off supplementary benefits. Any fine, therefore, will claim a proportionately large share of his income; he can literally ill afford to take the risk of increasing it. In such circumstances it can hardly be found surprising if he 'plays it cool'.

The recent and presumably continuing growth in the use of drugs, particularly marihuana, makes little difference to this situation. There are at least two reasons why this should be so. First, like any form of deviance which originates in a disreputable subculture but which exhibits what may be termed 'centrifugal' characteristics over time, the tendency for pot smoking to be publicly viewed as a symbolic act of defiance has diminished as it has increasingly spread to respectable middle-class and professional groups whose members do not share the bohemian values and radical ideology of its progenitors. Such people are likely to have little interest in canvassing public support for a change in the law, particularly if they can live within it. This leads on to the second point, for it should be obvious that the very respectability of such groups is correlated with a high degree of immunity from police action; their drug use, in other words, is of low visibility. Consider for example the following extract from a statement which the magazine *Nova* obtained from 'Timothy', a forty-year-old property developer who inhabits 'an exquisite £35,000 Georgian house in Kensington':

> To be quite frank, we've never really thought much about getting busted, although of course from time to time one does get a touch of what's known as pot-smoker's paranoia: this feeling that someone out there is watching you. ... But let's face it, people who look like us and live in a house like this just don't give rise to police suspicion. It's terribly unfair I know, and one feels dreadfully sorry for pot smokers who happen to look freaky and get picked up all the time. One's just very grateful it's not us.[34]

In view of this, there is little need for any radical change in the strategy of police surveillance or the criteria for apprehension of suspects, for even if the hippie regards his drugtaking as any the less a symbol of righteous protest (which is unlikely), the continuing disreputable character of his life-style and appearance ensures that he will remain the primary target of police harassment.

Seldom, then, will the kind of respectable person who does have the financial resources to withstand a heavy fine appear in court. Even if he does, he is highly unlikely to challenge popular conceptions of the kind described. The reasons here are not economic in the crude sense of the term, but moral; in general terms, the more respectable a person is, the greater the stigma attached to any conviction and the greater, correspondingly, the commitment to at least appearing to be on the right side of the law.[35] Such a person, indeed, may be even more anxious to play it safe than his hippie counterpart.

There are of course certain groups whose members are in a position to be relatively free from either economic or moral constraints of this kind. One may cite pop stars, showbusiness celebrities and publicly recognised spokesmen of the 'alternative society' as cases in point; these are all people who have sufficient financial resources to be able to air their views with a certain disregard for the threat of a heavy fine, yet whose unconventional way of life or celebrity status leaves them relatively unaffected by any imputations of moral stigma. Yet it would be misleading to suppose that such unconventionality is entirely free from stigma in the public arena; the fact of being considered unconventional at all is sufficient to undermine the ability of such people to act effectively as moral entrepreneurs in favour of a public redefinition of drug use. Being by definition extra-ordinary, they tend to be regarded as 'a law unto themselves', enjoying a life-style far removed from that of the 'vast majority of ordinary folk' with whose humble fortunes they are contrasted. Their views tend thus to be simultaneously accepted as a half-legitimate accompaniment of public renown and dismissed as evidence of the kind of moral corruption which such renown is commonly thought to involve.[36] As such, they are unlikely to effect any significant change in the tenor of public opinion about drugs. Moreover, even if they do make active attempts in this direction, they are likely to find things made difficult for them. In a recent court case, for example, Richard Neville (ex-editor of Oz and one of the most outspoken public critics of the present drug laws) was stopped from making a speech in mitigation by Old Bailey judge Bernard Gillis, QC, before being fined £25 for possessing cannabis. 'I will not let the court be used as a platform', the judge informed him.[37]

One might not attribute such importance to the character of statements made by drug users themselves were it not for the existence of other constraints upon a redefinition of the moral status of drug use. But the explanations of deviant or even criminal behaviour in terms of the effects of drugs have created just such a constraint. Irrespective of their origins (since deviants and control agents have an almost equal interest in maintaining their credibility), such explanations now appear to have entered our everyday vocabularies of motive. Their increasing public acceptability has only been matched by the increasing likelihood of their featuring in the inferential processes whereby people make sense of one another's behaviour.

Perhaps in one sense this may best be understood in terms of the commonsense observation that in any society which is as complex and morally heterogeneous as our own there will be a large—and probably increasing—amount of behaviour which from at least somebody's viewpoint is unusual or deviant and thus requires explaining. Now the motives for such behaviour may be as unusual or as unpalatable to the observer as the behaviour itself. But whether this is the product of a reluctance or an inability to do otherwise, a common solution to this problem is to deny that such motives actually exist. As Stanley Cohen puts it, 'the only way of making sense of some actions is to assume that they do not make sense. Any other assumption would be threatening.'[38] Consequently, there is a great deal of behaviour in our society which is seen as determined or 'compulsive', the external manifestation of some inner sickness or inadequacy. Concrete expressions of this perspective draw upon (and are in turn legitimated by) the large stock of culturally given imagery about mental illness and insanity; at both a public and a private level, our repertoire of moral classifications abounds with descriptions of others as 'foolish', 'crazy', or 'out of their heads'.[39] The very term 'common sense', to which so much appeal is made in the settling of public conflicts of any kind, presupposes the existence of values and beliefs which are shared by those who claim it. Those whom it patently fails to embrace are typically dismissed by the invocation of such labels as the 'irrational minority' or the 'lunatic fringe'.

In a situation such as this, explanations of deviant behaviour in terms of the effects of drugs are likely to hold a peculiar appeal. This is partly a product of the fact that the attribution of such behaviour to mental illness has become increasingly problematic over the last few years, particularly when it has occurred on a large scale. But there are also other reasons for this, and some of these ought to be distinguished. First, since drug use has traditionally been associated with significant (and usually unpleasant) changes in behaviour, such explanations provide a publicly acceptable motive for the behaviour: the search for any deeper understanding of its meaning is cut short, the notion that 'he's behaving like that merely because he's on drugs' reaffirmed. Second, drug use is generally known to be widespread—particularly among the young, whose behaviour is likely to be regarded as being the most in need of explanation. Third, and perhaps most important, drug use is a concrete problem which, hopefully, can be dealth with. To label someone as a madman or a lunatic is to undertake an implicit commitment to cure him, with all the status ambiguities, practical problems and —most important—lasting stigma that this involves;[40] however, to label his behaviour as the product of drug use is merely to commit oneself to weaning him off the drug: by eliminating his drug use, one can hope to restore him to normality.[41]

So pervasive in fact are stereotyped ideas about the effects of drugs that the underlying reality may be almost completely obscured. Consider for example the following extract of a letter to the *Daily Mail* of 15 June 1972, in which a mother discusses the behaviour of her teenage son:

We look back on a childhood of non-conformity, violent outbursts and, later, foul language. His behaviour so resembled that of a drug addict that we were convinced that this was the reason for it. We were wrong... we have learned from our own experience that the root of his unhappiness has been frustration.

A similar tale appeared in the *Yorkshire Post* of the same date, prefacing a full-page report characteristically headed 'Could *you* tell if your child was taking drugs?'

The Yorkshire father of a rather wild teenage boy was worried. His son, 17, had been staying out late at night and would not say where he had been. According to the parent a search of the youth's room revealed what seemed to be the reason—a few dried leaves. The man feared the worst: 'My son is on drugs'. But he was wrong. A psychiatrist who specialises in treating young addicts had the little haul checked and was able to report that the hunt had turned up old beech leaves and not marihuana.

Since most of us lack the opportunity to verify our accounts of other people's behaviour, the fact that in both these examples the parents concerned were proved wrong in their suspicions is of little significance. Indeed, it is perhaps a measure both of their faith in the prevailing ideas about the effects of drugs and of their lack of confidence in their children that so much attention should apparently be given by parents to advice upon how to find out whether their moody or rebellious teenage son or daughter is *really* a secret drugtaker. To the extent that it succeeds in reducing the range of behaviour which is considered a normal reflection of the individual's personality and circumstances, such advice may be highly insidious. It does, however, have the merit of providing a basis for an acceptable definition of the situation where none might otherwise exist. In this sense, it is hardly surprising that drugs should be regarded animistically; for in so far as *they* are the source of the trouble, conflicts over the reality of life within the family (and the society of which it is a part) can be safely ignored. In this context at least, the pathological associations of drug use are likely to strongly resist redefinition.

In conclusion, then, I should like to suggest that one cannot form accurate judgements—as many studies have tried to do—about the relative harmfulness of illegal drugs such as marihuana and LSD in isolation from a consideration of the important social and political functions which their continued illegality performs. So long as, for example, a significant proportion of population has no first-hand experience of the effects of these drugs, such effects will continue to be romanticised and it will continue to remain possible for various groups to exploit this ignorance to their own advantage. One of the dangers arising from this is that the true character and meaning of the important social and political changes which contemporary society is at present undergoing may be obscured in favour of a tendency to denounce them as in some way a consequence of the effects of drug use. From this point of view it may well be argued that what people most fear is not drug use *per se* but the kinds of social change which drug use is invoked to explain. Such an argument would throw some light both on the reasons why drug use figures so prominently in public debates on crime and deviant behaviour and why—despite the sustained attempts of liberal opinion to change it—the law prohibiting the activity has if anything been made more severe. I would suggest that if the law comes to reflect a more lenient approach in the near future, this is unlikely to occur in response to any immediate change in public attitudes about the causes and likely consequences of drug use.

Notes

[1] For what is probably the original statement of this perspective, see Wilkins, Leslie *Social Deviance: Social Policy, Action and Research* (Tavistock, London 1964).

[2] See, for example, Halloran, James D., Elliott, Philip, and Murdock, Graham *Demonstrations and Communication: A Case Study* (Penguin, Harmondsworth 1970); Cohen, Stanley *Folk Devils and Moral Panics: The Creation of the Mods and Rockers* (MacGibbon & Kee, London 1972); Young, Jock *The Drugtakers: The Social Meaning of Drug Use* (Paladin, London 1971); Rock, Paul, and Cohen, Stanley, 'The Teddy Boy', in *The Age of Affluence: 1951–1964* ed. Bogdanor, V. and Skidelsky, R. (Macmillan, London 1970).

[3] The most systematic treatment of these issues is provided by Young, op. cit., and Young, Jock, 'Mass Media, Drugs and Deviancy', paper presented at the 1971 Conference of the British Sociological Association, London.

[4] Mills, C. Wright 'Situated Actions and Vocabularies of Motive', *American Sociological Review* vol. V (December 1940), pp.904–13.

[5] See, for example, Matza, David *Delinquency and Drift* (Wiley, New York/ London 1964); Box, Stephen *Deviance, Reality and Society* (Holt, Rinehart & Winston, London 1971), ch.4. A useful account of the differing strands of

debate on the subject is provided by Laurie Taylor in 'The Significance and Interpretation of Replies to Motivational Questions: The Case of Sex Offenders', *Sociology* vol. VI (January 1972), pp.23–39.

6 The term is used in the sense suggested by Scott and Lyman. See Scott, Marvin B., and Lyman, Stanford M., 'Accounts', *American Sociological Review* vol. XXXIII (February 1968), pp.46–62.

7 For an interesting but often neglected discussion of possible sources for this anomaly see Blum, Richard 'On the Presence of Demons', in Blum, R. *et al.*, *Society and Drugs* (Jossey-Bass Inc., San Francisco 1969), vol.1.

8 In other cases where editorial bias of this kind is not so immediately apparent, I have reproduced rather more of the original report. An important *caveat* is in order at this point, for unfortunately I can claim neither representativeness nor geographical specificity for my selection of press material. But in a situation where several hundred court cases alone involving drugs are reported annually by the press, and where both enforcement and sentencing policies, news values and public opinion over that period are subject as much to intraregional variations as interregional ones, to obtain anything like a representative sample is almost impossible. The value of the analysis which follows must therefore be considered to be primarily of a heuristic nature.

9 Young, *The Drugtakers*, op. cit., p.188.

10 Becker, Howard 'History, Culture and Subjective Experience: An Exploration of the Social Basis of Drug-Induced Experiences'. *Journal of Health and Social Behaviour* vol. VIII (Spring 1967), pp.163–76.

11 Blum, Richard, *et al.*, *Utopiates: The Use and Users of LSD 25* (Tavistock, London 1965), p.227.

12 This of course distinguishes the so-called soft drugs from the physically addictive drugs such as heroin, where repetition is normally conceded to have the specific purpose of avoiding the kind of 'unpleasantness' associated with withdrawal.

13 Becker, op. cit.; see also the essay 'Becoming a Marihuana User' in his *Outsiders* (Free Press, Glencoe 1963).

14 Cressey, Donald R. 'Role Theory, Differential Association and Compulsive Crimes', in *Human Behavior and Social Processes* ed. Rose, A. M. (Houghton Mifflin, Boston/Routledge & Kegan Paul, London 1962).

15 Ibid. On this point see also Hartung, Frank E. *Crime, Law and Society* (Wayne State University Press, Detroit 1965). This is not to say, however, that in the case of those offences whose motives are difficult to comprehend this claim will not be favoured by magistrates. See Laurie Taylor, op. cit.

16 See Millett, F. N. 'Criminal Responsibility of Drug Users', *Journal of Drug Issues* (July 1971), p.192; Mansfield, Michael 'I Didn't Know What I Was Doing', *Drugs and Society* vol. I (March-May 1972), pp.6–8.

[17] There appears, however, to be some controversy as to the conditions under which this may legitimately occur. See Millett, op. cit., pp.195–7. In such circumstances the outcome in any particular case will presumably depend much upon the predilections and beliefs of the individual magistrate.

[18] McHugh, Peter, 'A Common Sense Perception of Deviance', in *Deviance and Respectability: The Social Construction of Moral Meanings* ed. Douglas, Jack (Basic Books, New York 1970).

[19] Schofield, Michael *The Strange Case of Pot* (Penguin, Harmondsworth 1971), p.122.

[20] Reich, Charles *The Greening of America* (Penguin, Harmondsworth 1972), p.217.

[21] Quoted in *The Times*, 1 April 1971.

[22] Blum, *On the Presence of Demons*, op. cit. p.336.

[23] For example Lipton, Lawrence *The Holy Barbarians* (W. H. Allen, London 1960); Yablonsky, Lewis *The Hippie Trip* (Pegasus, New York 1969).

[24] Scheff, Thomas *Being Mentally Ill* (Aldine, Chicago 1966).

[25] Cohen, op. cit., p.77.

[26] Szasz, Thomas Stephen *The Myth of Mental Illness: Foundations of a Theory of Personal Conduct* (Secker & Warburg, London 1962), p.71.

[27] For related examinations of the ways in which conventional explanations for deviance conceal such meanings, see, for example, Cohen, Stanley, 'Hooligans, Vandals and the Community: Studies of Social Reaction to Juvenile Delinquency' (unpublished PhD thesis, University of London 1969); Taylor, Laurie and Walton, Paul 'Industrial Sabotage: Motives and Meanings', in *Images of Deviance* ed. Cohen, Stanley (Penguin, Harmondsworth 1971).

[28] See 'Hope Exposes Commie Plot', *International Times* no. 93 (December 1970), p.2.

[29] The 'widening of the net' effect which this refers to is a signficant by-product of the fabrication and manipulation of deviant stereotypes by the media, and may be an important source of deviance-amplification. See Cohen (1972) op. cit., pp.83–5.

[30] For a related example, in which the American press gave headline publicity to a claim to the effect that LSD causes blindness, but almost totally ignored the subsequent confession by its author that it was without foundation, see Braden, William 'LSD and the Press', in *Psychedelics* ed. Aaronson, B., and Osmond, H. (Doubleday, New York 1970).

[31] For a similar recommendation see Abrams, Steve, 'Dope Hope', *Oz* no. 27 (April 1970), p.17.

[32] Cohen, *Hooligans, Vandals and the Community* op. cit., ch.11.

[33] See the Report by the Advisory Committee on Drug Dependence *Cannabis* (HMSO, London 1968).

34 'When it's Harvesting Time in Trendy NW1...', *Nova* August 1971. On this point see also Chapman, Dennis *Sociology and the Stereotype of the Criminal* (Tavistock, London 1968).

35 For a recent discussion of the concept of commitment see Box, *Deviance, Reality and Society* op. cit., pp.144–7.

36 There is an interesting double-bind at work here, inasmuch as such people are also frequently charged with corrupting the morals of precisely those people with whose help they have presumably achieved notoriety in the first place. This may appear paradoxical, but the notion that pop stars, for example, have a 'responsibility' toward their fans was clearly evident in the public reaction to the celebrated trial of the Rolling Stones in 1967.

37 See Des Wilson's 'minority report': 'The Unspoken Plea', *The Observer* 13 January 1972.

38 Cohen, *Images of Deviance* op. cit., p.19.

39 Cf. Scheff, *Being Mentally Ill* op. cit.

40 On these issues see Goffman, Erving, 'The Insanity of Place', appendix to his *Relations in Public* (Allen Lane the Penguin Press, London 1971).

41 For a recent critique of this perspective see Szasz, Thomas 'The Ethics of Addiction', *Harper's Magazine* (April 1972).

Going Missing

Mike HEPWORTH and Mike FEATHERSTONE

> For at bottom, whatever we may say, we cannot live a lie or a falsehood without corroding and dividing the self.[1]

The case of sudden physical disappearance

Sudden physical disappearance is by no means a remote feature of our society:

> My husband said 'Excuse me, I'm going to the loo'. He never came back.[2]

Each year, it has been estimated, at least 100,000 people are classified as missing in Great Britain; one writer has suggested that only 40 per cent of this number reappear or are traced.[3] Evidence concerning the 'real' extent and nature of this behaviour is hard to come by since, excluding certain officially designated vulnerable categories such as the young,[4] the mentally ill, the retarded or those incarcerated in institutions, going missing is not considered a 'social problem' and therefore the focus of organised statistical or any other kind of analysis.[5]

Clearly people go missing from a whole range of social situations and in response to a wide variety of pressures.[6] The central preoccupation of this essay is with those who 'suddenly' and 'inexplicably' remove themselves from a 'settled' way of life. In other words we are not concerned here with individuals, from whatever social background, who go missing following a major disagreement or altercation with some others with whom they habitually interact; nor shall we be giving much attention to issues of forcible abduction, kidnapping and the like. Our substantive interest rests largely with certain problematic actions on the part of a specific category of members of society: those defined as adult members of 'respectable' families. It is with this group that the following discussion is primarily occupied.

One accessible everyday source of evidence about going missing comes from essentially 'truncated' or abbreviated newspaper reports effectively representing a sense of mystified concern and unease.[7] Just to take two examples: In 1972 the *News of the World* contained five paragraphs describing

171

the apparently voluntary disappearance of an unmarried clergyman from his parish, leaving behind him a newsletter stating his intention of absenting himself for a period of time;[8] a second much longer article referred to the inability of the police and the Salvation Army Missing Persons Bureau to discover a middle-aged man and a younger woman both of whom suddenly left their separate homes and scenes of employment.[9] Combining these two newspaper accounts to offer a generalisation, we can see that the sense of concern receiving expression in the media pertains both to the perceivedly problematic motivations underlying an act of social disengagement and the fact that it is still possible in our organised social world for people who are alive and well to pass 'out of reach' of others; to all intents and purposes, to be untraceable.

As with certain pertinent 'great mysteries' of our time—of especial interest is the unexplained disappearance of the passengers and crew of the *Marie Celeste*—the general concern already noted hovering around the missing persons issue is focused most sharply upon the actual situated act of going missing. The motives of those who have gone are usually inferred from whatever information is available about the mode and manner of their disappearance: the more this complex of factors is represented as routinely commonplace, the more mysterious does the act of going missing become. Progressively those left behind invite us to view the behaviour as 'out of character'. In the case of children and adolescents, anguished parents are frequently reported as hopefully ransacking their memories of the last known moments of their missing children and retracing their steps in an effort to find some clue to their disappearance.[10]

However, the quite widely reported phenomenon of going missing cannot be viewed in all instances, even where youngsters are concerned,[11] as a uniquely mysterious and isolable act understandable in its own terms. Defining going missing as a sudden and apparently inexplicable break in what are taken for granted as predictably on-going and crucial relationships, we can conveniently, though artificially, compartmentalise the patterns of interaction within which such events occur and through which they are interpreted or 'explained' as follows:

1   Interactional patterns and life-styles prior to the break.
2   Immediate circumstances and events (last moments) against which the break occurred.
3   The break.
4   Reactions of those left behind and efforts made to communicate the fact of the break and their reactions to this to others.
5   Reactions of the now-incorporated wider audience.
6   Institution or non-institution of search procedures.

172

7 The nature and persistence of the search and attendant publicity.
8 Subsequent patterns of 'flight', patterns of association and life-styles of the person missing.
9 Subsequent patterns of association and life-styles of those left behind.
10 Return (voluntary or otherwise) of the individual who went away and self-presentation of the erstwhile missing person.
11 Reactions of those to whom the person who went missing has returned.
12 Communication of reactions 10 and 11 to a wider audience by whatever parties.
13 Reactions of the wider audience drawn in as witnesses.

As the events formalised here unfold, a situated action of physical disappearance may or may not lead to the identification *in absentia* of the individual concerned as a missing person. Whether or not an act of *going missing* will come to be perceived and described as the act *of a missing person* depends upon the nature of the reaction by those remaining to the break itself. In certain respects a person going missing draws unto himself a 'transitional status';[12] outwardly and visibly, whether or not he becomes a missing person or ceases to be a missing person, will by no means be dependent entirely on his own actions. A crucial factor here, of course, is the passage of time.[13]

Once, therefore, the possible interaction ramifications and their implications for patterns of communication (regardless of the *substance* of the communication) are spelt out we can see immediately that the act of going missing is but one amidst a complex social context and any interpretation of the nature and significance of this behaviour is directly dependent upon a sociological analysis of this context. Furthermore, and this is the feature we particularly wish to enlarge upon, the possibility and actuality of sudden physical disappearance afford a pointed comment on certain facets of society.

John O'Neill has written:

> Every need of ours involves someone else. The great tissue of human involvement which is woven out of our inability to live without the love and labour of others arouses a constant wonder in us. It is the framework of everything that is relevant to us.[14]

A sense of belonging and personal worth may well depend on the untroubled persistence of apparently intimately informed interaction, where the validity knowledge of the others is ratified by their unfailing presence.

In such a context, going missing may be experienced by those remaining as a shocking violation of their sense of status and identity and thus the ability to retain their customary position in the moral order. In this sense the deliberate disengagement of a family member resembles the experience of bereavement; it can be similarly disruptive for those remaining because the process of adjustment involves possibly undesirable changes in social status and identity.

Whether or not an act of physical disengagement will be regarded as problematical (both for those left behind and a wider social milieu), will depend upon a variety of social factors. At the same time there is no doubt that going missing is interpreted in many quarters as socially damaging or at least as a matter which ought to be the target of legitimate investigation. There are two pointers to this conclusion:

1   The existence of a diffuse collection of sociological writings defining, discussing and empirically exploring issues of 'disaffiliation' in modern societies (particularly the United States).[15]
2   Coincidental with the emergence of a descriptive and analytical literature on disaffiliation, a recognition that going missing creates a series of personal problems for those left behind to whom some sort of official response should be made. Accompanying this concern is a tendency to accord, to some individuals at least, the deviant status of missing persons. Such missing persons may well, of course, be defined as themselves in need of help.[16]

Historically, organised concern over those who disappear is a relatively new feature of the social scene, the result in this country of pioneering work by the Salvation Army towards the end of the last century. Originating in the Army's concern over the moral threat posed by the well-known connection between poverty and prostitution in the larger urban centres, the search for missing persons has always advertised itself as a family service geared towards the restoration of such relationships.[17] Thus, the Army has tended to define as generally problematic behaviours in which other agencies such as the police and formal social services have evinced only a specific interest when particular incidents of going missing relevant to their organisational concerns have been brought to their attention. In turn the sociological literature has tended to reflect this special preoccupation so that our knowledge of processes of disaffiliation or disengagement has been distorted through too great an emphasis (predictable in a competitive society) on social groups struggling to handle the perils and dangers of downward social mobility.[18] Disaffiliation—and here we can include going missing—has become synonymous with disgraceful personal or social disintegration.

Broadly, then, those who go away, fell into two groups:

1   The unofficially problematic: that is, people who have gone away and are defined as missing by what was their immediate circle.
2   The officially problematic: people whose absence is of pressing concern

to formal agencies of social control.[19] This category includes those whose actual act of physical disengagement may be of no immediate concern but who may augment the membership of social groups whose appearance in a particular location is seen as potentially offensive to or disruptive of public order. Potential recruits to this armoury of 'folk devils'[20] include communitarians, members of pop festivals, migratory hippies and the like.

From all that has gone before it will be obvious that our concern is with the first group of people who go missing: the unofficially problematic.[21] This does not mean, of course, that discussion of officially problematic acts of going missing is totally precluded. Our central point is that a major distinction can be drawn between an act of going missing and the process of becoming a missing person and this can only effectively be brought about by a consideration of the varying interactional possibilities previously outlined. Because these interactional possibilities, with all their implications for communication work are the vehicle of a historical cultural framework (a 'societal stock of knowledge'), the interpretation of an act of going missing must take place against some analysis of the conventionally accredited social settings left behind. An appreciation of the ideological significance of these settings—in our case 'respectable' family relations—involves their consideration approved images of the ordered society and appropriately settled personal identities. To draw on Erving Goffman, though not necessarily to reflect him, we are asking: what is the overall 'symptomatic significance of situational improprieties'[22] revealed when a sense of concern is expressed over the unofficially problematic disappearance of what is conventionally considered to be a 'free' man or woman? Putting it another way: what kind of social order is suggested?

Finally in this section, we note the existence of at least two sets of evidence or perspectives on going missing. Students of the sociology of deviance have clearly demonstrated that any notion of withdrawal from interaction with some other members of society (whether enforced or through personal choice) is by no means a clearly understood or simple process. Certainly, such alleged withdrawal by no means signals the total rejection of conventional values let alone meaningful social relationships. James F. Rooney writes on contemporary skid-row residents in the United States that they 'accept the ultimate validity of the values of the middle class'. Moreover, he asserts that whereas selection for skid row was formerly the result of almost ineluctable structural forces—particularly economic pressures—'today psychological factors seem most important.' One need not uncritically accept Rooney's analysis to advertise that, rightly or wrongly, interest is shown by researchers in two analytically separated elements considered conducive to social disaffiliation:

1 'Mental', psychological or subjective elements.
2 External social pressures.

One thing can be said, and that is that this oversimplified dichotomy leaves us with behavioural indices reflecting features endemic to the organisation of our society.

Public world and private places

It has been stated already that people disappear or make a break from all kinds of situations; the only apparent link between them very often being the fact of their precipitous physical disappearance. Many people are categorised as missing in the aftermath of natural disasters such as earthquakes, hurricanes and floods not to mention as a result of man-made disasters such as warfare.[23] In all these cases the missing individual is generally regarded as having unwillingly been removed from his customary situation. Against the background of such frequently unpredictable happenings it is not difficult for those left behind to hope that the missing person will return, especially since it is unlikely that he chose to go.

By contrast, the term 'going missing' implies intentionality. It is for this reason that we earlier drew a distinction between going missing and 'becoming' a missing person. The two need not be the same. How can we best set out to understand the overall significance of going missing for those unofficially problematic groups whose members are commonly considered to 'know their own minds'? What is the relationship between this form of deviance (in the sense of relational rule-breaking) and respectability?—since it is with disappearances from what are perceived as primarily respectable and, moreover, desirable social settings that we are concerned.

In this section we shall examine the overall implications of unsettling sudden physical disappearance from settled private settings in an attempt to determine more precisely the sociological links between such private issues and public troubles. In the final two sections of our essay we shall discuss the nature of imputations of deviance directed at some of those who go missing and the problematic status of these imputations *vis-à-vis* the liberal model of the citizen as essentially self-determining.

We begin with the assumption that physical disappearance is mysterious: it is 'baffling' or 'defies explanation'. In his foreword to Noel Timm's study of 'rootless' girls drifting around London, R. Huys Jones indicates the *general problem* facing us here:

The report describes some very vulnerable young people in great trouble whose difficulties may be *all the more baffling because we cannot label* them as we have labelled the problems of drugs or drunkenness, mental disorder, prostitution or crime.[24] (Emphasis ours.)

By 'mysterious' we refer to a categorisation applied by observers other than the person who actually disappears; although someone who is found may apparently have difficulty in explaining his actions to his interrogators. In other words, as with certain cases of suicide, these are situations in which there seems to those left behind to be no adequate reason for a person to leave a settled and outwardly rewarding way of life.[25]

From the United States comes a human document—a diary—written by a white girl aged 15 and now dead from an overdose of drugs. She became involved in the 'drug scene' and went missing from her pleasant upper-middle-class home and concerned parents on at least two occasions. The diary reveals a sense of uncertainty over her identity; although she loves her parents and appreciates the advantages of her home—particularly security—she is aware of other experiences and possibilities and these simultaneously attract and repel her. She wrote:

> I'm partly somebody else trying to fit in and say the right things and do the right thing and be in the right place and wear what everybody else is wearing.

A few days later:

> 'Oh dear God, help me adjust, help me be accepted, help me belong, don't let me be a social outcast and a drag on my family.'[26]

In our research with social workers we have encountered similar cases where teenage girls who have gone missing express in intense and concentrated form a sense of ambiguity towards conventionally approved relationships through which self-fulfilment is appropriately directed in our society. In a general sense the act of going missing and the reactions it provokes sheds new light upon facets of the social bond in 'today's world'.

Richard Williams describes what seems to be one of the very few analyses of missing persons records available in this country, by researchers from Bedford College.[27] A sample of cases in the records of the Salvation Army in London revealed that 'a greater number of men leave home between the ages of 40 and 45.' Furthermore, of 111 inquiries selected for analysis from the transactions filed by the Family Services and Inquiry Department in 1963, '54 women gave reconciliation as the reason for tracing a husband, 28 inquiries were for maintenance, and 15 to determine the woman's legal status as a wife or widow.'[28] Following this analysis members of the Investigation Department staff which handles inquiries for missing relatives other than husbands or putative fathers undertook a survey of 1,000 consecutive cases (30 per cent of total inquiries for 1966). The largest number of cases involved inquiries for wives, brothers, sons and daughters; all other cases involved family relations with the exception of an 'unallotted' category of 'special inquiries'. With regard to the ages of the people sought, the greatest percentage indicated the age group 35–49 (29.7 per cent).[29]

Disappearance from some sort of family setting is obviously considered a major issue not only by the relevant departments of the Salvation Army but also by those seeking help.[30]

Ralph H. Turner has indicated that as far as family interaction is concerned, contemporary folklore places great emphasis on the importance of 'person bonds' which, he states, have the function of 'linking family members as persons'. Summarising various theoretical writings and relevant empirical research, Turner stresses that person bonds are forged through interaction processes which provide 'identity gratification' for the members concerned. These 'identity-oriented aspects of social interaction' serve to bring about a system of interpersonal bonds or dependencies of a kind not produced through the mere accomplishment of various social tasks (such as a man functioning as a competent wage-earner). Within the family unit it is possible for members to experience a necessary confirmation of the image they hold of themselves—their identity—whenever other members reveal their awareness and acceptance of this desired self-image.[31]

The relevant point that Turner is making is not that such identity gratifications are present at all times, nor for some any of the time, since person bonds, just like any other form of social bond, are vulnerable and may be fractured by a whole range of possible occurrences. What he is underscoring is that family life is increasingly coming to be viewed as an important arena for the confirmation and maintenance of the individual's view of himself over and above the accomplishment of the everyday business of living, which has traditionally been viewed by sociologists at any rate as the key *raison d'être* of this institution. It is our argument that the processes both of going missing and becoming a missing person shed light on this contemporary issue of 'identity gratification'. In what is, structurally speaking, an increasingly family-centred society where emphasis is placed on the privacy of private property and privately intimate relationships,[32] such gratifications come to be seen not only as a possibility but as a right.

The privatisation of family life presented as an ideal supportive unit in a competitive society clearly creates pressures for members to maximise identity gratifications within these partially concealed settings. For this reason, going missing violates the rules conducive to private situational order and can attract the attention of a wider circle to family misfortune.[33] Some time ago a journalist, Philip Smith, interviewed separately a husband who had gone missing and his wife who was still searching for him and ignorant of his whereabouts. He noted that the two accounts of the marriage prior to the break differed in certain respects and that when each was told the main points of the other's story contradictions remained. The article was prefaced with a statement to the effect that every year 'thousands' of husbands, hitherto quiet ordinary men who apparently have experienced few if any dissatisfactions with their lot, suddenly disappear never to be seen again.[34]

With regard to the interpretation of going missing as a deviant act and the potential of the break to assume the dimensions of a social problem, two major theoretical statements are in order.

First, people who go missing and individuals who become known to those remaining as missing persons need not necessarily be 'outsiders'. As we have observed, the status 'missing person' usually constitutes an index of the imputed potential of the absent figure to return and resume interaction without undue fuss and with customary competence. ' "Don't tell my husband where I am," pleaded a woman tearfully to the detective standing at the door of her bedsitter. "I want to stay missing"'.[35] When a teenage girl, absent for five months returned home following her recognition by a fellow worker as a missing person, her parents were reported as saying: 'We're delighted to have her home. She picked up the threads as if she had just gone out on an errand'.[36] Again, time is an important factor,[37] as convicted men facing prison sentences of 20 or 30 years know to their cost.[38] Those waiting for someone to return appear to discount the possibility of identity changes[39] in the person who has gone missing or at least to push these disquieting thoughts to the back of their minds.

Second, those who go missing are nicely poised between exclusion and acceptance, and by examining the social matrix of their activities and the ideologies informing the interpretation of their disquieting actions we can obtain clues of central importance to an understanding of some of the processes underlying the emergence, attribution and acceptance of deviant or nondeviant identity.[40]

It follows that one important source of ambiguity over the whole issue is the reaction to those who go missing. This reaction, as far as it has been recorded, is selectively informed by traditional notions of English liberalism and a generally romantic ambiguity towards those on the move who cut away from organised society. Conventional explanations of going missing and becoming a missing person can be interpreted in terms of the tension between popular conceptions of social stability (the 'ordered' life and its general desirability) and notions of the liberty of the adult individual (especially the male) which include the right to move around the country both physically and socially without let or hindrance. Indeed he may be positively encouraged to do so in response to economic pressures such as the need for labour elsewhere[41] or, more respectably, in managerial pursuit of company policy.

At the same time a problem remains, and is neatly stated by Kellow Chesney commenting on Victorian England: 'God-fearing men and woman lived between four walls....'[42] Motives for going missing must be understood as part of the structures they indicate and to which they lend persistence.

The construction of explanations by those left behind

A major concern of those left behind is to explain the missing individual's act of social disengagement to themselves and a wider audience. In some cases the circumstances surrounding the disappearance appear to offer a clear indication of why the individual went missing. However, in many cases it would seem that those left behind have to construct explanations of the disappearance in the absence of clear-cut or at least *acceptable* evidence about the motive of the individual. Thus the accounts put forward may emerge from a process of negotiation in an ambiguous situation in which consideration may be given to the acceptability of the account to those still involved, as well as to the missing individual should he return. In such situations those types of accounts which de-emphasise individual volition— accounts which are popular and acceptable in our society—may be cited.

In cases where there is some ambiguity about the reason for the disappearance, the type of account that invokes the motive of abduction or cites the influence of 'bad company' could be seen to be attractive to those who remain: it directs attention away from the contribution they may have made to the interactional situation which existed before the disengagement. Those who return may confirm conventional assumptions that going missing is *essentially a temporary state of disengagement* prefacing the resumption of former nondeviant relations. The following letter to the *News of the World* drives this point home:

> I am now 23, happily married with a two-year-old son. Four years ago I was a 'missing person', one of the thousands of teenagers who ran away from home. ... When I left home I thought it was going to be a wonderful adventure. The longer I stayed away the harder it became to swallow my pride and return. ... To all decent parents whose child has run away from home I say this: you must not blame yourselves. And never lose hope that you will hear from the child one day.[43]

Teenage girls are seen as being particularly vulnerable to the enticements of unscrupulous predators who 'charm away their fears' and lure them away from their accustomed circle.[44] In one newspaper report about a missing teenage girl who was thought to have disappeared in the company of an older man, the father was said to have commented: 'I don't think she went entirely willingly. I think someone must have some kind of hold over her'.[45]

Another report about the disappearance of a fourteen-year-old girl on a train journey to her boarding school, states that the police were seeking a 'woman in red' who was thought to have been in the same compartment. The girl's mother is quoted as having remarked: 'She would be too naive to know what to do had she run away on her own. We are worried in case she might have fallen into the hands of some unscrupulous people.'[46]

Whereas the line of argument we are pursuing here suggests that in some cases nonvolitional accounts of going missing may seem more acceptable to those left behind, it needs to be emphasised that the reverse situation may occur: an individual's account of abduction may not be believed. The scepticism of conventional wisdom to unusual accounts of abduction is echoed in this newspaper headline: 'Three women forced me to make love— he says.'[47] The report goes on to describe the story of a 22-year-old man who claimed he was abducted and raped by three young women. At the same time the awareness that abduction occurs in our society can be considered as part of our 'stock of knowledge at hand' out of which those left behind seek to construct explanations.[48]

We would stress that we do not intend to imply that those left behind deliberately and rationally attempt to cover up the interactional setting from which the person has disappeared although, inevitably, they are presenting a partial explanation. We would suggest that accounts such as 'she went unwillingly', and 'someone had a hold over her' are prevalent and readily understandable in our society, especially when applied to children and young people. Such accounts can be seen as providing a basis for ordering a potentially complex situation in directing attention away from the total interactional setting in which the absent individual was involved, that is away from those others (real or symbolic) with whom he or she may have interacted unknown to those left behind. In addition, the nonvolitional account may be functional for the missing person returned to his previous company in that it may appear to clarify a motive which the individual has not clearly articulated to himself, and facilitate the resumption of the 'normal' relations prior to the break as it may seem a convenient and acceptable bridge which both parties can latch on to.

As with abduction, amnesia is used in explanations of going missing that de-emphasise the intentionality of missing persons. The inability to remember aspects of one's life experience—a 'blackout' or 'memory block'—

is generally regarded as a medical condition.[49] Cases in which we have encountered amnesia cited as a possible explanation are those in which the relatives left behind and those involved in the search are at a loss to find a motive for the individual's disappearance. Such cases are frequently described as a 'riddle' or a 'mystery' in newspaper reports.[50] A police spokesman commenting on the disappearance of a magistrate is quoted as saying: 'We're baffled. There's nothing to suggest this was just another person walking out of his home.' The report adds that: 'The police are now working on the theory that he may have lost his memory.'[51]

Failure at work or overdue stress are sometimes associated with amnesia. A wife in attempting to account for her husband's disappearance is reported as stating that he made a mistake at work and was demoted. The reporter wrote: 'She believes her husband may have worried so much that "something snapped" and he may now be suffering from a loss of memory.'[52] In this context, than, the amnesia is conceived as a processual affair reaching into the past.

Those immediately concerned who are confronted by the 'inexplicable' disappearance of a relative will have to give explanatory accounts to their immediate circle and any others whose attention is drawn to the absence. Their concern here will usually be to maintain existing relationships by ascribing a motive which is acceptable to those around them. Because those remaining are the immediate focus of attention and concern, individuals who suddenly and inexplicably disengage themselves may well be labelled 'selfish' or 'heartless'. Thus, in crediting the missing person with intentionality those left behind may find themselves confronted with an unacceptable account of the disengagement which does not seem congruent with their knowledge of the missing person, and does not seem to augur a harmonious resumption of former relationships should the individual return. To invoke a nonvolitional account therefore—loss of memory or a blackout—may seem more plausible and acceptable. Furthermore, such accounts are popular and legitimate within our society—they conveniently hold criticism of conventional social arrangements at bay.[53]

Another widely used nonvolitional explanation of social disengagement emphasises the 'inadequacy' of certain individuals in coping with their life situations. The alleged inability to act 'rationally' in a troublesome situation is regarded as leading some individuals to seek to escape from their responsibilities by abandoning the situation. This predisposition to act emotionally rather than rationally is emphasised by Richard Williams who asserts that: 'People do not deliberately disappear for the sake of so doing, generally the cause is emotional strain, or an overriding necessity to escape from responsibilities and obligations.'[54]

While such notions are frequently used in conjunction with the disappearance of teenage boys and girls,[55] they are also applied to adults. Discussing deserting husbands Dennis Marsden writes:

> Half of the husbands who deserted were suspected by their wives not of mental illness, but of some kind of 'immaturity' or 'personality defect' for which their wives had been prepared to make allowances. Often these suggestions of 'immaturity' had the effect of transferring the blame from the husband to his kin or some impersonal force such as heredity.'[56]

One wife tells of her determination not to wait and allow such a character trait to emerge in her husband: 'And every time his father put his mother in the family way he used to bugger off. That's why I threw him out when I did. He wasn't going to follow in his father's footsteps.[57] An individual's 'inadequacy' is, therefore, sometimes regarded as having a biological origin, or as having resulted from a process of 'incomplete socialisation'.[58]

Accounts that draw upon variants of the inadequacy syndrome and invoke notions such as 'immaturity', 'biogenetic forces' and 'emotional strain' can be seen as oversimplifying a complex interactional situation in shifting attention away from the individual as initiator of his action, to contemplating him as responding to forces which he is either unwilling or unable to master.[59] Consequently, explanations of this kind can be seen as providing a mandate for those left behind to assume control over the person concerned or to pass the problem over to others in the expectation of a solution.

However, not all explanations of going missing seek to de-emphasise the individual's intentionality. Attention may be focused on types of situations that allow the individual little choice but to depart. Here the individual's volition is acknowledged, but in such a way as to stress that the line of action taken was the only one that could have been selected. In a situation of extreme economic hardship the explanation of the person's departure may seem immediately understandable and self-evident to those left behind.[60] One social worker we spoke to explained that some working-class wives confronted by a home situation which characteristically involved poverty, debt and unemployment often concluded that the only option for them was to abandon the situation and try to make a fresh start elsewhere.[61] But it would seem that economic deprivation or serious reversals of fortune are seldom sufficient to explain a person's total disengagement. What seems significant is that most people tend to stay in spite of constraining circumstances. Dennis Marsden writes that a separated wife who was describing her marriage which lasted nine years told him: 'It ought to have broken up in the first week'.[62] The very constraints that can be regarded as an explanation of why a person leaves may also be perceived as providing strong reasons why the person cannot leave. Working-class wives may find themselves in a situation where disengagement seems impossible:

> 'The wife's lack of freedom to leave cannot be overstressed as an influence in prolonging marriage. Wives with children are economically dependent upon their husbands. They did not know about alternative income from national assistance, nor would it have been easy to find other accommodation. They feared that if they left they might lose custody of the children.'[63]

Typically, we can suggest, the response to some perceived situations is for members to temporarily disengage themselves perhaps once or on several occasions, in order to relieve a 'crisis'.

In our experience the types of account of going missing which implies that severe economic deprivation offers the individual no choice but to leave—whether temporarily or permanently—are constructed by social workers or commentators when they are not directly acquainted with those involved in the situation. In such contexts the distance of the social workers from the case concerned enables them to bypass the complexities embodied in a consideration of the accounts of those left behind, and may lead to what has the appearance of a more objective statement of the relation of cause to effect. Further freedom to proffer such an analysis may also be afforded by the absence of organisational or other pressures to take some sort of official action.

Social disengagement and the search for subjective experience

Finally we turn from a consideration of the explanations proffered by those left behind to the subjective experience of going missing. Social disengagement can be regarded, like other types of social action, as involving a project on the part of the individual concerned. That is, actors mentally construct their anticipated action before carrying it out. In many cases the contemplated action, social disengagement, is but one link in a chain of projects or the individual's plans. However, as Alfred Schutz has said, the kind of knowledge the person has of his project 'can be of any degree of clarity from one of total vagueness to one of maximum detail.'[64]

If we consider an imaginary individual contemplating going missing there would appear to be a number of possibilities. His project may be clearly defined only as far as the interactional break itself, his aims and plans after the break may be totally vague. On the other hand it is possible that the initial project, social disengagement, may be but one step in a series of

184

clearly worked out plans. It is therefore possible to imagine a whole range of replies to the question, 'What was your intention in going missing?' from 'to get away' (the project is the break) to 'I wanted to go somewhere where I could be myself so I decided to go to London and join the hippies' (the break is only the initial step in a series of plans). The type of replies given to such a question would of course be dependent on the stage in the sequence at which the question is posed. Settled in a new situation the individual who looks back on his completed action may perceive stronger continuities between his actions and a greater clarity of intention than was actually the case.[65]

Given these complexities we would like to look all too briefly at a limited number of publicly affirmed projects involving an act of social disengagement.

For many individuals the intention to leave may come suddenly, for example in the aftermath of a family crisis. The main concern here is just to leave, to disengage oneself from the present company. A fifteen-year-old girl who had just been located, explained that she had left home when aged thirteen after a row with her mother about pocket money; she commented: 'I didn't care where I was going. It could have been Manchester, Glasgow— anywhere. I just wanted to get away.'[66] In such cases the act of going missing does not seem to involve a planned search for new experiences or a conscious attempt to change one's identity. This is supported by an examination of the type of new situation which the missing person enters into. A social worker informed us that working-class wives who leave home are generally located in similar areas of other northern industrial towns, and are engaged in social relationships similar in form to those they have left. For them it would seem that the acceptability of the type of relationship they have left is not in question, rather it is the personally perceived failings of the specific individuals involved in the relationship from which they seek to disengage themselves.

However, the individual may view the act of disengagement as a necessary step in enabling him to enter a situation in which he can work out his life projects. As Alfred Schutz notes:

> Undoubtedly there are situations in which each of us sits down and thinks over his problems. In general he will do so at critical points in his life when his chief interest is to master a situation.[67]

The quest for such an interstitial break is illustrated by the remarks of E. G. Love:

> 'A few years ago I was caught up in a whirlwind of my own. When it all ended I found myself walking the streets. I needed more than just

185

a job. I needed to reassess life. ... It seemed to me at the time that the reassessment was more important than the material side of things, I had to think. I had to have time to think. So I drifted.'[68]

The project of the individual may be more closely defined when disengagement is seen as a necessary step in the process towards the formation of a different personal identity in a new situation among new others. The individual in this case constructs his project in the knowledge of the existence of other situations which are perceived as offering a possibility of subjective self-development (an important theme in modern society)[69] which is not feasible in the present situation. The individual's prior knowledge of the existence of groups such as tramps, hippies and communes—groups in which the search for new experience and individual self-development are articulated themes[70]—may have a major influence on the construction of his plans.

Of course, it is possible for the individual to stop and review his project and change his plans at any stage prior to and after the disengagement. Our intention in examining social disengagement as planned is not to emphasise an exclusive overt rationality underlying going missing. While such rationality may be evident in cases where the individual has a clear notion of the situation he is going to—such as a life of self-development in a hippie commune— in many cases it would seem that the span of the project goes only so far as the act of disengagement itself. Once the act of disengagement has taken place the individual who has left 'just to get away' may then start reviewing the alternative situations which seem open to him. It is at this point that the status 'missing person' becomes dependent on a series of social and psychic processes that are, in varying degrees, independent of the actual act of sudden physical disappearance.

Notes

[1] O'Neill, J. *Sociology as a Skin Trade: Essays Towards A Reflexive Sociology* (Heinemann, London 1972).

[2] Letter to the *News of the World* 22 October 1972.

[3] Smith, P. Gladstone *The Crime Explosion* (Macdonald, London 1970).

[4] Paulette Pratt has reported six cases of children who 'inexplicably' disappeared without warning during the course of their conventional daily rounds. She notes that when children mysteriously disappear an explanation, or the child in question, is eventually found. 'The Children Who Vanish Without Trace', *Observer Magazine*, 29 October 1972.

[5] An overall concern with those who go missing is confined to voluntary social welfare agencies; predominantly the Salvation Army which considers

that the annual failure of certain individuals to appear predictably in their normal surroundings is 'an uncomfortable social fact'. Williams, R. *Missing: A Study of the World-wide Missing Persons Enigma and Salvation Army Response* (Hodder & Stoughton, London 1969).

[6] For a discussion of the themes and variations permeating the overall analysis of the missing persons phenomenon see Hepworth, J. M., and Featherstone, J. M. 'Persons Believed Missing: A Search for a Sociological Interpretation', in *Deviance and Social Control*, ed. Rock, P., and McIntosh, M. (Tavistock, London 1972).

[7] For a discussion of the symbolic content of newspaper reports of deviant or criminal acts see Hepworth, J. M. *Blackmail: Publicity and Secrecy in Everyday Life*, (MacGibbon & Kee, forthcoming).

[8] 'Village Vicar's Absence', *News of the World* 23 January 1972.

[9] Barry, J. 'Couple Who Vanished "From Face of the Earth"', *News of the World* 27 August 1972.

[10] Pratt, op. cit., quotes some particularly poignant instances.

[11] For example, a Bradford man has recently returned home after an absence of six years. At the age of fifteen he vanished from his paper round after what he is reported as describing as a conscious decision to change his life. 'Son Drops In After Six-year Absence' *The Guardian* 13 January 1972.

[12] The concept of status here employed is that elaborated by Glaser and Strauss in their theory of 'status passage'. As they put it, status 'is a resting place for individuals'. Nevertheless a status is not static, the possibility is always present for an individual to change his status or for others to change it for him. Glaser, B. G., and Strauss, A. L. *Status Passage* (Routledge & Kegan Paul, London 1971).

[13] Within a family setting a person's status as missing may be confirmed as a result of occasional communications by letter and the passage of time. Leslie, David 'Heartbreak Plea to Her Lost Son', *News of the World* 23 May 1971.

[14] O'Neill, op. cit.

[15] Much of this material is summarised conveniently in Bahr, H. M. (ed.) *Disaffiliated Man: Essays and Bibliography on Skid Row, Vagrancy and Outsiders* (Oxford University Press, London 1971).

[16] As far as the problem of 'homelessness' is concerned certain categories of homeless people which may well include some missing persons are defined as mentally ill and/or alcoholic. See, for example, the report on a survey carried out by the National Assistance Board, *Homeless Single Persons* (HMSO, London 1966). This report opens with the words:

> The origins of this Survey could be said to be twofold. In 1964 and 1965 a number of voluntary bodies expressed concern both to the govern-

ment and to government departments about what they regarded as the increasing problem of the misfits and drifters of society, particularly those who habitually live in lodging houses and hostels or sleep rough. This concern was not in itself by any means new, but it was clear that the problem was attracting increased public attention, and discussions were held among the government departments most concerned. ...

[17] Williams, op. cit. Also: Stafford, A. *The Age of Consent* (Hodder & Stoughton, London 1964).

[18] For instance, Nels Anderson's classic sociological study, *The Hobo: The Sociology of the Homeless Man* (University of Chicago Press, Chicago 1961).

[19] Not long ago an Under-Secretary of State for Health and Social Security informed the Commons that 66 out of every 100 girls in approved schools 'abscond'. The figures, he stated, had changed little in ten years. He also stressed that there were problems when it came to defining the meaning of the word 'abscond'. 'A Word is Running Wild', *The Guardian* 11 December 1971.

A recent study by the Home Office Research Unit absconding from approved schools largely by boys, but including some analysis of girl absconders, stressed that absconding behaviour, which has been little researched to date, was disquieting because 'it seems from the present research and also from work undertaken in probation hostels by Sinclair (1971) that it is a powerful measure of institutional climate and morale.'

Importantly for our overall discussion of the social significance of going missing, the researchers saw absconding as 'predictive of failure' after release (that is, it is intimately linked statistically with an unwillingness to go straight) athough personality tests revealed that in terms of individual characteristics 'absconders differ very little from other boys'. It was thus a strategic issue in the debate over the efficacy of approved school treatment for juvenile delinquents. Clarke, R.V.G., and Martin, D. N. *Absconding From Approved Schools* (HMSO, London 1971).

[20] For an extended discussion of the part played by 'moral panics'—a sense of threatened social values evinced by certain legitimated members of society—in the construction of 'folk devils' (those who symbolise the threat), see Cohen, S. *Folk Devils and Moral Panics: The Creation of the Mods and Rockers* (MacGibbon & Kee, London 1972).

[21] Wider issues concerning the problems of defining missing persons and the processes underlying these definitional difficulties have been discussed in Hepworth and Featherstone, op. cit.

[22] Goffman, E. *Behavior in Public Places: Notes on the Social Organization of Gatherings* (Free Press, New York/Collier-Macmillan, London 1963).

See also his *Relations in Public: Microstudies of the Public Order* (Allen Lane the Penguin Press, London 1971).

23 Lloyd's Intelligence Department reports that 71 ships have disappeared in the last ten years. 'There were no survivors, very little flotsam and no bodies. They simply disappeared, taking with them 1,034 men, women and children.' 'Three Women and Child in Ship that Vanished', *The Weekly News* 24 July 1971.

24 R. Huys Jones introducing Timms, N. *Rootless in the City*, (National Institute for Social Work Training, London 1968).

25 Not surprisingly, great concern is expressed when a middle-aged man 'of precise habits' who is not seen to be 'in trouble of any sort' fails to return home from work. Pritchard, Nicholas 'He Walked Right Out of Her Life', *News of the World* 18 October 1970.

26 Anonymous *Go Ask Alice* (Eyre Methuen, London 1972).

27 Williams, op. cit.

28 From time to time, judges are asked by interested relatives to declare a missing person legally dead in order to facilitate the transfer of property or so that those remaining may adopt a new status. The time factor, to which we have previously referred, looms up significantly here, particularly in those cases where there is no other evidence of death.

29 Williams, op. cit.

30 Whether or not the noticeable incidence of inquiries for persons in middle age confirms the psychoanalytical theory of the 'mid-life crisis' is a moot point. Elliot Jacques feels that many people experience a mid-life crisis around the age of 35. This mid-life crisis is experienced as a period of transition (of status passage) informed by an increased awareness by those concerned that, chronologically speaking, death is creeping closer. Jacques, E. 'Death and the Mid-Life Crisis', *International Journal of Psychoanalysis*, vol. XLVI (1965).

31 Turner, R. H. *Family Interaction* (Wiley, New York 1970).

32 O'Neill, op. cit. (ch.3, 'Public and Private Space') describes this as 'the ethic of individualistic-familism'. Slater, Philip E. *The Pursuit of Loneliness: American Culture at the Breaking Point* (Allen Lane the Penguin Press, London 1971) refers to the interrelationships between the search for an increasingly private family home life and participation in the competitive occupational world.

33 Going missing can be compared with Goffman's discussion of the symptomatic significance of behaviour labelled as mental illness within 'American middle-class' family settings. Such behaviour indicates primarily that the individual breaking the situational rules of interpersonal conduct has failed to appreciate his place in the scheme of things—thus transforming him or her into a threat to a hitherto stable life-style:

The maintenance of the internal and external functioning of the family is so central that when family members think of the essential character, the perduring personality of any one of their numbers, it is usually his habitual pattern of support for family-organised activity and family relationships, his style of acceptance of his place in the family, that they have in mind. Any marked change in his pattern of support will tend to be perceived as a marked change in his character. The deepest nature of an individual is only skin-deep, the deepness of his others' skin.

Goffman, E. 'The Insanity of Place' in *Relations in Public*, op. cit.
[34] Smith, P., 'The Runaway Husband', *The Sunday Times Magazine* 29 November 1970.
[35] 'Missing Wives Who Lead Secret Lives', *The Weekly News* 23 October 1971.
[36] 'We help Find a Missing Girl', *News of the World* 22 March 1970.
[37] On which the clearest statement can be found in Irwin, J. *The Felon* (Prentice-Hall, Englewood Cliffs 1970).
[38] Cohen, S., and Taylor, L. *Psychological Survival: The Experience of Long Term Imprisonment* (Penguin, Harmondsworth 1972).
[39] 'Two Faces of a Missing Girl', *Sunday Mirror* 22 August 1971, in which was reproduced two quite different photographs of the same girl. 'And a detective said: "The two moods transform her. They show two different girls."'
[40] Lofland, C. J. *Deviance and Identity* (Prentice-Hall, Englewood Cliffs 1969). Especially interesting in his conceptualisation of an initial act of deviance as either 'defensive' or 'adventurous'.
[41] Chambliss, W. J., 'A Sociological Analysis of the Law of Vagrancy', *Social Problems*, vol. XII (1964).
[42] Chesney, K. *The Victorian Underworld* (Temple Smith, London 1970).
[43] *News of the World*, 15 March 1970.
[44] Part of the prominence accorded to cases of abduction in the media derives from and fosters the belief that there are dangerously ill-balanced people around constantly on the lookout for innocent women and children. This anxiety is expressed by M. Ellison who writes: 'No one is more completely the victim of circumstances than the young child. There is always the terrible fear that so small a being could fall an easy prey to a maniac's fury, with neither the strength to struggle nor the voice to cry out.' *Missing from Home* (Pan, London 1966).
In addition, commentators such as Ellison and Williams (op. cit.) emphasise the evilly rational exploitation of young girls who end up in enforced prostitution. 'Ponces' and 'madams' are apparently always on the lookout for the innocent young girls who arrive alone seeking accommodation in the city.

In a feature article about the notorious 'chocolate-drop girls' of Middles-brough, Frank Greig informs us of 'Mother Fagins' who, in offering help to young girls on the run, persuade them into prostitution (*Middlesbrough Evening Gazette* 21 September 1971).

[45] *Middlesbrough Evening Gazette* 8 October 1970.

[46] *News of the World* 31 January 1971. Not only parents of young girls are disposed to considering abduction as an explanation of going missing. There may be legal definitions involved, and damages at stake. Under the headline 'Man who stole a wife gets a bill for £12,000 it' was reported that a husband claimed that a man had debauched and carnally known his wife. The judge informed the jury that a wrong had been done to the husband 'for his wife had been seduced and kept from him' and damages were awarded accordingly. Yet the 'stolen wife' appeared in court to defend her 'seducer' and cast doubts upon the reputation of her 'wronged' husband. *Daily Mirror* 22 June 1972.

[47] *News of the World* 27 October 1970.

[48] 'Since it first came into being', writes Edgar Morin, 'the white-slave trade has always exercised a twofold fascination on people.' Researching into a rumour circulating in 1969 in Orleans, that girls were being abducted into the white-slave trade via the fitting rooms of certain Jewish-owned dress shops, Morin and his team indicated that the rumour ('pure and absolute', because it was totally unsupported by fact—no one disappeared) was built primarily upon models of actual white-slave incidents reported in the press and other sources from time to time.

So, therefore, although white slaving has occurred and may still occur, this does not mean such an explanation fits all cases but rather that we also have to explore the underlying social reasons leading individuals to draw, on the 'stock of knowledge at hand' and proffer such explanations. Morin E. *Rumour in Orleans: Jews Accused of White Slaving: A Modern Myth Examined* (Anthony Blond, London 1971).

[49] '... a farmer who had been missing since Saturday, was found by the police yesterday wandering in Inverness, dazed and apparently suffering from loss of memory.' 'Missing Farmer Found "Dazed"', *The Guardian* 18 July 1972.

[50] 'Riddle of the Silent Woman', *News of the World* 5 March 1972. 'Mystery of a Father Who is Missing', *Middlesbrough Evening Gazette* 25 February 1972. 'Riddle of Missing Magistrate', *News of the World* 20 December 1970 'Missing Baronet—the Mystery Grows', *News of the World* 20 December 1970.

[51] *News of the World* 20 December 1970. Unfortunately this case ended tragically, the magistrate's body was found in a reservoir: 'Missing JP's body is found', *News of the World* 10 January 1971.

[52] 'Mystery of a Father who is Missing', *Middlesbrough Evening Gazette*

25 February 1972. In another case 'Man "Back from the Dead" Goes Home', *The Guardian* 12 November 1971, a businessman disappeared after a boating accident and was believed drowned. 77 days later he turned up at his home exhausted 'and apparently suffering from a memory block'. In the course of a further report (*The Guardian* 15 November 1972) describing the fall from the window of the psychiatric ward in which he was staying, it was 'mentioned that a creditors' meeting was to be held to discuss debts incurred at his garage.

[53] On the acceptability to magistrates of accounts by offenders of reasons for committing sex offences see Taylor, L., 'The Significance and Interpretation of the Replies to Motivational Questions: The Case of Sexual Offenders', *Sociology*, vol. VI (1972).

[54] Williams, op. cit.

[55] As far as teenage girls are concerned many of the accounts we encountered while examining social-work records emphasised that girls were 'impulsive', 'irresponsible', 'defeated by the need for self-discipline', 'immature', 'self-centred', etc. Such descriptions, of course, reflect certain organisational imperatives and ideologies underpinning the definition of socially problematic individual 'needs'. Cicourel, A. V. *The Social Organisation of Juvenile Justice* (Wiley, New York 1968) (especially ch. 4 'Conversational Depictions of Social Organisation').

[56] Marsden, D. *Mothers Alone: Poverty and the Fatherless Family* (Allen Lane the Penguin Press, London 1969). Marsden goes on to say that 'some wives referred to their husbands as "mother's boys" implying a psychological dependence and character immaturity or weakness.'

[57] Marsden, op. cit.

[58] Contemporary adult society includes many persons who are inadequately socialised and who are at least vaguely aware of their inadequacies. They are dissatisfied, but do not know what to do about the situation. Some of them create major problems for the community.'

Those who are 'inadequately socialised' are individuals or groups of individuals 'who may not have an *opportunity to learn* all of the things' which would make them able to participate fully in the manner approved in the social environment in which they live. See Rose, A. M. 'Incomplete Socialisation', *Sociology and Social Research*.

[59] Lee Rainwater and his research team have demonstrated that the structure of a community, responsibe to overall socioeconomic processes—in this case a lower-working-class Negro ghetto in St Louis—can order life chances in such a detrimental way that the resultant separation of male and female roles produces specific and not necessarily creditable notions concerning the *essential nature of masculinity* as a psycho-biological 'given.' One Negro male characteristic in this context is that of persistent unreliability

and a tendency to renege on family commitments and to seek satisfactions productive of a sense of self-esteem in associations with men and women outside the home. As a consequence family life is unstable for many members of this community and temporary or permanent physical absence of the father is not a rare occurrence. Overall economic deprivations—particularly the absence of stable work opportunities—lead to behavioural responses on the part of men faced with threats to their conventionally accredited status of masculine breadwinner. These behavioural responses confirm the cultural stereotype that fundamentally men as beings are flawed by certain inadequacies. Rainwater, Lee *Behind Ghetto Walls: Black Families in a Federal Slum* (Allen Lane the Penguin Press, London 1971).

[60] Many commentators have noted the relationship between major economic depressions and the increase in the number of tramps, hobos and wandering people. Kenneth Allsop, for example, emphasises that poverty forced many unemployed young men to leave their families in the Great Depression: 'The ordinary uncomplicated fact was that the young boy shuttling about... was either in flight from actual starvation or had taken a Captain Scott decision to relieve the pressure on a family in extremity by removing one stomach.' Allsop, K. *Hard Travellin: The Hobo and His History* (Hodder & Stoughton, London 1967)

[61] A case described to us involved a woman who had left behind her an unemployed husband, ten children and a house in which there was no food or coal. These deprivations were interpreted as in themselves constituting a situation in which it was practically impossible for the mother to solve the problems facing her. The social worker's terse comment about such cases was: 'The women just get pig sick.' Hepworth and Featherstone, op. cit.

[62] She went on to outline her marriage in the following terms:

> He started knocking me about. There was other women as well. And the drink! I knew that he drank before we got married, but nothing like that. He used to come home blind drunk at four o'clock in the morning, and he didn't care what he did when he was drunk. Anything that I'd got he smashed it all up and he broke all the windows. And he just didn't care how he was. He used to wet the beds and mess in the beds when he was like that. And when David was only little he used to kick him out of his bed so he could get in there and do it. (Marsden, op. cit.)

[63] Marsden, op. cit.

[64] For a clear discussion of acting and planning see: Wagner, H. (ed.) *Alfred Schutz on Phenomenology and Social Relations* (Chicago University Press, Chicago 1970), (especially section 3, 'Acting in the Life-World')

[65] Further complexities occur around the question of the individual's motivational account. The degree of clarity the individual has when looking back on the motive for his project depends on the vocabularies of motive available to him. Some motivational accounts are more appropriate to some situations than others. See Mills, C. Wright 'Situated Actions and Vocabularies of Motive', *American Sociological Review* vol. V (1940).

[66] *News of the World* 7 November 1971

[67] Wagner, op. cit.

[68] Love, E. G. *Subways are for Sleeping* (Gollancz, London 1958).

[69] This view is emphasised by Berger, Peter Ludwig, and Luckmann, Thomas *The Social Construction of Reality* (Allen Lane the Penguin Press, London 1967) and Luckmann, T., and Berger, P. 'Social Mobility and Personal Identity', *Archives Européennes de Sociologie* (1964).

[70] In the literature by and about tramps, 'the pull of other places', 'freedom from the ties of conventional life' and 'the absence of monotony' seem to be prominent themes. See, for example, Allsop, op. cit., and Phelen, J. *We Follow the Roads*, Phoenix House, 1949. The hippie world view seems to revolve around 'the perpetual search for pleasure' and 'the conscious concern to find oneself'; see Hall, S. *The Hippies: An American Moment* (University of Birmingham, 1968) and Young, J. *The Drugtakers: The Social Meaning of Drug Use* (Paladin, London 1971).